Pathway
Advanced

Vorschläge für Klausuren mit kombinierten Aufgabenformaten

Qualifikationsphase Sekundarstufe II

Herausgegeben und erarbeitet von:
Iris Edelbrock

Sprachliche Betreuung:
Simone Duxbury-Ziemer

Schöningh
westermann

Begleitmaterialien zum Lehrwerk

Pathway Advanced Audio-CDs
4 CDs mit Hörtexten und Songs, Transkripte im Booklet
Best.-Nr. 062532-6

Pathway Advanced Skills and Language Trainer
Best.-Nr. 040162-3

Pathway Advanced Abi *kompakt*
Thematic Vocabulary – Important Facts – Relevant Skills
Best.-Nr. 040164-7

Pathway Advanced Teachers' Manual
Best.-Nr. 040165-4

Pathway Advanced Comprehension
Reading – Listening – Viewing. Kopiervorlagen für neue Aufgabenformate
Best.-Nr. 040157-9

Pathway Advanced Mündliche Prüfung
Kopiervorlagen
Best.-Nr. 040159-3

Pathway Advanced Mediation
Kopiervorlagen
Best.-Nr. 040163-0

westermann GRUPPE

© 2015 Bildungshaus Schulbuchverlage
Westermann Schroedel Diesterweg Schöningh Winklers GmbH
Braunschweig, Paderborn, Darmstadt

www.schoeningh-schulbuch.de
Schöningh Verlag, Jühenplatz 1–3, 33098 Paderborn

Druck A³ / Jahr 2017
Alle Drucke der Serie A sind im Unterricht parallel verwendbar.

Umschlaggestaltung: Nora Krull, Bielefeld
Druck und Bindung: westermann Druck GmbH, Braunschweig

ISBN 978-3-14-**040158**-6

Contents

Vorwort

Liebe Kollegin, lieber Kollege,

die vorliegende Materialsammlung bietet Ihnen eine Auswahl an Vorschlägen für die schriftliche Leistungsüberprüfung entsprechend den Vorgaben der **Kernlernpläne für NRW**.

Die **20 Klausuren** sind inhaltlich auf die Themenvorgaben der Kernlehrpläne sowie die Units der Neubearbeitung des Schülerbuches *Pathway Advanced* abgestimmt und können z. B. zur schriftlichen Leistungsüberprüfung zum Abschluss einer Unit oder einer Sequenz eingesetzt werden.

Darüber hinaus sind die Prüfungsmaterialien auch lehrbuchunabhängig einsetzbar, da sie den **Schwerpunktthemen der Qualifikationsphase der Sekundarstufe II** Rechnung tragen. Alle Aufgabenapparate folgen der Systematik *comprehension – analysis – comment/(re-)creation of text* und entsprechen damit in ihrer Struktur und den standardisierten Formulierungen (Operatoren) den Anforderungsbereichen des Zentralabiturs. Darüber hinaus werden bei den Auswahlaufgaben zu *(Re-) Creation of Text* die **Zieltextvorgaben** berücksichtigt.

Die Klausuren bieten **Materialkombinationen zur Überprüfung der folgenden Kompetenzen**:
- Lesen/Schreiben (integriert) + Hörsehverstehen (isoliert)
- Lesen/Schreiben (integriert) + Hörverstehen (isoliert)
- Lesen/Schreiben (integriert) + Mediation (isoliert)
- Lesen/Schreiben (integriert)

Die Aufgabenformate für die **Teilkompetenzen Hörsehverstehen und Hörverstehen** umfassen sowohl **geschlossene** als auch **halboffene Aufgaben**, z. B.:
- (four-option) multiple choice
- true-false-not given with correction
- sequencing
- sentence completion
- matching

Die Textauswahl bietet ein breites Spektrum an Textsorten und umfasst fiktionale Texte wie z. B. Textauszüge einer *Short Story*, einer *Novel* oder eines *Screenplays* sowie nicht-fiktionale Texte wie beispielsweise Auszüge aus Magazin- oder Zeitungsartikeln, die in ihrer Länge/Wortzahl den prozentualen Vorgaben entsprechend der jeweiligen **Gewichtung der Einzelkompetenzen entsprechen**.

Alle Texte/Materialien sind sorgfältig annotiert und ermöglichen damit den Schülern zeitökonomisches und zielgerichtetes Arbeiten.

Die die Klausuren ergänzenden Informationskästen geben schnellen Aufschluss über den thematischen Zusammenhang, die anzuwendenden bzw. zu überprüfenden Teilkompetenzen, Textlänge, Textsorte sowie Materialkombination.

Jeder Klausur ist das aktuelle **NRW Bewertungsraster inklusive Erwartungshorizont** beigefügt. Im Anhang des Bandes finden Sie **Kopiervorlagen** für die Bewertungsraster für die Darstellungsleistung/sprachliche Leistung, die Orientierungsangaben für die Sprachrichtigkeit sowie die Zuordnung der Notenstufen zu den Punktzahlen.

Die dem Band beigefügte **CD-ROM** enthält:
- Filmausschnitte (2),
- Audiodokumente (8),
- alle Bewertungsraster sowohl als editierbare Worddokumente wie auch als pdf-Dateien,
- die Lösungen.

Ihr Pathway Team

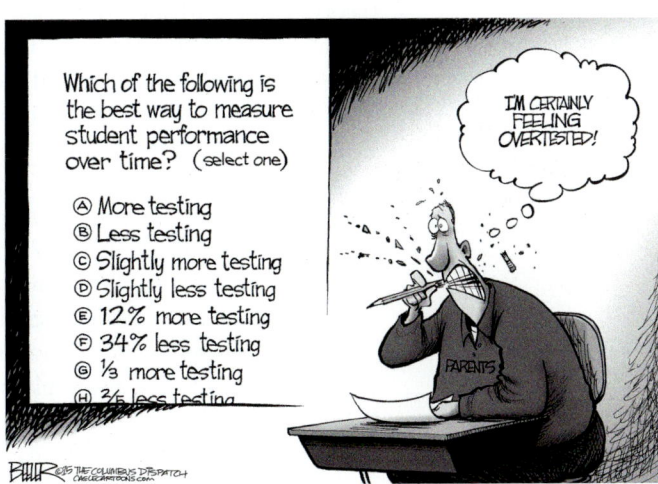

> **Topic:** Shakespeare – The Impact of Shakespearean Drama on Young Audiences Today
>
> **Skills:** Analysis of a non-fictional text (newspaper article); writing a letter to the editor (*Zieltextformat*); viewing comprehension
>
> **Texts:** **Part A:** Jonathan Bate: Shakespeare's 450th Birthday: Now All the World Is His Stage. Telegraph, April 2014 (500 words)
> **Part B:** Kevin Spacey: Now – Richard III documentary (03:18 mins)

Part A: Reading/Writing

Jonathan Bate

Shakespeare's 450th Birthday: Now All the World Is His Stage

This week, it is a racing certainty[1] that every major news outlet in the world will have something to say about the Bard of Avon's 450th birthday, which falls on Wednesday. And this is only prologue to the wall-to-wall[2] programme of celebrations, productions, exhibitions and documentaries being planned for 2016, the quatercentenary[3] of his death. Shakespeare has become a global icon, not
5 merely a local heritage[4] product whose presumed birthday conveniently coincides with St George's Day[5].
At the time of his death, he was a much admired dramatist. But Francis Beaumont, who passed away a few weeks before him, was equally admired, on the basis of far fewer plays. The centenary of Shakespeare's birth fell soon after the theatres reopened with the Restoration of the monarchy, fol-
10 lowing the period when the Puritans had closed them down for the duration of the Civil War[6]. His plays formed a staple[7] part of the repertoire, but those of Beaumont[8] and John Fletcher[9] were performed more frequently. Shakespeare only pulled ahead of the pack[10] in the Georgian Era[11]. It was around his 200th anniversary, under the auspices[12] of the great actor David Garrick, that he took on his status as National Poet and exemplar of artistic genius. [...]
15 But an even more important turning point was the triumph of Shakespeare in Love at both the box office[13] and the Oscars. Tom Stoppard's brilliant screenplay drew such strong parallels between the Elizabethan theatre and modern Hollywood that the film contrived[14] to turn Shakespeare into a celebrity. It made him our contemporary at precisely the moment when culture was taken over by a rage[15] for the now, a cult of the new. [...]
20 How knowledgeable should we expect our schoolchildren to be about Shakespeare?
During the Government's recent overhaul[16] of GCSEs[17], I was asked to join a consultative group advising on the English Literature syllabus[18]. It quickly became clear that the minister wanted to prescribe two Shakespeare plays for every 16-year-old in the land. I argued, to the contrary, that there should be one Shakespeare play and one play by anybody except Shakespeare. It cannot be in
25 Shakespeare's interest for teenagers to associate him with compulsion[19], for his plays and his alone to have the dreaded[20] status of set books[21]. [...]
In a verse preface to the First Folio[22] of the complete plays, his friend and rival Ben Jonson predicted that there would come a time when Shakespeare would be held in as high regard as the great

---

[1] **racing certainty** (*BE, infml.*) sth. that is certain to happen – [2] **wall-to-wall** continuous, completely-filled – [3] **quatercentenary** 400 years after an important event – [4] **local heritage** *heimatliches Erbe* – [5] **St George's Day** national holiday marking the feast day of St. George, England's patron saint – [6] **British Civil War** (1642–1651) internal battle between Parliamentarians and Royalists – [7] **staple** basic, main – [8] **Francis Beaumont** (1584–1616) English Renaissance dramatist – [9] **John Fletcher** (1579–1625) British playwright – [10] **to pull ahead of the pack** (*infml.*) to be considered better than the rest – [11] **Georgian Era** (1740–1830) period in British history spanning the reigns of four kings named George (I–IV) – [12] **under the auspices of sb./sth.** with the protection or support of sb./sth. – [13] **box office** the place in a theatre/cinema where the tickets are sold – [14] **to contrive** to manage to do sth. – [15] **a rage** an exciting or entertaining event – [16] **overhaul** improvement, *Revision* – [17] **GCSC** General Certificate of Secondary Education, *mittlere Reife* – [18] **syllabus** curriculum – [19] **compulsion** *Zwang* – [20] **dreaded** *gefürchtet* – [21] **set books** *Pflichtlektüre* – [22] **First Folio** *Erstausgabe*

writers of antiquity[23]. "Triumph, my Britain, thou hast one to show," he wrote, "To whom all Scenes
30 of Europe homage owe." Shakespeare's Britain stood on the threshold[24] of the modern world. Britain's Shakespeare was a creation of the 18th and 19th centuries, an era when the nation and thus the
national poet moved on the world stage. [...]
Now it is not just "all scenes of Europe" but almost all countries in the world that pay homage to
William Shakespeare. His works are our most enduring cultural export. *(500 words)*

www.telegraph.co.uk/culture/theatre/william-shakespeare/10777409/Shakespeares-450th-birthday-Now-all-the-world-is-his-stage.html, 20 April 2014 [04.04.2015]

ASSIGNMENTS

1. Outline Jonathan Bate's reflections on Shakespeare's 450th birthday and the reasons he considers to be relevant for Shakespeare's ongoing success and popularity.
   (Comprehension)

2. Analyse the stylistic and rhetorical devices and show how they convey the message of the text
   and the author's perspective.
   (Analysis)

3. You have a choice here. Choose **one** of the following tasks:

   3.1 Keeping in mind your own experiences of studying Shakespeare's works, comment on
   ll. 21–26.
   In your opinion, how important is it to study (at least one of) Shakespeare's plays in class?
   (Comment/Evaluation)

   3.2 Write a "Letter to the Editor" in response to the article, in which you explain your point of
   view.
   Do you share the author's view that Shakespeare would have probably fallen into oblivion[1] if
   England had not "moved on the world stage" as the British Empire in the 18th and 19th
   centuries?
   ((Re-)Creation of text)

---

[23] **antiquity** *die Antike* – [24] **threshold** *Schwelle*

[1]**to fall into oblivion** *in Vergessenheit geraten*

Part B: Viewing Comprehension

Kevin Spacey

Now – Richard III Documentary

The documentary that this excerpt is taken from follows 20 British and American actors on a 10-month international stage production tour of William Shakespeare's drama *Richard III*, which they undertook in 2013. The British director Sam Mendes and all of the actors, including American actor Kevin Spacey, share their thoughts about their roles, personal life and the tour project with the viewer.

Source: www.kevinspacey.com/nowthefilm (03:18 mins)

Annotations »»»

simpery *einfältig lächelnd* ■ **to shift** here: to change from one state to another ■ **to get away with sth.** (*phr.v.*) to do sth. bad without being punished for it ■ **to bear** to carry ■ **the corpse** dead body ■ **hedgehog** *Igel* ■ **mortal** causing death ■ **tango** here: a complex and energetic choreography between two people ■ **daring** brave and willing to take risks ■ **to go for sth.** (*phr. v.*) to put the maximum effort into doing sth. ■ **humor** here: mood, state ■ **to woo sb.** [wuː] *um jdn. werben* ■ **cojones** (*Spanish: infml.*) balls, *Eier* (i. e. courage) ■ **to egg sb. on** (*infml.*) to strongly encourage sb. to do sth.

ASSIGNMENT 1

Watch the scene from the documentary, and decide on the correct completion for the following sentences. Only one of the answers is correct for each statement.

1. The British actress, Annabel Scholey, plays …

☐ a) … Lady Anne, Richard's wife.

☐ b) … Lady Anne, Richard's fiancée.

☐ c) … Lady Anne, whose husband was killed by Richard III.

2. Lady Anne …

☐ a) … accuses Richard III of having murdered her husband.

☐ b) … curses the murderer of her husband.

☐ c) … cannot believe that her husband was murdered.

3. Annabel Scholey understands Lady Anne …

☐ a) … as a soft and easily-broken woman.

☐ b) … as an unstable woman with mental problems.

☐ c) … as a strong woman who can handle emotional extremes.

4. Kevin Spacey believes that Richard III …

☐ a) … is very much influenced by the Lady Anne scene.

☐ b) … is surprised by Lady Anne's reaction.

☐ c) … is overconfident about what he can get away with.

5. Richard III and Lady Anne ...

☐ a) ... flatter each other.

☐ b) ... provoke and insult each other.

☐ c) ... are scared of each other.

6. Dominic Fraser thinks that the Lady Anne scene ...

☐ a) ... is absurd and funny.

☐ b) ... provokes the audience.

☐ c) ... is one of the best scenes of the play.

7. When she first got the role of Lady Anne, Annabel Scholey ...

☐ a) ... was worried about playing this role and going on a long, international tour.

☐ b) ... was excited about acting in a sexy scene with Kevin Spacey.

☐ c) ... was insecure about acting in such an intimate scene with Kevin Spacey.

8. Kevin Spacey ...

☐ a) ... wanted the Lady Anne scene to focus on sex and seduction rather than love.

☐ b) ... wanted to make the audience sympathize with Richard III.

☐ c) ... wanted the Lady Anne scene to be magical.

9. Annabel Scholey explains that ...

☐ a) ... she initially felt very shy around Kevin Spacey and could not really act the scene well.

☐ b) ... the scene is only believable because it is so physical and energetic.

☐ c) ... Sam Mendes advised her to speak loudly.

10. Kevin Spacey communicates with the audience ...

☐ a) ... in order to draw them into the action.

☐ b) ... so as to make them hate his character.

☐ c) ... because he wants to show them that Richard III is a strong character.

ASSIGNMENT 2

After watching the scene a second time, give examples that prove and support the statements below. Refer to textual, as well as visual elements and cinematic devices.

1. King Richard III provokes and woos Lady Anne at the same time.

_____

_____

_____

2. Lady Anne is "a rock of a woman".

_____

_____

_____

3. The scene is more about sex than about love.

_____

_____

_____

4. Richard III and Lady Anne are equally strong characters.

_____

_____

_____

5. Kevin Spacey plays Richard III as a witty and strong character.

_____

_____

_____

Bewertungsbogen für: _____	Kurs: _____

Part A: Teilaufgabe 1 (Comprehension)

	Anforderungen **Der Schüler/die Schülerin ...**	maximal erreichbare Punktzahl	erreichte Punkte
1	... umreißt **das Ausmaß der** von Jonathan Bate **genannten Feierlichkeiten** im Zusammenhang mit Shakespeares 450. Geburtstag und nennt z. B. • die außerordentliche Medienpräsenz und Berichterstattung (*every major news outlet in the world ...*), • die umfassenden Feierlichkeiten und geplanten Aktivitäten (*wall-to-wall programme of celebrations, productions ...*), • den glücklichen terminlichen Zusammenfall der Shakespeare-Feierlichkeiten mit dem englischen Nationalfeiertag (*conveniently coincides with St George's Day ...*).	3	
2	... skizziert die **historisch bedingten Gründe** für Shakespeares Erfolg und Popularität und verweist z. B. auf • die bereits bestehende Popularität Shakespeares zum Zeitpunkt seines Todes (*at the time of his death ..., he was ...*), • die Wiedereröffnung der Theater nach dem Bürgerkrieg im 17. Jahrhundert (*his plays formed a staple part ...*), • Shakespeares Aufstieg zum „National Poet" in der *Georgian Era* (*under the auspices of David Garrick ..., status as National Poet, example of artistic genius ...*).	3	
3	... spezifiziert die genannten **Gründe für Shakespeares heutige Popularität** und benennt z. B. • den triumphalen Erfolg des Films *Shakespeare in Love* (*both at the box office and the Oscars ...*), • Tom Stoppards brilliantes Sccreenplay, das elisabethanisches Theater und modernes Hollywood verbunden hat (Z. 15 ff.), • die zeitgemäße Adaption des „alten" Stoffes (*our contemporary, a rage for the now, a cult of the new ...*).	3	
4	... legt die vom Autor genannte **Beziehung zwischen Großbritanniens wirtschaftlichem bzw. geopolitischem Aufstieg und Shakespeares Popularität** dar, indem er darauf verweist, dass ... • Großbritannien zur Zeit Shakespeares im Begriff war, eine der führenden Weltmächte zu werden (*on the threshold of ...*), • Shakespeare im 18./19. Jahrhundert internationalen Ruhm erlangte, weil Großbritannien zum britischen Empire aufstieg (*creation of the 18th and 19th centuries ... and era when the nation and thus the national poet moved on the world stage ...*), • Shakespeare heute ein „globales Exportprodukt" Großbritanniens darstellt (*almost all the countries ... most enduring cultural export ...*).	3	
5	... erfüllt ein weiteres aufgabenbezogenes Kriterium. (2) •	2	
		12	

Part A: Teilaufgabe 2 (Analysis)

	Anforderungen **Der Schüler/die Schülerin ...**	maximal erreichbare Punktzahl	erreichte Punkte
1	... arbeitet **strukturelle Stilmittel** heraus und weist deren Funktion nach, z. B. • die Vorwegnahme der Darstellung der globalen Bedeutung Shakespeares in der Überschrift (*Now all the world ...*), • die Rahmenstruktur des Aufbaus des Artikels (Überschrift: *Now ...*; abschließender Abschnitt: *Now it is ...*), • die klare lineare Struktur des Artikels, bedingt durch die (historische) Chronologie (*now* → *2016; at the time of this death* → *centenary; 200th anniversary* → *18th and 19th centuries* → *now*).	5	
2	... analysiert **sprachliche Stilmittel** und stellt dar, wie diese den (expositorischen) Charakter des Textes unterstützen. Er/sie verweist z. B. darauf, dass • Bates Englisch zwar verständlich ist, aber er insgesamt einen gehobenen Sprachgebrauch hat und Umgangssprache weitgehend vermeidet (*prologue to, quatercentenary, presumed, conveniently coincides, passed away, auspices, the film contrived, pay hommage to ...*, etc.), • Bates Wortfelder zu den Bereichen „history", „education" und „culture" einarbeitet, • Bates sich durch den Gebrauch von Fachausdrücken (*expert language*) und bestimmten Formulierungen als „expert" in Bezug auf Geschichte und Literatur ausweist (*whose presumed birthday; Restoration of the monarchy; Puritans ...; Civil War; I was asked to join a consultative group advising on ...*, etc.).	5	

3	... analysiert **rhetorische Stilmittel** und verdeutlicht deren Funktion, z. B. • den durchgehenden Gebrauch von „allusions" und „references" auf die britische Geschichte und deren Einfluss auf die Kultur generell und das Theater im Besonderen, • den Gebrauch von „positive emotive words" und Hochwertwörtern im Zusammenhang mit Shakespeare, seinem Können und seinem kulturellen Einfluss (*global icon, admired, a staple part, ahead of the pack, his status as National Poet, exemplar of artistic genius, the triumph of ..., celebrity, the world stage ...,* etc.), • den Gebrauch von Komparativen, Superlativen und „antithesis/contrast" sowie „parallelism",„chiasmus" und „climax" (*global icon – local heritage; much admired; far fewer ...; more frequently; national poet – artistic genius; more important; Elizabethan theatre – modern Hollywood; a rage for the now – a cult of the new; Shakespeare's Britain – Britain's Shakespeare*).	5	
4	... kommt zu einer **Darstellung der „text message" und „author's perspective"** und verdeutlicht z. B. • die von Bate herausgestellte historische Dimension von Shakespeare und seinem Werk, • den zusammenfassend von Bate hervorgehobenen globalen Einfluss von Shakespeares Werk (*but all countries in the world ...*), • die Identifikation Bates mit Shakespeare und seinem literarischen Werk (*use of personal und possessive pronouns: I, we, our*).	5	
5	... erfüllt ein weiteres aufgabenbezogenes Kriterium. (4) •	4	
		20	

Part A: Teilaufgabe 3.1 (Evaluation/Comment)

	Anforderungen Der Schüler/die Schülerin ...	maximal erreichbare Punktzahl	erreichte Punkte
1	... **kommentiert** Bates Ausführungen und verweist z. B. auf • die Parallelen des britischen und deutschen Curriculums, z. B. den umfangreichen Literaturkanon im Deutschunterricht der Oberstufe (Goethe etc.), • die offenbar ähnlich ambitionierten Bildungsziele deutscher und britischer Politiker, die die Situation von Jugendlichen nicht berücksichtigen.	3	
2	... nimmt **vor dem Hintergrund eigener Erfahrungen kritisch Stellung** und stellt z. B. dar, dass • Filme wie *Shakespeare in Love* das Interesse von Jugendlichen an Shakespeare und seinem Werk wecken bzw. steigern können, • es wichtig ist, neben Shakespeare auch noch zeitgenössische Literatur zu lesen.	3	
3	... führt vor dem **Hintergrund seines/ihres Kontextwissens** aus, dass • die schulische Lektüre von literarischen Klassikern selbstverständlich sein sollte, • die schulische Lektüre von Shakespeare mit dem Englisch der modernen Welt wenig zu tun hat und daher wenig „alltagstauglich" ist, • bereits der Begriff „Pflichtlektüre" den Spaß am Lesen nimmt.	5	
4	... kommt vor dem Hintergrund seiner persönlichen Meinungsbildung zu einer **begründeten Schlussfolgerung**, in der er/sie z. B. anführt, dass • die Lektüre von Shakespeare im Englischunterricht durchaus Bedeutung hat, aber in der heutigen Zeit medial vermittelt werden sollte, • man im Unterricht einen zeitgemäßen Umgang mit historischen Autoren und Stoffen finden sollte, um Schüler nicht zu demotivieren, z. B. durch moderne Theater- und Filmadaptionen, • die Lektüre von Shakespeare-Stücken viele Schüler sprachlich überfordert und man stattdessen im Unterricht auf sprachlich einfachere und modernere Literatur zurückgreifen sollte.	5	
5	... erfüllt ein weiteres aufgabenbezogenes Kriterium. (4) •	4	
		16	

Part A: Teilaufgabe 3.2 ((Re-)Creation of text)

	Anforderungen Der Schüler/die Schülerin ...	maximal erreichbare Punktzahl	erreichte Punkte
1	... stellt vor dem **Hintergrund seines/ihres Kontextwissens** über britische Kolonialgeschichte und ausgehend von der Information des Textes dar, dass • die Aussage des Autors nur bedingt zutrifft, da Shakespeares Werk (in der jeweiligen Übersetzung) auch in Ländern erfolgreich ist, die nicht zum britischen Empire gehörten, • die Themen und Motive in Shakespeares Werk so zeitlos und universal sind, dass es keines Empires bedurfte, um Shakespeare berühmt und populär zu machen.	3	
2	... bezieht sich auf weitere **Werke der Weltliteratur** und verweist z. B. auf • deutsche oder französische Dichter der Weltliteratur, die „globalen Status" erlangt haben, obwohl weder Frankreich noch Deutschland jemals einen dem britischen Empire vergleichbaren Status erlangt haben, • die moderne Film- und Medienwelt, die offenbar großes Interesse an historischen Stoffen und Werken hat, weshalb schon deshalb Autoren wie Shakespeare nicht in Vergessenheit geraten.	3	
3	... verarbeitet die **formal-stilistischen Elemente eines „Letter to the Editor"**, z. B. • die persönliche Anrede und die Grußformel zum Schluss des Briefes, • die persönliche Vorstellung und Benennung des Anliegens/Anlasses; die Themenverknüpfung und Argumentation, • die sprachlichen Normen/Formal English/Höflichkeitsfloskeln/Small Talk etc.	5	
4	... kommt zu einem **begründeten Resümee** und führt z. B. an, dass • sich „gute Literatur" immer durchsetzt, unabhängig von politischen Strukturen, • das britische Empire möglicherweise sogar eine Gegenreaktion auf Shakespeare hätte zur Folge haben können, als Reaktion auf die aggressive Politik der Briten, • Shakespeares Stücke so populär geworden sind, weil sie nicht „Britishness" exportieren, sondern universal menschliches Verhalten darstellen und hinterfragen, sowie zeitlose Themen und Motive.	4	
5	... erfüllt ein weiteres aufgabenbezogenes Kriterium. (4) •	4	
		16	

Part B: Viewing Comprehension

	Anforderungen	maximal erreichbare Punktzahl	erreichte Punkte
1	**Viewing Comprehension 1** – je richtige *sentence completion* ein Punkt	10	
2	**Viewing Comprehension 2** – je richtiges Beispiel vier Punkte	20	
		30	

Part B: Viewing Comprehension – Solutions

ASSIGNMENT 1

1c, 2b, 3c, 4a, 5b, 6a, 7c, 8a, 9b, 10a

ASSIGNMENT 2

1. Richard provokes Lady Anne by being aggressive and disrespectful and playing down the murder of her husband, but at the same time, he flirts with her and makes it clear that he wants to kiss her and feels sexually attracted to her.

2. Lady Anne is able to manage the extreme situation of dealing with the sexual advances of her husband's killer while facing her husband's corpse; she is also able to stand her ground against Richard's insults and provocations and to fire back offensive remarks of her own.

3. The scene is very physical because Richard and Lady Anne insult and attack each other verbally, but at the same time, get very close to each other physically and are able to play with the aggressive energy and sexual tension of the scene

4. Richard and Lady Anne are equally strong

   a) verbally because both are able to dish out insults and provocations while dealing with the affronts that the other person is throwing at them,

   b) although Lady Anne is a widowed woman and therefore has a lower status, socially speaking, she nevertheless manages to remain on par with Richard, because he is physically disabled and has a lower status, morally speaking.

5. Kevin Spacey's body language and facial expressions reveal irony and sarcasm; he seems to move backwards and forwards like a crab, but at the same time, confidently laughs, smiles and directly addresses the audience. Despite his aggressiveness, he makes fun of the situation and of himself.

Part B: Viewing Comprehension – Transcript

Kevin Spacey

Now – Richard III Documentary

LADY ANNE Set down, set down your honourable load.

ANNABEL SCHOLEY Quite often she is played as simpery* and a soft, broken woman, and I just didn't see how the scene could work because it's so unbelievable that a woman can go from being so um ... such a mess and in love to being with him at the end of the scene.

5 LADY ANNE O curséd be the hand that made these holes; curséd the heart that had the heart to do it.

KEVIN SPACEY It's the Lady Anne scene that I think shifts* everything for him. Because he's that kind of character that looks at the audience and says 'This is what I'm gonna do.' And then he goes and does it and he's like amazed that he got away with* it.

RICHARD III Stay, you that bear* the corpse*, and set it down. Villains, set down the corpse, or by
10 Saint Paul, I'll make a corpse of him that disobeys.

LADY ANNE Didst thou not kill this king?

RICHARD III I grant you, yeah ...

LADY ANNE Dost grant me, hedgehog?

DOMINIC FRASER (production manager) The absurdity of it makes it funny. And, he just has got such
15 a brilliant way of establishing a relationship with an audience ... a dialogue with an audience ...

ANNABEL SCHOLEY When I got the part, I had that amazing burst of 'Oh my God, I can't believe I've got it ... and like, oh yeah, we're going ...'. And then I suddenly thought 'O fuck, now I actually have to do the job.'
How am I ever gonna do this really intimate scene with, with Kevin? Like I just thought, I mean,
20 I'm never ever gonna be able to do it. And I know, Kevin wanted the scene to be really hot and more about sex than about love.

LADY ANNE Where is he?

RICHARD III Here. [she spits at him] Why dost thou spit at me?

LADY ANNE Would it were mortal* poison, for thy sake!

25 RICHARD III Never came poison from such sweet a place.

ANNABEL SCHOLEY It took a long time in rehearsals because the scene is really a tango*. It's a really physical scene. And, until we found each other's energy, it sort of ... it was quite ... it was bumpy. Sam gave me a note. He said, 'Drop your voice.' Because she's like this rock of a woman, you know. And that, just that note, really helped me, because I realized 'Okay, you're not playing little
30 girls anymore, Annabel. You're ... She's a woman'. And that thought brought strength for me to the part.
As we get to know each other better, we're more daring* with each other physically and really go for* it. And it's just so fun, every night. It's brilliant.

RICHARD III Was ever woman in this humor* wooed*? Was ever woman in this humor won? I'll
35 have her, but I will not keep her long.

KEVIN SPACEY He's talking to the audience; he's making them his co-conspirators. They love it, against their better judgment. And I think that gives him bigger cojones* to go out and try even ... 'Well, if I can get away with that, what else can I get away with?' I think that eggs him on* and gives him more internal power. *(555 words)*

taken from http://www.kevinspacey.com/nowthefilm, transcript by Iris Edelbrock

*vocab given along with the assignments

Topic: Shakespeare – The Impact of Shakespearean Drama on Young Audiences Today

Skills: Analysis of a non-fictional text (play); continuation of a fictional text (*Zieltextformat*); viewing comprehension;

Texts: **Part A:** William Shakespeare: Othello. Act III, Scene 3 (614 words)
Part B: Kenneth Branagh: Othello. Act III, Scene 3 (02:59 mins)

Part A: Reading/Writing

William Shakespeare

Othello

OTHELLO
Villain[1], be sure thou prove my love a whore,
Be sure of it; give me the ocular[2] proof:
Or by the worth of mine eternal soul
Thou hadst been better have been born a dog
5 Than answer my waked wrath[3]!

IAGO
Is't come to this?

OTHELLO
Make me to see't; or, at the least, so prove it,
That the probation[4] bear no hinge nor loop[5]
To hang a doubt on; or woe[6] upon thy life!

IAGO
10 My noble lord, –

OTHELLO
If thou dost slander[7] her and torture me,
Never pray more; abandon all remorse[8];
On horror's head horrors accumulate[9];
Do deeds to make heaven weep, all earth amazed;
15 For nothing canst thou to damnation[10] add
Greater than that.

IAGO
O grace! O heaven forgive me!
Are you a man? have you a soul or sense?
God be wi' you; take mine office[11]. O wretched[12] fool.
20 That livest to make thy honesty a vice[13]!
O monstrous world! Take note, take note, O world,
To be direct and honest is not safe.
I thank you for this profit[14]; and from hence[15]
I'll love no friend, sith[16] love breeds such offence.

OTHELLO
25 Nay, stay: thou shouldst be honest.

---

[1] **villain** an evil person – [2] **ocular** visual – [3] **waked wrath** [rɒθ] aroused anger – [4] **probation** trial, testing process –
[5] **to bear no hinge nor loop** *weder Haken noch Aufhänger haben* — [6] **woe upon thy life** may you live to regret it –
[7] **to slander sb.** to damage sb.'s reputation by telling lies about them – [8] **to abandon all remorse** to act without
mercy or pity – [9] **to accumulate** *anhäufen* – [10] **damnation** *Verdammung* – [11] **office** here: job – [12] **wretched** unfortunate, miserable – [13] **vice** a moral fault or weakness in sb.'s character – [14] **profit** here: valuable lesson – [15] **hence**
now on – [16] **sith** (*old*) since

IAGO
I should be wise, for honesty is a fool
And loses that it works for.

OTHELLO
By the world,
I think my wife be honest and think she is not;
30 I think thou art just and think thou art not.
I'll have some proof. Her name, that was as fresh
As Dian's[17] visage[18], is now begrimed[19] and black
As mine own face. If there be cords[20], or knives,
Poison or fire, or suffocating[21] streams,
35 I'll not endure it. Would I were satisfied!

IAGO
I see, sir, you are eaten up with passion:
I do repent[22] me that I put it to you.
You would be satisfied?

OTHELLO
Would! nay, I will.

IAGO
40 And may: but, how? how satisfied, my lord?
Would you, the supervisor[23], grossly[24] gape on[25] –
Behold[26] her topp'd[27]?

OTHELLO
Death and damnation! O!

IAGO
It were a tedious[28] difficulty, I think,
45 To bring them to that prospect[29]: damn them then,
If ever mortal eyes do see them bolster[30]
More than their own! What then? how then?
What shall I say? Where's satisfaction?
It is impossible you should see this,
50 Were they as prime[31] as goats, as hot as monkeys,
As salt[32] as wolves in pride[33], and fools as gross[34]
As ignorance made drunk. But yet, I say,
If imputation[35] and strong circumstances,
Which lead directly to the door of truth,
55 Will give you satisfaction, you may have't.

OTHELLO
Give me a living[36] reason she's disloyal.

IAGO
I do not like the office:
But: sith I am enter'd in this cause so far,
Prick'd[37] to't by foolish honesty and love,
60 I will go on. I lay with Cassio lately;
And, being troubled with a raging[38] tooth,

---

[17] **Dian** = Diana: Roman virgin goddess of the moon, hunting and childbirth and protector of women – [18] **visage** face – [19] **begrimed** *beschmutzt* – [20] **cord** rope or string – [21] **suffocating** *erstickend* – [22] **to repent** [rɪˈpent] (*fml.*) to regret, be sorry – [23] **supervisor** sb. who watches over sb. or sth. – [24] **grossly** extremely – [25] **to gape on** *gaffen* — [26] **to behold sb./sth.** to look at sb./sth. – [27] **topp'd** here: having sex with sb. – [28] **tedious** [ˈtiːdɪəs] *langwierig* – [29] **prospect** here: *Perspektive* – [30] **to bolster** to share the same pillow – [31] **prime** (*infml.*) *geil* – [32] **salt** (*infml.*) *geil* – [33] **in pride** in heat – [34] **gross** vulgar, unrefined – [35] **imputation** (*fml.*) a suggestion that sb. is guilty – [36] **living** here: real, genuine – [37] **prick'd** instigated, *aufgewiegelt* – [38] **raging** here: extremely painful

I could not sleep.
There are a kind of men so loose of soul,
That in their sleeps will mutter their affairs:
65 One of this kind is Cassio:
In sleep I heard him say 'Sweet Desdemona,
Let us be wary[39], let us hide our loves,'
And then sir, would he gripe and wring[40] my hand,
Cry 'O sweet creature!' and then kiss me hard,
70 As if he pluck'd up[41] kisses by the roots
That grew upon my lips: then laid his leg
Over my thigh[42], and sigh'd, and kiss'd; and then
Cried: 'Cursed fate that gave thee to the Moor!'

OTHELLO
O monstrous! monstrous!

IAGO
75 Nay, this was but his dream.

OTHELLO
But this denoted[43] a foregone conclusion:
'Tis a shrewd[44] doubt, though it be but a dream.

IAGO
And this may help to thicken[45] other proofs[46]
That do demonstrate thinly.

OTHELLO
80 I'll tear her to pieces. (*614 words*)

William Shakespeare: Othello. Ed. Brainerd Kellogg. Clark & Maynard, New York 1892

---

[39] **wary** careful, alert – [40] **to gripe and wring sth** to grab hold of sth. and twist it with your hands – [41] **to pluck sth. up by the roots** *etw. an den Wurzeln packen* – [42] **thigh** *Oberschenkel* – [43] **to denote** to indicate sth. – [44] **shrewd** ominous, bitter – [45] **to thicken** here: to support – [46] **proof** *Beweis*

ASSIGNMENTS

Othello, the story of a Moorish (*maurisch*) general, is set in Venice against the backdrop of the military conflict between Venice and Turkey.

Othello and the beautiful Desdemona have married secretly against the will of her father, Brabanzio. Othello's major antagonist in the play, Iago, hates him because Othello recently passed him over for the position of a grip lieutenant in favour of the inexperienced soldier Cassio.

In an act of revenge, Iago deceives Othello into believing that his wife is unfaithful and that she is having an affair with Cassio.

1. Give an outline of the conversation between Othello and Iago, stating
    a) how Iago discredits Desdemona and
    b) Othello's reaction to it.
    (*Comprehension*)

2. Characterize Iago's behaviour and the strategy he uses to incite Othello's jealousy and suspicions against Desdemona by analysing the stylistic and rhetorical devices that are employed in his speech.
    (*Analysis*)

3. You have a choice here. Choose **one** of the following tasks:

    3.1 Most scholars consider Shakespeare and his works to be "ageless" and "universal".
        Comment on this thesis by referring to
        a) relevant aspects and motifs in the scene at hand, and
        b) your knowledge of Shakespeare and his works and relevant aspects that you dealt with in
           class.
        (*Comment/Evaluation*)

    3.2 After the conversation with Iago, Othello is furious and takes Desdemona to task, demanding that she declares her position.
        Write a dialogue between Othello and Desdemona, in which you take into account that
        a) Othello is a very jealous and passionate man, and
        b) Desdemona is, in fact, innocent and is a faithful, devoted and loving wife to her husband.
        (*(Re-) Creation of text*)

Part B: Viewing Comprehension

William Shakespeare

Othello (Act III, Scene 3)

The scene at hand depicts a heated conversation between Othello and Iago, who is trying to make Othello suspect that his wife, Desdemona, is unfaithful and deceitful and that she is having an affair with Iago's good friend Cassio.

Source: Warner Bros. USA 1995 (02:59 mins)

Annotations ⟫

I prithee (*old*) from "I pray thee", here: *ich bitte dich* ■ **to ruminate** to think deeply about sth. ■ **to utter** to express ■ **vile** terrible, disgusting ■ **whereinto** (*old*) into which ■ **to intrude** *eindringen* ■ **apprehension** suspicion ■ **to keep leets** (*old*) *Hof halten* ■ **to sit in session** *tagen* ■ **meditations lawful** here: *zugelassene Gedanken* ■ **to conspire against sb.** *sich gegen jdn. verschwören* ■ **to beseech sb.** *jdn. flehentlich um etwas bitten* ■ **perchance** (*old*) perhaps ■ **vicious** *boshaft* ■ **it is my nature's plague** it is a bad habit of mine ■ **to conceit** (*old*) to imagine ■ **scattering** *zerstreut* ■ **observance** observation ■ **quiet** here: peace of mind ■ **good** here: well-being ■ **purse** *Geldbeutel* ■ **to filch** to steal ■ **custody** *Obhut* ■ **beware** watch out! ■ **to mock** to make fun of, to disrespect ■ **cuckold** (*old*) husband whose wife is unfaithful ■ **bliss** *Seligkeit* ■ **certain of his fate** here: knowing for sure that his wife is cheating on him ■ **wronger** here: the unfaithful wife ■ **to dote** to care deeply for sb. ■ **fineless** infinite, without end ■ **tribe** family ■ **to defend sb. from sth.** *jdn. vor etw. bewahren* ■ **resolved** set free from doubt ■ **exsufflicate and blown** overblown, puffed up ■ **surmise** *Mutmaßung* ■ **matching** similar to ■ **inference** hint, suggestion ■ **fair** here: beautiful ■ **merit** (*fml.*) good and praiseworthy characteristic ■ **revolt** betrayal, change of heart ■ **frank** honest, sincere ■ **to bind sb. to do sth.** (*phr. v.*) to force sb. to keep a promise ■ **to wear one's eye** (*old*) to look a certain way ■ **self-bounty** kindness ■ **disposition** nature, character ■ **pranks** here: shameful and excessive behaviour ■ **to shake and fear sb.'s looks** *von jdm. eingeschüchtert sein* ■ **seeming** pretence, *Schein* ■ **Why, go to then** *Na, da hast du es!* ■ **humbly** *bescheiden* ■ **to dash sb.'s spirits** to discourage, depress sb.

ASSIGNMENT 1 ⟫⟫⟫

1. Watch the scene and decide whether the following statements are true, false or not given in the text.

	True	False	Not given
a) Othello wants Iago to tell him his worst thoughts.	☐	☐	☐
b) Iago tells Othello about his suspicions right away.	☐	☐	☐
c) Othello wants to know what Desdemona told Iago about Cassio.	☐	☐	☐
d) Iago at first refuses to speak to Othello frankly because he is worried about making wrong accusations.	☐	☐	☐
e) Iago thinks that losing one's good name is worse than being robbed.	☐	☐	☐
f) Iago tells Othello that there is no reason to be jealous.	☐	☐	☐
g) Othello wants to confront his wife with the accusations.	☐	☐	☐

	True	False	Not given
h) Othello says that he can trust his wife and wants Iago to prove his accusations.	☐	☐	☐
i) Iago wants Othello to make Desdemona stay at home because people in Venice are gossiping about her affair.	☐	☐	☐
j) Iago implies that Desdemona cannot be trusted in general because she deceived her father by secretly marrying Othello.	☐	☐	☐

(10 x 2 points)

ASSIGNMENT 2

Before watching the scene a second time, study the following assignments. Afterwards, take notes related to the correct answers.

1. Name four cinematic devices that are used in the scene to highlight the characters' emotions.

   1 _____

   2 _____

   3 _____

   4 _____

2. Jealousy is a green-eyed monster, which …

   _____

3. According to Iago, losing one's good reputation is …

   _____

4. Othello thinks that he has no reason to be jealous because his wife is …

   _____

5. In Othello's view, having exact proof of something helps to …

   _____

6. Iago advises Othello to keep an eye on Desdemona because he thinks Venice is a place …

   _____

7. At the end of the scene, Iago has "dashed Othello's spirits" because …

   _____

(10 points)

Bewertungsbogen für: _____ Kurs: _____

Part A: Teilaufgabe 1 (Comprehension)

	Anforderungen **Der Schüler/die Schülerin ...**	maximal erreichbare Punktzahl	erreichte Punkte
1	... arbeitet die **Struktur und den Verlauf der Dialogszene** heraus und benennt z. B. ● Iagos deutlich höheren Redeanteil, ● Othellos von Anfang an aggressive Grundhaltung im Gegensatz zu Iagos eher vorsichtiger Vorgehensweise (*Is't come to this?, My noble lord* ...), ● dass Iago am Ende der Szene sein Ziel erreicht hat: Othello zweifelt an Desdemonas Treue und ist noch aggressiver (*'Tis a shrewd doubt; I'll tear her to pieces* ...).	3	
2	... skizziert **Iagos „Strategie"**, mit der er Othello beeinflusst und stellt z. B. dar, dass ● Iago zunächst seine Ehrlichkeit und seine uneingeschränkte Treue/Dienstbarkeit gegenüber Othello hervorhebt (*take mine office; I thank you* ...), ● Iago Othello gewissermaßen dahingehend ausfragt, was ihn als Beweis zufriedenstellen würde (*how? how satisfied?; you, the supervisor, grossly gape on ...; where's satisfaction?*), ● Iago vorschlägt, Desdemona sozusagen „in flagranti delicto" zu überführen (*were they ... as hot as monkeys ... strong circumstances ... which lead directly to the door of truth ... you may hav't ...*).	3	
3	... beschreibt **Iagos „Beweise"**, die Desdemonas Untreue und verräterischen Charakter belegen sollen, z. B. ● Iagos Verweis auf Cassios „losen Charakter", ● dass er Cassio im Schlaf belauscht hat, ● Cassios offensichtliche sexuelle Affäre mit Desdemona, ● Cassios Hass auf Othello.	3	
4	... zeigt **Othellos Reaktionen** auf Iagos Verdächtigungen und Beschuldigungen auf, z. B. ● sein aggressives Verhalten gegen Iago und seine Verdächtigungen eingangs der Szene (*Villain ... be sure ... answer my waked wrath* ...), ● seine zunehmend emotionalen Ausbrüche, ● sein anfängliches Schwanken zwischen Eifersucht, verletztem Stolz und den daraus resultierenden Forderungen nach Gewissheit und Beweisen (*my wife be honest ... she is not; thou art just ... thou art not ...* ➔ *I'll have some proof; Give me a living reason* ...), ● Othellos zunehmende Aggression und Zweifel (*a foregone conclusion ... a shrewd doubt ... I'll tear her to pieces*).	3	
5	... erfüllt ein weiteres aufgabenbezogenes Kriterium. (2) ●	2	
		12	

Part A: Teilaufgabe 2 (Analysis)

	Anforderungen **Der Schüler/die Schülerin ...**	maximal erreichbare Punktzahl	erreichte Punkte
1	... charakterisiert **Iagos Verhalten** und erläutert z. B. ● Iagos hinterlistige und hinterbriebene Schmeichelei Othello gegenüber (*My noble lord; O heaven forgive me!; God be with you; thine honesty ...; I do repent me that I put it to you* ...), ● Iagos Spiel mit Halbwahrheiten und Andeutungen (*to be direct and honest is not safe; if ever mortal eyes do bolster ...; if imputation and strong circumstances ... you may hav't ...; this was but his dream; this may help* ...), ● Iagos Fähigkeit, gezielt Othellos „wunden Punkt" zu treffen: die Sorge um seinen guten Ruf und seine Emotionalität und Neigung zu Eifersucht (*Are you a man?; you are eaten up with passion ...; they as prime goats, as hot as monkeys ...; men so loose of soul* ➔ *one of this is Cassio* ...).	5	
2	... untersucht **Iagos persuasive Strategien**, indem er/sie z. B. verdeutlicht, dass ● Iago Othellos anfängliche Drohungen geschickt abmildert, indem er den Unwissenden und Unschuldigen spielt (*Is't come to this?; My noble lord ...; O grace! O heaven forgive me!; O wretched fool* ...), ● Iago Othellos Emotionalität aufgreift und den Leidenden bzw. Entrüsteten spielt (*O Grace ...! O monstrous world! ...; love breeds no such offence* ...), ● Iago Othellos Bemerkungen konkret aufgreift und ihm damit das Gefühl vermittelt, nicht der aktive Part zu sein, sondern durch Othello bedrängt zu werden (*Othello: heaven weep ... earth amazed* ➔ *Iago: O heaven forgive me! ... O monstrous world!; Othello: thou should be honest* ➔ *Iago: honesty is a fool* ...).	5	

3	... benennt und analysiert **rhetorische Stilmittel und deren Funktion** und benennt z. B. • den Gebrauch von (rhetorischen) Fragen zur Lenkung von Othellos Reaktionen (*Is't come to this?; Are you a man? Have you a soul or sense?; You would be satisfied? ...*), • den Einsatz von *contrast/antithesis* zur Verstärkung des Verrats durch Desdemona und Cassio (*honesty – vice; love – offence; vice – God; honest/just – dishonest/unjust; fresh – begrimed ...*), • den Einsatz von Wortfeldern zu den Themen und Leitmotiven *honesty, sexuality/desire, deception, emotion/passion.*	5	
4	... untersucht *weitere Stilmittel*, die Iagos manipulatives Verhalten hervorheben und weist sie am Text nach, z. B. • den Gebrauch von Konjunktionen, die Aussagen ganz oder teilweise zurücknehmen (*But yet, I say ...; I do not like ... But: sith I am ...*), • den Gebrauch von Steigerung/Klimax (*goats ... monkeys ... wolves ... fools; gripe ... wring ... kiss ... sigh'd ... cried*) und Metaphern (*monstrous world; honesty is a fool; the door of truth ...*) sowie Personifikationen (*love breeds ...; ignorance made drunk ...*), • Iagos *gossiping* im Zusammenhang mit *eavesdropping* (*I will go on. I lay with Cassio ... in their sleep will mutter their affairs ...*).	5	
5	... erfüllt ein weiteres aufgabenbezogenes Kriterium. (4) •	4	
		20	

Part A: Teilaufgabe 3.1 (Evaluation/Comment)

	Anforderungen	maximal erreichbare Punktzahl	erreichte Punkte
	Der Schüler/die Schülerin ...		
1	... nimmt Bezug auf **zentrale Motive/Leitmotive des Textausschnitts** und führt dabei z. B. an, dass • Themen wie Eifersucht, Beziehungsprobleme, Ehebruch etc. zeitlos und universal sind, • Iagos Verhalten (Betrug, Verrat, Lauschen etc.) ebenfalls zeitlos ist und beispielsweise zentraler Stoff von modernen Filmen, Fernsehserien, *soap operas* etc. ist, • Themen wie „verletzter Stolz, Ehre, Rache" etc., die im Drama mit Othello verknüpft sind, auch im 21. Jahrhundert „modern" sind.	3	
2	... greift das **Gesprächsverhalten der beiden Figuren** auf und stellt z. B. dar, dass • Iagos hinterlistige Strategie durchaus „modern" ist und sozusagen zeitgemäße Rhetorik darstellt, • die generell von Iago verwendeten rhetorischen Mittel, z. B. seine Anspielungen und Andeutungen und das „Weitertratschen" von Belauschtem, sowohl zeitgemäße Mittel z. B. der heutigen Werbung als auch „typisch" menschliches Verhalten widerspiegeln.	3	
3	... nimmt Bezug auf **weitere zentrale Aspekte von Shakespeares Werk**, die auch im 21. Jahrhundert aktuell sind, z. B. • *sex and betrayal vs. honour and virtue,* • *betrayal ➔ occular proof,* • *revenge/vengeance.*	5	
4	... kommt zu einer **begründeten Stellungnahme**, die sich schlüssig aus den Ausführungen ergibt, z. B. • stimmt er/sie dieser These zu, auch mit Blick darauf, dass Shakespeare-Aufführungen immer noch Publikumsmagnete sind, d. h. die heutigen Zuschauer thematisch/emotional ansprechen, • schränkt er/sie die These ein, z. B. mit einem Verweis darauf, dass nur moderne Shakespeare-Adaptionen eine gewisse Zeitlosigkeit garantieren, • lehnt er/sie die These ab und benennt dafür z. B. Shakespeares (veraltete) Sprache, veränderte Beziehungen der Menschen in der heutigen Zeit, veränderte Lebensbedingungen etc.	5	
5	... erfüllt ein weiteres aufgabenbezogenes Kriterium. (4) •	4	
		16	

Part A: Teilaufgabe 3.2 ((Re-)Creation of text)

	Anforderungen	maximal erreichbare Punktzahl	erreichte Punkte
	Der Schüler/die Schülerin ...		
1	... versetzt sich in **Othellos Situation** und berücksichtigt dabei z. B. • seine glühende Eifersucht und Emotionalität, • sein verletztes Ehrgfühl/Schamgefühl, • die „Information", die ihm Iago gegeben hat.	3	
2	... versetzt sich in **Desdemonas Lage** und führt z. B. an, dass • sie von den Vorwürfen vollkommen überrascht – und entsprechend schockiert und entsetzt ist, • sie versucht, ihren Mann zu beruhigen und die „Beweise" zu entkräften, • sie ebenfalls einen *emotional outburst* hat, verzweifelt ist etc.	3	
3	... greift den **Dialogcharakter der Situation** auf, indem er/sie ... • beide Figuren abwechselnd zu Wort kommen lässt, • die Redeanteile der beiden Figuren situations- und rollengemäß anpasst, • die Dialogpartner aufeinander eingehen lässt.	5	
4	... berücksichtigt die der **Situation und der Position der Figuren entsprechende Sprache**, z. B. • greift er/sie Othellos Sprachstil aus der Szene auf, • lässt er/sie die Figuren sprachlich „interagieren" (Verwendung von Ausrufen, Interjektionen, Unterbrechungen etc.), • die *gender roles* vor dem Hintergrund des Elisabethanischen Zeitalters (Dominanz des Mannes, Devotheit der Frau etc.).	5	
5	... erfüllt ein weiteres aufgabenbezogenes Kriterium. (4) •	4	
		16	

Part B: Viewing Comprehension

	Anforderungen	maximal erreichbare Punktzahl	erreichte Punkte
1	**Viewing Comprehension 1** – 10 x 2 Punkte	20	
2	**Viewing Comprehension 2** – je Antwort 1 Punkt	10	
		30	

Part B: Viewing Comprehension – Solutions

a = true; b = false; c = not given; d = true; e = true; f = false; g = not given; h = true; i = false; j = true

1. 1) high angle ➜ Othello's physical dominance
   2) close-up on eyes ➜ emotional reaction; aggression; fear
   3) establishing shot ➜ orientation for the viewer
   4) reverse angle shots ➜ Iago's/Othello's reactions to each other
2. … falsifies and distorts people's perception of reality.
3. … worse than being robbed or being poor.
4. … fair, feeds well, loves to play, is free of speech.
5. … drive away doubt, jealousy, or end a relationship/marriage.
6. … full of deception where people cover up affairs.
7. … he has made Othello suspicious of his wife/… he has reminded Othello of Desdemona's deception of her father.

Part B: Viewing Comprehension – Transcript

William Shakespeare

Othello

OTHELLO
Nay, yet there's more in this:
I prithee*, speak to me as to thy thinkings,
As thou dost ruminate*, and give thy worst of thoughts
The worst of words.

IAGO
5 Good my lord, pardon me:
Though I am bound to every act of duty,
I am not bound to that all slaves are free to.
Utter* my thoughts? Why, say they are vile and false;
As where's that palace whereinto foul things
10 Sometimes intrude* not? who has a breast so pure,
But some uncleanly apprehensions*
Keep leets* and law-days and in session sit*
With meditations lawful*?

OTHELLO
Thou dost conspire* against thy friend, Iago,
15 If thou but think'st him wrong'd and makest his ear
A stranger to thy thoughts.

IAGO
I do beseech you –
Though I perchance am vicious* in my guess,
As, I confess, it is my nature's plague*
20 To spy into abuses, and oft my jealousy
Shapes faults that are not – that your wisdom yet,
From one that so imperfectly conceits*,
Would take no notice, nor build yourself a trouble
Out of his scattering* and unsure observance*.
25 It were not for your quiet* nor your good*,
Nor for my manhood, honesty, or wisdom,
To let you know my thoughts.

OTHELLO
What dost thou mean?

IAGO
Good name in man and woman, dear my lord,
30 Is the immediate jewel of their souls:
Who steals my purse* steals trash; 'tis something, nothing;
'Twas mine, 'is his, and has been slave to thousands:
But he that filches* from me my good name
Robs me of that which not enriches him
35 And makes me poor indeed.

OTHELLO
By heaven, I'll know thy thoughts.

IAGO
You cannot, if my heart were in your hand;
Nor shall not, whilst 'tis in my custody*.

OTHELLO
Ha!

IAGO
40 O, beware, my lord, of jealousy;
It is the green-eyed monster which doth mock*
The meat it feeds on; that cuckold* lives in bliss*
Who, certain of his fate*, loves not his wronger*;
But, O, what damned minutes tells he o'er
45 Who dotes*, yet doubts, suspects, yet strongly loves!

OTHELLO
O misery!

IAGO
Poor and content is rich and rich enough,
But riches fineless* is as poor as winter
To him that ever fears he shall be poor.
50 Good heaven, the souls of all my tribe* defend*
From jealousy!

OTHELLO
Why, why is this?
Think'st thou I'ld make a lie of jealousy,
To follow still the changes of the moon
55 With fresh suspicions? No; to be once in doubt
Is once to be resolved: exchange me for a goat,
When I shall turn the business of my soul
To such exsufflicate and blown surmises,
Matching thy inference. 'Tis not to make me jealous
60 To say my wife is fair, feeds well, loves company,
Is free of speech, sings, plays and dances well;
Where virtue is, these are more virtuous:
Nor from mine own weak merits will I draw
The smallest fear or doubt of her revolt;
65 For she had eyes, and chose me. No, Iago;
I'll see before I doubt; when I doubt, prove;
And on the proof, there is no more but this,–
Away at once with love or jealousy!

IAGO
I am glad of it; for now I shall have reason
70 To show the love and duty that I bear you
With franker spirit: therefore, as I am bound,
Receive it from me. I speak not yet of proof.
Look to your wife; observe her well with Cassio;
Wear your eye thus, not jealous nor secure:
75 I would not have your free and noble nature,
Out of self-bounty, be abused; look to't:
I know our country disposition well;
In Venice they do let heaven see the pranks
They dare not show their husbands; their best conscience
80 Is not to leave't undone, but keep't unknown.

OTHELLO
Dost thou say so?

IAGO
She did deceive her father, marrying you;
And when she seem'd to shake and fear your looks,
She loved them most.

OTHELLO
85 And so she did.

IAGO
Why, go to then;

She that, so young, could give out such a seeming*
To seal her father's eyes up close as oak -
He thought 'twas witchcraft – but I am much to blame;
90 I humbly do beseech you of your pardon
For too much loving you.

OTHELLO
I am bound to thee forever.

IAGO
I see this hath a little dash'd your spirits.

(728 words)

William Shakespeare: Othello. Ed. Brainerd Kellogg. Clark & Maynard, New York 1892

*vocab given along with the assignments

Topic: The UK – Between Tradition and Modernity

Skills: Analysis of a non-fictional text (newspaper article); writing a letter to the editor (*Zieltextformat*)

Text: Royal Reform: The Royal Family Must Modernise in Order to Endure, The Times, 2015 (565 words)

Reading/Writing

Royal Reform: The Royal Family Must Modernise in Order to Endure

It is 14 years since the Duke of York[1] left the navy, and four since he stood down as the UK's special representative for international trade and investment. Since 1996 he has been unmarried. He is now under the intense pressure to respond personally and forcefully to allegations[2] that in 2001 he had sex with a 17-year-old girl procured[3] for money and his amusement by a friend.

5 Whatever the veracity[4] of these claims, it is clear that while Prince Andrew's life out of uniform has not been short of entertainment, it has been short of structure. He has been content to craft for himself the portfolio[5] existence of a freelance[6] royal.

He has depended too much on his friends to help to support a lifestyle that, even as a scion[7] of one of Britain's richest families, he could not fund himself. And he has chosen those friends poorly.

10 As a result he is caught up in a scandal that will infuriate the Queen because of its potential to tarnish[8] not merely his own reputation but that of the royal family, so painstakingly[9] restored over the past two decades.

In the early 1990s the Queen acted decisively after what she called her annus horribilis[10] to end the perception of a royal family gallivanting[11] at public expense. She promised to pay income tax. Time

15 was called[12] on the civil list[13]. Plans were drawn up to decommission[14] the Royal Yacht Britannia at considerable personal anguish for herself.

A series of lawyers' claims on behalf of a woman identified as Virginia Roberts do not yet constitute a crisis of confidence for the royals. Even so, a decisive response is needed. Put bluntly[15], the royal family, as an institution, is too big.

20 Too many of its members have official roles or spend time seeking them for want of[16] conventional occupations. For the sake of the family, and for the country, it should be streamlined.

As elected leaders wrestle with tight budgets and taxpayers struggle to fund them, it is only right that the royal family cuts its cloth accordingly[17]. This is not only a question of funds, but of expectations and an evolving[18] sense of what the monarchy stands for.

25 It has endured as a symbol of constancy and as a ceremonial focal point at times of national mourning and celebration. To go on enduring it must become more like the royal families that co-exist comfortably with modernity elsewhere in Europe, and less like the retrograde[19] clichés foisted[20] on it by an endlessly fascinated media.

The monarchy's official duties should be performed by the Queen and those in direct line to suc-
30 ceed her. Their siblings and cousins have often set inspiring examples. The Princess Royal's[21] role

---

[1] **the Duke of York** Prince Andrew (*1960), the 2nd son and 3rd child of the Queen – [2] **allegation** (*fml.*) *Beschuldigung* – [3] **to procure** (*fml.*) to get a prostitute for sb. else to have sex with – [4] **veracity** (*fml.*) truth – [5] **portfolio** (*BE*) a particular area of responsibility, esp. of a member of parliament – [6] **freelance** able to work freely for many different organizations rather than being officially employed by a single organization – [7] **scion** ['saɪən] (*lit.*) a young member of a rich and famous family – [8] **to tarnish** *beflecken* – [9] **painstaking** involving great care and effort – [10] **annus horribilis** [ˈænəs həˈrɪbɪlɪs] (*Lat.*) a horrible year filled with extremely bad events – [11] **to gallivant** (*infml.*) to go from one place to another looking for fun and entertainment without worrying about other things you should be doing – [12] **to call time** (*BE, idiom*) to decide to end sth. – [13] **the Civil List** a sum of money granted by British Parliament each year to help the British royal family cover expenses; officially abolished in 2011 – [14] **to decommission** here: to take a ship out of active use – [15] **blunt** *unverblümt* – [16] **for want of sth.** because of the need for sth. – [17] **to cut one's cloth accordingly** (*idiom*) to live within one's means – [18] **evolving** developing gradually – [19] **retrograde** returning to earlier and worse conditions – [20] **to foist sth. on sb.** to force sb. to accept sth. they do not want – [21] **Princess Royal** Anne (*1950) the only daughter of the Queen

as Olympic competitor and ambassador, Prince Harry's service in Afghanistan and his uncle Andrew's in the Falklands[22] come to mind. [...]

Britain's royal family has 18 official members, according to its website. Sweden's and Belgium's have nine, Denmark's seven and Norway's five, all keeping official numbers low by making clear

35 distinctions between those with representative duties and those without.

The House of Windsor needs more clarity among these lines. More importantly, it needs a clearer vision of itself, not as a crisis-prone[23] family business but as a family led by the head of state. Last year Spain's king abdicated; this year his daughter could face trial for fraud[24]. No royal family is indispensable[25], or permanent. (*565 words*)

The Times, 7 January 2015

ASSIGNMENTS

1. Point out the British royal family's appearance and conduct in the public eye, as well as the conclusions the author draws from his observations.
   (*Comprehension*)

2. Analyse the linguistic and rhetorical means the author employs to get across his message and view of Britain's royal family.
   (*Analysis*)

3. You have a choice here. Choose **one** of the following tasks:

   3.1 Discuss the overall message of the article, taking into consideration information given in the article itself, as well as work done in class on the British monarchy and modern democracy.
       (*Comment/Evaluation*)

   3.2 Imagine you are a British citizen who is
       a) critical of the monarchy and the royal family *or*
       b) in favour of the monarchy and the royals.

       Write a letter to the editor in response to the article and state your views.
       In addition to the aspects depicted in the article itself, take further aspects into consideration that you have dealt with in class.
       ((*Re-*)*Creation of text*)

[22]**the Falklands** British Overseas Territory; reference to the Falklands War (April to June 1982) – [23]**prone** likely to show a particular negative characteristic – [24]**fraud** [frɔːd] *Betrug* – [25]**indispensable** *unverzichtbar*

<table>
<tr><td>Bewertungsbogen für: _____</td><td>Kurs: _____</td></tr>
</table>

Part A: Teilaufgabe 1 (Comprehension)

	Anforderungen Der Schüler/die Schülerin ...	maximal erreichbare Punktzahl	erreichte Punkte
1	... umreißt das **dargestellte Verhalten des Duke of York** (Prince Andrew) und benennt z.B., dass • Prince Andrew seit seinem Austritt aus der Royal Navy in zahlreiche Skandale verwickelt war, • Prince Andrew sich (finanziell) von falschen Freunden abhängig gemacht hat und offenbar einen zweifelhaften Lebenswandel führt(e), • Prince Andrew trotz der umfangreichen finanziellen Mittel, die er als Mitglied des Königshauses erhält, seinen (verschwenderischen) Lebenswandel nicht eigenständig finanzieren kann.	4	
2	... beschreibt die **Rolle der Queen** und ihre Reaktion auf die Situation und verweist z.B. darauf, dass • die von ihr durchgeführten umfangreichen „Reparaturmaßnahmen" am Image des Königshauses durch neue Skandale zunichte gemacht wurden, • die Queen versprochen hat, Einkommensteuer zu zahlen, um das Image der Königsfamilie mit Blick auf deren Verschwendungssucht aufzubessern, • die Queen sogar bereit war, die von ihr geliebte *Royal Yacht Britannia* stillzulegen.	4	
3	... beschreibt das **Auftreten und Verhalten anderer europäischer Königsfamilien** – im Gegensatz zu den britischen Royals – und erwähnt z. B. • deren deutlich begrenzte Anzahl auf einen unmittelbaren „harten Kern", • die dort vorgenommene deutliche Differenzierung zwischen Mitgliedern der Königsfamilie mit und ohne repräsentative Pflichten (und entsprechender Finanzierung), • das deutlich modernere und den öffentlichen Medien entsprechende und nicht skandalträchtige Auftreten der anderen europäischen Königshäuser.	4	
4	... arbeitet das **Resümee des Autors** heraus, indem er/sie z.B. • eine Reduktion der (finanziell geförderten) Mitglieder des britischen Königshauses fordert, • ein skandalfreies und den Gegebenheiten des modernen Lebens angepasstes Auftreten und einen entsprechenden Lebensstil der Royals fordert, • darauf hinweist, dass ein Königshaus auch abgeschafft werden könnte.	4	
5	... erfüllt ein weiteres aufgabenbezogenes Kriterium. (2) •	2	
		16	

Part A: Teilaufgabe 2 (Analysis)

	Anforderungen Der Schüler/die Schülerin ...	maximal erreichbare Punktzahl	erreichte Punkte
1	... untersucht die **Struktur des Textes** und verweist z. B. auf • den progressiven Aufbau des Artikels (*problem → solution, arrangement*), • die inhaltlich klare Strukturierung (Einleitung – Hauptteil – Schluss/*topical order*), • die thematische Fokussierung (*The Royal Family Must Modernise ... No royal family is indispensable ...*).	6	
2	... analysiert **sprachliche Stilmittel**, die die kritisch-distanzierte Perspektive des Autors betonen, z. B. • den durchgehenden Gebrauch von *Standard* bzw. *Formal English*, um die Seriosität des Autors zu betonen (*allegations, veracity, annus horribilis, decommission* etc.), • die z. T. ironisch-kritische und pointierte Zusammenfassung und Kommentierung der Situation (*Prince Andrew's life out of uniform has not been short of entertainment; a freelance royal; ... so painstakingly restored ...; portfolio existence*), • den gezielten, z. T. kontrastiven Einsatz von Wortfeldern zu *royals/monarchy vs. the country; economy/finances; (public) duty/ceremony/institutions*).	6	
3	... untersucht und erklärt **rhetorische Stilmittel**, z. B. • das Nennen von konkreten Zahlen/Fakten zur Untermauerung der Seriosität, • den Gebrauch von Antithese sowie Parallelismus zur Verstärkung (*Prince Andrew's life has not been short ... it has been short of ...; for want of ... for the sake of; to tarnish ↔ restore*), • den Gebrauch von Klimax zur Darstellung des (enormen) Ausmaßes der Fehlleistung und Verschwendung (*the Queen acted ... to end the perception ... promised to pay ... time was called ... plans were drawn up ...; leaders wrestle ... taxpayers struggle ... it is right that the royal family cuts its cloth accordingly*).	6	

4	... benennt **weitere Stilmittel**, die die Aussage des Artikels hervorheben, z. B. • die implizite Androhung des Endes der Monarchie (*... to go on enduring ...; No royal family is indispensible ...*), • konkrete Verweise auf positiv-/negativ-Beispiele zur Verdeutlichung und Kontrastierung (*the Duke of York; the Queen; the Princess Royal; Prince Harry; other European monarchies ...*), • die pointierte Schlussfolgerung aus den genannten Beispielen, bzw. die daraus resultierende implizite Drohung (*a decisive response is needed; the royal family ... is too big; it should be streamlined; what the monarchy stands for; official duties should be performed by ... ; the House of Windsor needs more clarity ...*).	6	
5	... erfüllt ein weiteres aufgabenbezogenes Kriterium. (4) •	4	
		24	

Part A: Teilaufgabe 3.1 (Evaluation/Comment)

	Anforderungen **Der Schüler/die Schülerin ...**	maximal erreichbare Punktzahl	erreichte Punkte
1	... nimmt **konkreten Bezug auf die „message"** des Artikels und stellt z. B. dar, dass • gerade in Zeiten wirtschaftlicher Rezession symbolträchtige Institutionen wie z. B. das Königshaus besondere Vorbildfunktion haben, • vor allem das britische Königshaus, einerseits vor dem Hintergrund vergangener Skandale, andererseits mit Blick auf seine Erfahrung und Professionalität, zur (selbst-)kritischen Reflexion, Evaluation und Modernisierung in der Lage sein sollte.	4	
2	... nimmt **vor dem Hintergrund unterrichtlicher Ergebnisse** kritisch Stellung und benennt z. B. • den (rechtlichen) Status des Königshauses im Rahmen einer „constitutional monarchy" sowie die damit verbundenen Rechte und Pflichten, • die i.W. repräsentative Funktion der *Queen* (und der *Royal Family*), die der britische Staat jährlich mit hohen Millionenbeträgen unterstützt.	4	
3	... nimmt **vor dem Hintergrund seines Kontextwissens** Stellung zur britischen Monarchie sowie evtl. anderen europäischen Monarchien und führt z. B. an, dass • die Windsors schon aufgrund des enormen historischen Hintergrundes eine besondere Stellung innerhalb der europäischen Königshäuser einnehmen, • sich in Teilen bereits ein Generationswechsel vollzogen hat (→ *William and Kate*) und damit auch Modernisierungen zu erwarten sind, • die Royals nur noch von einem Teil der Bevölkerung wirklich wahr- und ernst genommen werden und eher von den Hochglanzmagazinen und der Klatschpresse vermarktet werden.	6	
4	... kommt in Abwägung der verschiedenen Aspekte und Argumente **zu einer begründeten und logischen Schlussfolgerung** und stellt z. B. heraus, dass • es/sie sich der kritischen Haltung des Autors anschließt, • er/sie demgegenüber darstellt, dass die Royals z. B. den Tourismus ankurbeln und damit in vielen Wirtschaftsbereichen auch Geld und Einnahmen generieren, • er/sie eine deutliche Beschränkung der staatlichen Ausgaben für das Königshaus fordert.	6	
5	... erfüllt ein weiteres aufgabenbezogenes Kriterium. (4) •	4	
		20	

31

Part A: Teilaufgabe 3.2 ((Re-)Creation of text)

	Anforderungen **Der Schüler/die Schülerin ...**	maximal erreichbare Punktzahl	erreichte Punkte
1	... nimmt durchgängig die **vorgegebene Perspektive** eines Monarchie-Kritikers/-Unterstützers ein, indem er/sie z. B. • auf die Verschwendungssucht und die Skandales des britischen Königshauses verweist, • auf den „Glamour-Faktor" des britischen Königshauses hinweist, • das positive Beispiel von z. B. William und Kate hervorhebt sowie bereits vollzogene Verhaltensänderungen im öffentlichen Auftreten von vielen Mitgliedern des Königshauses (z. B. Harry, Charles und Camilla).	4	
2	... greift zur **Verdeutlichung seiner Position auf im Artikel genannte Zahlen/Fakten/Bespiele** zurück und benennt z. B. • das Negativbeispiel des Duke of York, • das intensive Bemühen der Queen um finanzielle Einsparungen und Schadensbegrenzung bzgl. des Images der Royals, • die positiven Gegenbeispiele anderer (moderner) europäischer Monarchien.	4	
3	... integriert die **formal-stilistischen Elemente eines „Letter to the Editor"**, z. B. • Anrede/Grußformal am Schluss, • klare Bezugnahme auf den Artikel/das Thema, • kurze Selbstvorstellung/eigene Position/Appell an die Leser etc.	6	
4	... kommt zu einem **die Ergebnisse berücksichtigenden Fazit**, indem er/sie z. B. • die kritische Haltung des Autors hinterfragt/unterstützt, • auf die Verpflichtung von demokratischen Staaten zum Wohle und im Sinne (der Mehrheit) des Volkes hinweist, • ein generelles Umdenken fordert, z. B. die Abschaffung der Monarchie bzw. der extrem privilegierten Stellung der Mitglieder des Königshauses oder aber einer deutlichen Verpflichtung der Königshäuser zu aktiver Verantwortungsübernahme und sozialem Engagement etc. durch den Staat.	6	
5	... erfüllt ein weiteres aufgabenbezogenes Kriterium. (4) •	4	
		20	

4

Topic: India: Democracy, Diversity and Determination

Skills: Analysis of a fictional text (modern novel); writing a newspaper article (*Zieltextformat*)

Text: Aravind Adiga: Between the Assassinations, London 2010 (720 words)

Reading/Writing

Aravind Adiga

Between the Assassinations

"There was an accident last night. Near Flower Market Street. A hit and run."

"I know the case," Gururaj said. It had not been his story, but he read the proofs[1] of the entire paper every day. "An employee of Mr Engineer's was involved."

"The newspaper said that. But it was not the employee who did it."

5 "Really?" Gururaj smiled. "Then who did it?"

The Gurkha looks right into the Gururaj's eyes. He smiled and then pointed the barrel[2] of the ancient gun at him. "I can tell you, but I'd have to shoot you afterwards."

Looking at the barrel of the rifle, Gururaj thought I'm talking to a madman. [...]

The Gurkha talks quietly. He explains to the newspaper editor that a network of nightwatchmen

10 passes information around Kittur; every nightwatchman comes to the next for a cigarette and tells him something, and that one visits the next one for a cigarette in turn. In this way, word gets around. Secrets get spread. The truth – what really happened during the daytime – is preserved.

This is insane, this is impossible – Guraraj wipes the sweat from his forehead.

"So what actually happened – Engineer hit a man on his way back home?"

15 "Left him for dead."

"It can't be true."

The Gurkha's eyes flashed. "You've lived here long enough, sir. You know it *can be.* Engineer was drunk; he was coming back from his mistress's home; he hit the fellow like some stray dog and drove away, leaving him there, with his guts[3] spilled out on the street. In the morning the newspa-

20 per boy found him like that. The police know perfectly who drives down that road at night drunk. So the next morning two constables go to his house. Hasn't even washed the blood off the front wheels of the car."

"Then why – "

"He is the richest man in this town. He owns the tallest building in this town. He cannot be arrest-

25 ed. He gets one of the employees of his factory to say that he was driving the car when it happened. The guy gives the police a sworn affidavit[4]. I was driving under the influence on the night of 12 May when I hit the unfortunate victim. Then Mr Engineer gave the judge six thousand rupees, and the police something less, perhaps four thousand or five, because the judiciary is of course more noble than the police, to keep quiet. Then he wants his Maruti Suzuki back, because it's a new car and a

30 fashion statement and he likes driving it, he gives the police another thousand to change the identity of the killer car to a Fiat, and he has his car back and he's driving around town again."

"My God."

"The employee got four years. The judge could have given him a harsher sentence, but he felt sorry for the bugger[5]. Couldn't let him off for free, of course. So' – the nightwatchman brought down an

35 imaginary gavel[6] – 'four years.'

"I can't believe it," Gururaj said. "Kittur isn't that kind of place." [...]

That evening, the editor-in-chief of the newspaper summoned[7] him to his room. He was a plump old man, with sagging[8] jowls[9] and thick white eyebrows that looked like frosting and hands that

---

[1] **proof** here: a printed copy of sth. that is examined and corrected before the final copies are printed – [2] **barrel** the long tube-shaped part of a gun; *Revolverlauf* – [3] **guts** *Eingeweide* – [4] **a sworn affidavit** [ˌæfəˈdeɪvɪt] *eine beeidete schriftliche Erklärung* – [5] **bugger** (*BE, infml.*) here: poor man that you feel sorry for – [6] **gavel** *Hammer (eines Richters oder Auktionators)* – [7] **to summon sb.** to order sb. to come to a particular place – [8] **to sag** *schlaff herunterhängen* – [9] **jowl** [dʒaʊl] *Unterkinn*

trembled as he drank his tea. The tendons[10] in his neck stood out in deep relief[11], and every part of
40 his body seemed to be calling out for retirement.

If he did retire, Gururaj would inherit his chair.

"Regarding the story you've asked Menon to reinvestigate ..." said the editor-in-chief, sipping the tea. "Forget it."

"There was a discrepancy over the cars – "

45 The old man shook his head. "The police made a mistake on the first filing[12], that was all." His voice changed into the quiet, casual tone Gururaj had come to recognize as final. He sipped more tea, and then some more.

The slurping sound of the tea being sipped, the abruptness of the old man's manner, the fatigue[13] of so many nights of broken sleep got on Gururaj's nerves and he said: "A man might have been sent
50 to jail for no good reason; a guilty man might be walking free. And all you can say is, let's drop the matter."

The old man sipped his tea; Gururaj thought he could detect his head move, as if in the affirmative[14]. (*720 words*)

Aravind Adiga: Between the Assassinations. Atlantic Books, London 2010, pp. 156 ff.

ASSIGNMENTS

Gururaj is an experienced Indian journalist, who works for a local newspaper in the industrial city of Kittur.
After being given a secret tip about an accident that happened in Kittur's commercial district, he begins to reinvestigate the case and questions the Gurkha, one of the city's numerous night watchmen.

1. Give an outline of Gururaj's investigation into the accident near Flower Market Street and his efforts to find out what really happened that night.
(*Comprehension*)

2. Examine the narrative and stylistic devices and explain how they
a) support the particular atmosphere depicted in the excerpt, and
b) emphasize the message the author wishes to convey.
(*Analysis*)

3. You have a choice here. Choose **one** of the following tasks:

3.1 Critically discuss the editor-in-chief's order to "forget" the reinvestigation of the (false) news report, taking into consideration
a) your knowledge of "modern India", and
b) democratic principles you have dealt with in class.
(*Comment/Evaluation*)

3.2 Put yourself in the position of Gururaj and write a newspaper article that reveals and depicts the truth of what happened near Flower Market Street that night, as well as the scandalous cover-up of the incident.
(*(Re-)Creation of text*)

---

[10] **tendon** *Sehne* – [11] **to stand out in deep relief** *sich deutlich abheben* – [12] **filing** ['faɪlɪŋ] *Archivierung, Ablage* – [13] **fatigue** [fəˈtiːg] extreme tiredness – [14] **affirmative** *Zustimmung*

| Bewertungsbogen für: _____ | Kurs: _____ |

Part A: Teilaufgabe 1 (Comprehension)

	Anforderungen Der Schüler/die Schülerin ...	maximal erreichbare Punktzahl	erreichte Punkte
1	... skizziert die **dargestellten Rahmenbedingungen** des Romanauszugs und benennt z. B. • Gururajs „reinvestigation" des tödlichen Verkehrsunfalls, über den offenbar in der Lokalzeitung Kitturs falsch berichtet wurde, • Gururajs Befragung des *nightwatchman*, „Gurkha", der ihm über den tatsächlichen Unfallhergang und dessen Folgen berichtet, • die strikte Anweisung des *editor-in-chief* über den Fall Schweigen zu bewahren.	4	
2	... legt die vom *nightwatchman* Gurkha gegebenen Informationen bezüglich der **Vertuschung und heimlichen Weitergabe von Informationen** in Kittur dar, z. B. • das Netzwerk der *nightwatchmen*, die untereinander Informationen/Nachrichten und Neuigkeiten austauschen, • die „Bewahrung der Wahrheit" durch die Heimlichkeit des Informationsaustausches, • die *nightwatchmen* als Quelle der Wahrheit in Kittur im Gegensatz zur korrupten und die Nachrichten verfälschenden Presse.	4	
3	... beschreibt den **tatsächlichen Hergang** des Unfalls und seiner Folgen und erwähnt z. B. • den wahren Unfallverursacher (*Engineer*), einen der reichsten Männer der Stadt Kittur, der betrunken war und Fahrerflucht begangen hat, • die Vertuschung der wahren Geschehnisse sowie die Übernahme der Schuld durch einen Angestellten des *Engineer*, • die Bestechung der Polizei und des Richters durch den *Engineer*.	4	
4	... legt die **(Hinter-)Gründe** für den dargestellten Betrug und die falsche Berichterstattung bzw. Zensur (durch den *editor-in-chief*) dar, z. B. • die Angst der Behörden vor dem reichsten Geschäftsmann der Stadt, • die Bestechlichkeit/Unehrlichkeit der Behörden und Medien, • die Kapitulation der Presse vor der lokalen „Wirtschaftsmacht" und Korruption.	4	
5	... erfüllt ein weiteres aufgabenbezogenes Kriterium. (2) •	2	
		16	

Part A: Teilaufgabe 2 (Analysis)

	Anforderungen Der Schüler/die Schülerin ...	maximal erreichbare Punktzahl	erreichte Punkte
1	... arbeitet die relevanten **narrative devices** heraus und weist sie am Text nach. Er/sie verweist z. B. auf • die Erzählperspektive des *3rd person omniscient narrators* (*looking at ... Gururaj thought ...; The Gurkha talks ... explains ... word gets around ...; the editor-in-chief was ...; If he did retire ...*), • die häufigen Tempuswechsel zur Spannungssteigerung (*past* (cover-up) → *present* (= truth/facts) → *past* (lies, fraud) ... etc.), • den alternierenden Gebrauch von „scenic" und „panoramic presentation"; i. W. Beschreibung des Erzählers; *interior monologue* (durch Gururaj).	6	
2	... analysiert **sprachlich-erzählerische Stilmittel** und weist deren Wirkung und Funktion nach, z. B. • die explizite Vermeidung von Begriffen wie *„fraud", „corruption", „crime", „bribery"* etc. (→ Vertuschung von Tatsachen, Vermeidung von Realität und Konfrontation), • den Gebrauch von *conditionals* zur Verstärkung der Indifferenz und Mehrdeutigkeit der Situation (*the judge could have given ...; A man might have been sent ... might be walking ...*), • den Gebrauch von Namen (*Gururaj, the Gurkha*) im Zusammenhang mit „truth" und die Vermeidung von Namensnennungen (*Engineer, employee, editor-in-chief* → anonymity) im Zusammenhang mit Unwahrheit, Betrug und Vertuschung.	6	
3	... arbeitet den durchgehenden Gebrauch von **contrast/antithesis** heraus und weist dessen Funktion mit Blick auf die message des Textes heraus, z. B. • *oral history* (→ truth) vs. *print media* (→ lies, censorship), • *justice* vs. *injustice*, • *money* vs. *morals*, • *vague formulations* (→ conditionals) vs. *precise information* (→ simple present) and orders.	6	

4	... untersucht **weitere Stilmittel** und verweist z. B. auf <ul><li>die spezifische *choice of words* im Bezug auf *truth* (*insane, impossible ... sweat ...*); *lies* (*a sworn affidavit, gave the judge ... the police ... to keep quiet ... to change the identity*); *media/newspaper* (*plump old man ... sagging jowls ... hands that trembled*),</li><li>die implizite Kritik, die durch die Reaktionen Gururajs deutlich wird (*I'm talking to a madman; It can't be true; My God; I can't believe it ...*),</li><li>den impliziten Hinweis darauf, dass es sich um keine Ausnahme, sondern eine permanente Problematik handelt (*the fatigue of so many nights of broken sleep ...*).</li></ul>	6	
5	... erfüllt ein weiteres aufgabenbezogenes Kriterium. (4) <ul><li></li></ul>	4	
		24	

Part A: Teilaufgabe 3.1 (Evaluation/Comment)

	Anforderungen **Der Schüler/die Schülerin ...**	maximal erreichbare Punktzahl	erreichte Punkte
1	... nimmt **Bezug auf die im Text dargelegten Hinweise** und führt dabei an, dass <ul><li>auf die „archaische" Kultur der „oral history" Bezug genommen wird (→ *Gurkha, nightwatchmen ...*),</li><li>es strenge (unsichtbare) gesellschaftliche Regeln/Grenzen gibt, die nicht überschritten werden (dürfen) (*I can tell you, but I'd have to shoot you ...; In this way, word gets around ...; You know it can be; He cannot be arrested; Forget it*),</li><li>es klare gesellschaftliche Hierarchien gibt, die nicht hinterfragt werden (*He gets one of the employees ...; Mr Engineer ... the judge ... the police ... the judiciary ...*).</li></ul>	4	
2	... **vergleicht** die im Text dargestellte Situation **mit Kontextwissen aus dem Unterricht** und diskutiert dabei z. B., dass <ul><li>Indiens Gesellschaft und Wirtschaftssystem unter Korruption, Bestechung etc. leidet und es kaum möglich scheint, dagegen vorzugehen,</li><li>Indien – bei aller Modernität in bestimmten Gebieten – in vielen Bereichen noch archaische Strukturen aufweist (*caste system, violence against women, patriarchal structures*, etc.), die notwendigen gesellschaftlichen Entwicklungen und Reformen im Wege stehen,</li><li>das v. a. im städtischen Umfeld das moderne Indien (*IT giant, international services ...*) dem ländlichen Indien (*illiteracy, oral history, social hierarchies ...*) gegenübersteht.</li></ul>	4	
3	... **kommentiert** die im Text gegebenen (indirekten) Hinweise auf **explizite Verstöße gegen fundamentale rechtliche und demokratische Grundprinzipien** kritisch, z. B. <ul><li>den Verstoß der Zeitung/des *editor-in-chief* gegen die grundsätzliche Verpflichtung der Presse zur wahrheitsgemäßen Berichterstattung,</li><li>die Korruptheit und das rechtsbrecherische Verhalten der staatlichen Organe (Polizei, Richter, die Judikative),</li><li>die Verletzung des Rechts der öffentlichen Rede- und Pressefreiheit als demokratisches Grundrecht.</li></ul>	6	
4	... kommt zu einer **die Ergebnisse berücksichtigenden Schlussfolgerung** und führt z. B. an, dass <ul><li>das Verhalten des *editor-in-chief* einer Zeitung in der (zumindest formal) größten Demokratie der Welt rechtsbrecherisch und undemokratisch ist,</li><li>die im Text dargestellte Widersprüchlichkeit mit den aktuellen Problemen Indiens (wirtschaftliche Probleme durch Korruptheit, Gewaltausbrüche etc.) korrespondieren.</li></ul>	6	
5	... erfüllt ein weiteres aufgabenbezogenes Kriterium. (4) <ul><li></li></ul>	4	
		20	

Part A: Teilaufgabe 3.2 ((Re-)Creation of text)

	Anforderungen	maximal erreichbare Punktzahl	erreichte Punkte
	Der Schüler/die Schülerin ...		
1	... versetzt sich **durchgängig in die Position von Gururaj**, indem er/sie z. B. anführt, dass • er unter der Situation in Kittur leidet (z. B. Schlaflosigkeit, Unruhe, Angst etc.), • er sich über die Korruptheit und Verlogenheit seiner Zeitung aufregt und sich selbst dem „*investigative journalism*" verpflichtet fühlt, • er fassungslos ist, dass in „seinem" Kittur solche skandalösen und verbrecherischen Zustände herrschen.	4	
2	... greift zur Darstellung der Wahrheit auf **im Text genannte Details** zurück und benennt z. B. • die Aussage eines „Zeugen" (→ *Gurkha, nightwatchmen* ...), • die Korruptheit des gesamten Rechtssystems, • die Verlogenheit der Medien (seiner Zeitung ...), • das verbrecherische Verhalten des *Engineers*.	4	
3	... integriert die **formal-stilistischen Elemente eines *newspaper article***, z. B. • eine klare Gliederung und thematische Schwerpunktsetzung (*headline, topical order, simple present*, etc.), • eine klare und argumentativ schlüssige Bezugnahme auf das Thema, • einen Appell an die Leserschaft, das Verhalten/Indien etc. zu ändern und sich einer Demokratie/demokratischen Standards entsprechend zu verhalten.	6	
4	... kommt zu einem **die Ergebnisse und Argumente berücksichtigenden Fazit** bzw. „message", indem er/sie z. B. • eine grundlegende Reform der indischen Gesellschaft und der staatlichen Institutionen fordert, • Bezüge zu anderen demokratischen Staaten herstellt, • Grundprinzipien demokratischen Denkens und Handelns darstellt.	6	
5	... erfüllt ein weiteres aufgabenbezogenes Kriterium. (4) •	4	
		20	

Topic: The American Dream – Reveries and Realities

Skills: Analysis of a non-fictional text (newspaper article); writing a letter to the editor (*Zieltextformat*); listening comprehension

Texts: **Part A:** Hank Sanders, Faya Rose Toure: Still Waiting in Selma, New York, 2015 (503 words)
Part B: Barack Obama, Selma Speech, 7 March, 2015 (04:59 mins)

Part A: Reading/Writing

Hank Sanders, Faya Rose Toure

Still Waiting in Selma

On March 25, 1965, tens of thousands of us gathered before the Alabama State Capitol, the endpoint of a five-day, 54-mile march from Selma to Montgomery. Dr. Martin Luther King Jr. called out, "How long?" and the crowd responded, "Not long!" The moment was electric. We believed it would not be long before the right to vote was deeply rooted and bearing fruit[1] in America.

5 In one sense, we were right. The Voting Rights Act[2], passed just months after the Selma marches, banned the discriminatory voting practices[3] that many southern states had enacted following the Civil War. Over time, the Act enabled millions of African-Americans to register to vote, and for decades following its passage, voting rights continued to slowly expand. But in another sense we are still waiting. Either Dr. King was wrong or "not long" is biblical, measured in generations.

10 We came to Selma in 1971, newly married and fresh out of Harvard Law School. Our intentions were to stay for five years. We were sure that by then Dr. King's vision of voting rights would have been realized. Over 40 years later, not only are the fruits scarce[4], but the roots are shallow[5] and feeble[6].

Celebrations, commemorations[7] and movies make people feel good, but the reality is that voting 15 rights have been rolled back dramatically in recent years. [...] Today, all Alabama voters must show photo identification. In Alabama and other states, this I.D. must be government-issued[8]. These policies, which disproportionately affect minority, poor and elderly voters who are less likely to possess government-issued I.D.s, are the 21st-century equivalent of the Jim Crow-era poll tax[9] and literacy test. Dr. King understood that voting would be the last right granted to African-Americans because it 20 was the most powerful. Indeed, if we had better understood our history, we would not have been surprised that "not long" has stretched into a half-century. [...]

But what of Selma, the worldwide symbol of voting rights and freedom?

As Dr. King urged[10], we marched on the ballot boxes. In 1965 there were 300 registered African-American voters and zero African-American elected officials in Dallas County, where Selma is located; 25 in 2015 there were 19,862 registered African-American voters and 19 African-American elected officials. But we greatly underestimated the power of those who control the voting process. [...]

Despite our city's fame as a cornerstone of the Civil Rights movement, African-Americans in Selma who dare to discuss these issues openly and honestly are called racists, haters and worse.

Yes, we marched on the ballot boxes[11]. But for the tens of thousands of African-Americans in Selma, 30 life, as Langston Hughes said, "ain't been no crystal stair." Better off is not equal.

We came to Selma over four decades ago; today we are both in our seventies. When we arrived, we agreed that every five years we would decide anew whether to stay or leave. Each time we chose to stay. The choice is coming up again next year. What shall we do? The struggle continues because the challenges remain great. (*503 words*)

http://www.nytimes.com/2015/03/07/opinion/still-waiting-in-selma.html?_r=0, 6 March 2015 [05.04.2015]

---

[1] **to bear fruit** (*fml.*) to produce successful results – [2] **Voting Rights Act of 1965** an act signed into law by President Lyndon B. Johnson that prohibited racial discrimination in voting – [3] **voting practices** a standard or accepted way of organizing the election process – [4] **scarce** not easy to find or get – [5] **shallow** ['ʃæləʊ] not deep – [6] **feeble** weak and unstable – [7] **commemoration** [kə,memə'reɪʃən] *Gedenkfeier, Gedenkveranstaltung* – [8] **government-issued** officially provided by the government – [9] **poll tax** here: money that had to be paid in order to be allowed to vote – [10] **to urge** [ɜːdʒ] to strongly advise sb. to do sth. – [11] **ballot box** *Wahlurne*

ASSIGNMENTS

1. Point out Hank Sanders' and Faya Rose Toure's reflections on and memories of the events in Selma in 1965, as well as the 50th anniversary and the situation of African-Americans in 2015.
   (*Comprehension*)

2. Examine the authors' comparison of Selma back in 1965 and nowadays in 2015 and explain their conclusions.
   (*Analysis*)

3. You have a choice here. Choose **one** of the following tasks:

   3.1 Comment on the authors' observation that "[o]ver 40 years later, not only are the fruits scarce, but the roots are shallow and feeble." (ll. 12 f.), taking into consideration the recurring racial tensions and unrest in America and the continued infringements of the civil rights of African-American citizens, for example in Ferguson, Missouri.
   (*Comment/Evaluation*)

   3.2 In the concluding paragraph of the article, the authors mention that they decide anew every five years as to whether (or not) they will stay in Selma.
   Based on your knowledge of American politics, as well as the racial unrest of recent years, write a letter to the editor in which you respond to this question.
   ((*Re-*)*Creation of text*)

Part B: Listening Comprehension

Barack Obama

Selma Speech

On 7 March 2015, President Obama honoured the civil rights activists who marched across the Edmund Pettus Bridge in Selma, Alabama 50 years ago.
In 1965, Alabama police clubbed down non-violent marchers who were crossing the bridge en route to Montgomery, Alabama's state capital. This brutal crackdown on the civil rights protestors, known as Bloody Sunday, helped to pave the way to the Voting Rights Act of 1965.

Source: www.youtube.com/watch?v=7SoG4KZOvRc (04:59 mins)

Annotations »»

to endure to tolerate sth. difficult or painful ■ **to fashion sth.** (*fml.*) to give shape or form to sth. ■ **the imperative of citizenship** the obligation and duty to actively participate in and contribute as a member of society ■ **deacon** *Dekan* ■ **aristocracy** [ˌærɪˈstɒkrəsi] the upper class; *der Adel* ■ **to endow sb. with sth.** [ɪnˈdaʊ] *jdn. mit etw. ausstatten* ■ **Lewis and Clark** Meriwether Lewis and Williams Clark led the first American expedition from St. Louis to the Pacific Coast (1804–1806) on behalf of President Thomas Jefferson ■ **Sacajawea** a Native American woman who accompanied the Lewis and Clark Expedition as an interpreter and guide ■ **stampede** *Ansturm* ■ **huckster** *Straßenhändler(in)* ■ **Sojourner Truth** (1797–1883) African-American abolitionist and women's rights activist ■ **Fanny Lou Hamer** (1917–1977) African-American voting rights activist and civil rights leader ■ **Susan B. Anthony** (1820–1906) American social reformer and feminist, who played a crucial role in women obtaining the right to vote ■ **to stow away** (*phr. v.*) *als blinder Passagier fahren* ■ **Rio Grande** large river in Texas that forms part of the border between the U.S. and Mexico ■ **stock photo** *Foto einer Bildagentur* ■ **feeble** weak and ineffective ■ **to pine for sth.** (*phr. v.*) to miss sb./sth. very much ■ **boisterous** noisy, energetic, rough ■ **John Lewis** (*1940) African-American politician and civil rights leader ■ **unconstrained** not limited or held back ■ **unencumbered** not weighed down, *unbelastet* ■ **to seize sth.** [siːz] to grab sth. quickly and hold on to it

ASSIGNMENT 1 »»»

The following phrases are taken from and relate to different sections of President Obama's speech. Read them before listening, and then, while listening, put them into the correct order.

☐ A. We shall overcome.

☐ B. America is exceptional.

☐ C. Americans are immigrants.

☐ D. Young Americans are unconstrained and unencumbered.

☐ E. It is the task of Americans to try to improve this great nation.

☐ F. America has endured war and fashioned peace.

☐ G. America is diverse and full of energy.

☐ H. The imperative of citizenship hasn't changed.

☐ I. Americans are the slaves who built the White House.

☐ J. The nation is waiting to follow the young and fearless at heart.

(10 points)

ASSIGNMENT 2

Listening for details: Listen to the speech again and complete the sentence starters given below. There will be a short stop after each relevant part so that you can take notes and complete the following tasks.

1. According to President Obama, much has changed since 1965 because …

_____

2. Loving and believing in America means …

_____

3. America is exceptional because …

_____

4. America is a nation of immigrants who …

_____

5. America is not stock photos, but …

_____

6. The American nation remains young in spirit because …

_____

7. Young Americans today must take away from the Selma anniversary that …

_____

8. The younger generation of America is characterized by …

_____

9. The most important aspect of American democracy is …

_____

10. The aim of Americans for the future is to …

_____

(10 x 2 points)

Bewertungsbogen für: _____ Kurs: _____

Part A: Teilaufgabe 1 (Comprehension)

	Anforderungen Der Schüler/die Schülerin ...	maximal erreichbare Punktzahl	erreichte Punkte
1	... beschreibt die **Erinnerungen der Autoren** an den **Selma-Montgomery Marsch** im Jahre **1965** und benennt z. B., dass • zehntausende *civil rights activists* und Afro-Amerikaner an dem Marsch teilgenommen haben, • die Stimmung damals insgesamt euphorisch war und die Erwartungshaltung der Teilnehmer sehr hoch, • die Teilnehmer (damals noch) glaubten, dass es bald grundlegende Änderungen und Verbesserungen in Bezug auf das Wahlrecht für Afro-Amerikaner geben würde.	3	
2	... zeigt demgegenüber **die tatsächlichen Entwicklungen und Verbesserungen** auf, z. B. • die gesetzliche Einführung des *Voting Rights Act* im Jahre 1965, • die Abschaffung von diskriminierenden *voting practices* für Afro-Amerikaner, • die schrittweise Ausweitung der *voting rights* und die daraus resultierende Registrierung und Wahlteilnahme von Millionen von Afro-Amerikanern.	3	
3	... legt dar, wie **die Autoren die Gedenkfeiern wahrnehmen und beurteilen** und erwähnt z. B., dass • die Feierlichkeiten, Gedenkfeiern und Filme anlässlich des Jahrestages den (afro-amerikanischen) Menschen ein gutes Gefühl geben (sollen), • laut den Autoren die amerikanische Realität anders aussieht und in den vergangenen Jahren die *voting rights* sogar reduziert wurden, • die neue Wahlpolitik, z. B. in Alabama, Minderheiten, Arme und ältere Menschen besonders benachteiligt.	3	
4	... arbeitet das von den **Autoren gezogene Resümee** heraus und stellt z. B. dar, dass • es zwischen 1965 und 2015 einen großen Zuwachs an afro-amerikanischen Wählern und politischen Repräsentanten gegeben hat (*300 voters* → *19,862 voters*; *0 elected officials* → *19 elected officials*), • die Macht derer, die die Wahlen steuern und kontrollieren, noch immer ungebrochen ist, • eine kritische Diskussion der Problematik – auch 2015 – nicht/kaum möglich ist, • es den Afro-Amerikanern zwar besser geht, sie aber nicht gleichberechtigt sind.	3	
5	... erfüllt ein weiteres aufgabenbezogenes Kriterium. (2) •	2	
		12	

Part A: Teilaufgabe 2 (Analysis)

	Anforderungen Der Schüler/die Schülerin ...	maximal erreichbare Punktzahl	erreichte Punkte
1	... untersucht die **positive Darstellung der Ereignisse im Jahre 1965** durch die Autoren und belegt dies z. B. durch • den Gebrauch von *positive emotive words and phrases* (*electric; deeply rooted; bearing fruit; millions of African-Americans register[ed] to vote ...*), • den Verweis auf die zentrale Figur der *Civil Rights Movement*, Martin Luther King (*"How long?" and the crowd responded, "Not long!"; Dr. King's vision ...*), • die Empathie und persönliche Einbeziehung der Autoren (... *tens of thousands of us; We believed ...; we were right ...*; → *personal pronouns*).	5	
2	... untersucht demgegenüber die Darstellung der **eher negativen Situation im Jahre 2015** und verdeutlicht dies z. B. durch • die Häufung von *negative emotive words and phrases* (*we are still waiting; scarce ... shallow ... feeble; but the reality is ...; have been rolled back dramatically ...; 21st-century equivalent of the Jim Crow-era ...*, etc.), • die kritische Betrachtung von Martin Luther Kings Visionen (*Either Dr. King was wrong ...; measured in generations; voting would be the last right ...*), • das eher frustrierende und weitgehend negative Resümee der Autoren (*we are still waiting; scarce ... shallow ... feeble ...; voting rights have been rolled back dramatically; policies disproportionally affect minority, poor and elderly voters ...; if we had better understood ...; greatly underestimated ...*).	5	

3	... analysiert von den Autoren **verwendete Stilmittel** und verdeutlicht deren **Funktion** und **Wirkung**, z. B. • die chronologische, aber kontrastiv gestaltete Struktur des Artikels (*1965 ... decades following ... 1971 ... 40 years later ... today; ... continued to slowly expand* ➔ *but ...; We were sure that* ➔ *but ...; ... make people feel good* ➔ *but ...; ... in 2015 there were ... voters ... elected officials* ➔ *But we ...,* etc.), • den Gebrauch von (rhetorischen) Fragen zur Verdeutlichung der Verunsicherung (*But what of Selma ...?; What shall we do?*), • die Zitate von/den Verweis auf Ikonen der *Civil Rights Movement* (z. B. Martin Luther King, Langston Hughes), • den Gebrauch von *personal and possessive pronouns* zur Darstellung der Empathie und der *personal identification* (*tens of thousands of us; We believed; we were right; we are still waiting; We came to Selma; Our intention ...,* etc.).	5	
4	... verdeutlicht die von den Autoren gezogenen überwiegend **kritischen und skeptischen Schlussfolgerungen** und belegt das z. B. durch • die *negative choice of words* (*slowly expanded; not only ... but ...; rolled back dramatically; disproportionately; Jim Crow-era; the power of those who control; racists, haters and worse ...,* etc.), • die grundsätzlich kritische (aber z. T. hoffnungsvolle) Haltung der Autoren bisher (*We came to Selma ... every five years we would decide ... Each time we chose to stay ...*), • die zunehmende Infragestellung einer möglichen Verbesserung und die (notwendige) Fortführung des Kampfes (*What shall we do?; The struggle continues ... the challenges remain great.*).	5	
5	... erfüllt ein weiteres aufgabenbezogenes Kriterium. (4) •	4	
		20	

Part A: Teilaufgabe 3.1 (Evaluation/Comment)

	Anforderungen Der Schüler/die Schülerin ...	maximal erreichbare Punktzahl	erreichte Punkte
1	... hinterfragt das **Statement der beiden Autoren** kritisch und verweist z. B. darauf, dass • es der Gesamtaussage des Textes entspricht (*The struggle continues ... the challenges remain great.*), • es trotz aller Rückschläge auch bemerkenswerte Fortschritte in der politischen Beteiligung von Afro-Amerikanern gibt (*19,862 voters ... 19 elected officials*), • die Situation auf gesellschaftlicher Ebene nach wie vor kontrovers ist (*African-American president vs. racial unrest* (*e. g. Ferguson ...*) etc.).	3	
2	... betrachtet vor dem Hintergrund unterrichtlicher Ergebnisse die **positiven wirtschaftlichen und gesellschaftspolitischen Entwicklungen** für Afro-Amerikaner und bezieht sich z. B. auf • eine vergleichsweise hohe Zahl von reichen und einflussreichen Afro-Amerikanern in den vergangenen Jahren (Barack Obama, Oprah Winfrey etc.), • die zunehmend große Gruppe der erfolgreichen afro-amerikanischen Künstler, z. B. im Bereich Musik, Film etc., • die insgesamt verbesserten Aufstiegsmöglichkeiten für Afro-Amerikaner, z. B. durch ein durchlässigeres Bildungssystem, Stipendien etc., • die weitgehende gesellschaftliche Selbstverständlichkeit und Akzeptanz von gemischt-rassigen Beziehungen und Ehen (im Gegensatz zu 1965).	3	
3	... kommt **demgegenüber zu der Einschätzung**, dass • v. a. im südlichen Teil der USA für die afro-amerikanischen Bürger die Situation – nach wie vor – wirtschaftlich und gesellschaftspolitisch problematisch ist (hohe Arbeitslosigkeit, fehlende/mangelhafte Ausbildung, Gewaltbereitschaft, Vorurteile etc.), • die sich in den letzten Jahren häufenden Übergriffe auf afro-amerikanische Jugendliche zeigen, dass die Autoren in weiten Teilen Recht haben, • auch der erhoffte Wandel durch Präsident Obama in vielen Bereichen gescheitert ist und die Menschen/Wähler frustriert sind.	5	
4	... kommt in Abwägung der verschiedenen Aspekte und Argumente zu einer **begründeten Schlussfolgerung** und führt dabei z. B. an, dass • er/sie der Sichtweise der Autoren zustimmt und die „Veränderungen" eher kritisch als positiv bewertet, • er/sie die Sichtweise der Autoren nicht/nur z. T. teilt und argumentiert, auf die positiven Dinge zu fokussieren und dies als Chance für weitere Veränderungen zu betrachten und zu nutzen.	5	
5	... erfüllt ein weiteres aufgabenbezogenes Kriterium. (4) •	4	
		16	

Part A: Teilaufgabe 3.2 ((Re-)Creation of text)

	Anforderungen	maximal erreichbare Punktzahl	erreichte Punkte
	Der Schüler/die Schülerin ...		
1	... bezieht sich **konkret auf die im Text genannten Aspekte** und stellt z. B. dar, dass • beide Autoren seit 1971 in Selma leben und ursprünglich nur 5 Jahre bleiben wollten, • sich seitdem beide Autoren immer wieder gefragt haben, ob es besser sei Selma zu verlassen, sich aber (bisher) – trotz aller Rückschläge – zum Bleiben entschieden haben, • im Jahre 2016 diese Entscheidung für die beiden Autoren wieder ansteht und sie (nun) nicht sicher sind, was sie tun sollen.	3	
2	... **rechtfertigt seine Darstellung argumentativ**, indem er/sie z. B. anführt, dass • man einen langen Atem und viel Geduld haben muss, um Dinge grundsätzlich zu verändern (*"not long" is biblical, measured in generations*), • es bereits viele (positive) Gründe gibt, den Kampf fortzuführen (*more voters and elected officials, African-American president*, etc.), • es zu viele gesellschaftspolitische Rückschläge gibt (*shootings, racism, Ferguson*, etc.), als dass die Autoren zu Lebzeiten (*we are both in our seventies*) noch grundlegende Änderungen erleben könnten, • die beiden Autoren 40 Jahre „ausgehalten" haben, es daher nun keinen Grund gäbe, aufzugeben.	3	
3	... integriert **die formal-stilistischen Elemente eines „Letter to the Editor"**, z. B. • Anrede/Grußformel am Schluss, • klare/eindeutige Bezugnahme auf den Artikel, • Darlegung der eigenen Position/des persönlichen Interesses/kurze Selbstvorstellung/Appell an die Leserschaft etc.	5	
4	... kommt in Abwägung der verschiedenen Aspekte und Argumente zu einer **Schlussfolgerung**, die sich **nachvollziehbar aus den zuvor entwickelten Gedanken** ergibt, z. B. • betont er/sie die Notwendigkeit, gerade in schwierigen Zeiten, dass Menschen mit Weitblick und Erfahrung weiterkämpfen, • es ein fatales Signal an die Gesellschaft insgesamt wäre, wenn sich Bürgerrechtsinitiativen etc. zurückzögen und damit signalisieren, dass der Kampf für eine gerechtere Gesellschaft und gegen Rassismus verloren oder hoffnungslos ist, • fordert er/sie eine stärkere Solidarisierung mit den Opfern von Diskriminierung und Gewalt etc.	5	
5	... erfüllt ein weiteres aufgabenbezogenes Kriterium. (4) •	4	
		16	

Part B: Listening Comprehension

	Anforderungen	maximal erreichbare Punktzahl	erreichte Punkte
1	**Listening Comprehension 1** – je richtigem *matching* Zuordnung 1 Punkt (10 x 1)	10	
2	**Listening Comprehension 2** – je richtiger *sentence completion* 2 Punkte (10 x 2)	20	
		30	

Part B: Listening Comprehension – Solutions

9 A. We shall overcome.

3 B. America is exceptional.

4 C. Americans are immigrants.

7 D. Young Americans are unconstrained and unencumbered.

10 E. It is the task of Americans to try to improve this great nation.

1 F. America has endured war and fashioned peace.

6 G. America is diverse and full of energy.

2 H. The imperative of citizenship hasn't changed.

5 I. Americans are the slaves who built the White House.

8 J. The nation is waiting to follow the young and fearless at heart.

1. According to President Obama, much has changed since 1965 because …
   … Americans have endured war, fashioned peace and seen technological wonders.

2. Loving and believing in America means …
   … risking everything to realize the nation's promise and fighting for one's rights and responsibilities with conviction and passion.

3. America is exceptional because …
   … its citizens were born of change, broke old aristocracies and consider themselves endowed by their Creator with certain unalienable rights, which they protect as a self-governing people.

4. America is a nation of immigrants who …
   … survived the Holocaust, the Soviet dictatorship, the war in Sudan and crossing the border between the USA and Mexico.

5. America is not stock photos but …
   … instead is made up of a large variety of former slaves, labourers, farmers and cowboys. Americans respect the past, but do not pine for it; they do not fear the future, but grab for it.

6. The American nation remains young in spirit because …
   … they are boisterous, diverse and full of energy.

7. Young Americans today must take away from the Selma anniversary that …
   … they are unconstrained und unencumbered by habits and conventions.

8. The younger generation of America is characterized by …
   … being fearless at heart as well as being the most diverse and educated generation in America's history.

9. The most important aspect of American democracy is …
   … the spirit of unity and the understanding that the Americans are a united people.

10. The aim of Americans for the future is to …
   … continually improve their great nation.

(10 x 2 points)

Part B: Listening Comprehension – Transcript

Barack Obama

Selma Speech

[...] Fellow marchers, so much has changed in fifty years. We've endured* war, and fashioned* peace. We've seen technological wonders that touch every aspect of our lives, and take for granted convenience our parents might scarcely imagine. But what has not changed is the imperative of citizenship*, that willingness of a 26-year-old deacon*, or a Unitarian minister, or a young mother
5 of five, to decide they loved this country so much that they'd risk everything to realize its promise. That's what it means to love America. That's what it means to believe in America. That's what it means when we say America is exceptional.

For we were born of change. We broke the old aristocracies*, declaring ourselves entitled not by bloodline, but endowed* by our Creator with certain unalienable rights. We secure our rights and
10 responsibilities through a system of self-government, of and by and for the people. That's why we argue and fight with so much passion and conviction, because we know our efforts matter. We know America is what we make of it.

We are Lewis and Clark* and Sacajawea* – pioneers who braved the unfamiliar, followed by a stampede* of farmers and miners, entrepreneurs and hucksters*. That's our spirit.
15 We are Sojourner Truth* and Fannie Lou Hamer*, women who could do as much as any man and then some; and we're Susan B. Anthony*, who shook the system until the law reflected that truth. That's our character.

We're the immigrants who stowed away* on ships to reach these shores, the huddled masses yearning to breathe free – Holocaust survivors, Soviet defectors, the Lost Boys of Sudan. We are the hope-
20 ful strivers who cross the Rio Grande* because they want their kids to know a better life. That's how we came to be.

We're the slaves who built the White House and the economy of the South. We're the ranch hands and cowboys who opened the West, and countless laborers who laid rail, and raised skyscrapers, and organized for workers' rights. [...]
25 That's what America is. Not stock photos* or airbrushed history or feeble* attempts to define some of us as more American as others. We respect the past, but we don't pine for* it. We don't fear the future; we grab for it. America is not some fragile thing; we are large, in the words of Whitman, containing multitudes. We are boisterous* and diverse and full of energy, perpetually young in spirit. That's why someone like John Lewis* at the ripe age of 25 could lead a mighty march.
30 And that's what the young people here today and listening all across the country must take away from this day. You are America. Unconstrained* by habits and convention. Unencumbered* by what is, and ready to seize* what ought to be. For everywhere in this country, there are first steps to be taken, and new ground to cover, and bridges to be crossed. And it is you, the young and fearless at heart, the most diverse and educated generation in our history, who the nation is waiting to fol-
35 low.

Because Selma shows us that America is not the project of any one person.

Because the single most powerful word in our democracy is the word "We." We The People. We Shall Overcome. Yes We Can. It is owned by no one. It belongs to everyone. Oh, what a glorious task we are given, to continually try to improve this great nation of ours. [...]

(572 *words*)

www.bloomberg.com/politics/articles/2015-03-07/transcript-of-president-obama-s-selma-speech [04.04.2015]

*vocab given along with the assignments

Topic: The UK – Between Tradition and Modernity

Skills: Analysis of a non-fictional text (interview); writing a formal letter; listening comprehension

Texts: Part A: Christoph Scheuermann: Interview with Hilary Mantel: "What Is Happening in Britain at the Moment Is Really Ugly", 2014 (652 words)

Part B: Sara Firth: Britain's Squeezed Middle Class (TV news coverage), 27 February, 2013 (03:55 mins)

Part A: Reading/Writing

Christoph Scheuermann

Interview with Hilary Mantel: "What Is Happening in Britain at the Moment Is Really Ugly"

Hilary Mantel's historical novels are celebrated in Britain, but her critiques of the establishment are widely feared. In a SPIEGEL interview, she says her country is retreating into insularity[1] and to attitudes prevalent in Victorian times.

SPIEGEL: How is the Britain of today different from the country you grew up in?

5 **Mantel:** I was born into a working class family in a village near Manchester. My grandmother worked as a weaver in a mill when she was 12, my mother at 14. That was what you did: As soon as you left school, you had to work in the mill. By the time I was a child, the mills were closing and I was lucky to get a government grant[2] for university. In the years after the war, both big parties, Labour and the Conservatives, were becoming ever-more centrist, drawing together on a social

10 democratic path – a period known as the postwar consensus. Maybe it couldn't have lasted, but we perceive Ms. Thatcher[3] as the person who knocked it down. Going to university is a seriously expensive business now.

SPIEGEL: It seems as though Britain today wants to retreat from the world, as though it has become war-weary[4], disinterested in global affairs and obsessed with immigration. Where does this

15 come from?

Mantel: It's a retreat into insularity, into a mood of harshness[5]. When people feel they're being mistreated, they lash out[6] against people who are weaker than themselves, immigrants for example. What's happening here at the moment is really ugly. The government portrays poor and unfortunate people as being morally defective. This is a return to the thinking of the Victorians. Even in the

20 16th century, Thomas Cromwell[7] was trying to tell people that a thriving economy has casualties[8] and that something must be done by the state for people out of work. Even back then, you saw the tide turning against this idea that poverty was a moral weakness. Who could have predicted that it would come back into style? It's myth making on a grand scale, and it's poisonous.

SPIEGEL: Is there a new form of nationalism emerging?

25 **Mantel:** I'm not sure it's nationalism pure and simple. But there is certainly a big turn to the right in government. The populist party UKIP[9] (*Ed.'s note: UKIP is demanding that Britain secedes[10] from*

---

[1] **insularity** the quality of being interested only in your own country or group and being unwilling to accept different or foreign ideas – [2] **grant** an amount of money, given esp. by a government to a person or organization for a special purpose, such as studying – [3] **Margaret Thatcher** (1925–2013) British prime minister (1979–1990) and leader of the Conservative Party (1975–1990), who was well known for her uncompromising politics and leadership style – [4] **war-weary** ['wɪəri] tired of war – [5] **harshness** unpleasantness, nasty behaviour – [6] **to lash out against sb.** (*phr. v.*) to suddenly attack sb. physically or verbally – [7] **Thomas Cromwell** (1485–1540) English lawyer and statesman and chief minister to Henry VIII; one of the strongest and most powerful advocates of the English Reformation – [8] **casualty** ['kæʒjuəlti] here: sb. who suffers or is harmed by a certain situation – [9] **UKIP** (*abbr.*) UK Independence Party; a right-wing populist political party in the UK – [10] **to secede** to formally break away from a country or stop being a member of an alliance, union, or other political entity

the European Union.) is on the rise; it's the party at the moment for people who are angry. They may not know what they're angry about, but they're going around declaring their intention to vote for UKIP as if that's going to make everyone terrified. It's like, I'm holding a hand grenade, can you see
30 it?

SPIEGEL: Where does this anger come from?

Mantel: Many people are poorer than they were five or six years ago. The last few years of austerity[11] after the banking crisis have opened up a wider gap between rich and poor. It has taken quite a while for people to see that it wasn't just a matter of a year or two. Transport, gas, electricity, hous-
35 ing: All those things that one must have are significantly more expensive. Wages remain low while the government is freezing and cutting benefits[12]. Traditionally, working class voters would have turned to the Labour Party for remedy[13]. But at the moment, they don't feel that they can do that. There's a mood of disaffection[14].

SPIEGEL: Austerity is the new dogma.

40 **Mantel:** What's put to the electorate[15] is: You can't have this, you can't have that, because there's no money in the pot. But it's not really a question of resources. It's a question of ideology, which is moving to the right. It wishes to reduce the role of government and it strives for a small state. Unfortunately, it's the very people who protest the loss of their public services that go to vote for the Conservatives, as if they don't see the tie-up[15]. (*652 words*)

www.spiegel.de/international/zeitgeist/hilary-mantel-in-an-interview-with-spiegel-on-the-britain-of-today-a-1002263.html,
12 November 2014 [02.04.2015]

ASSIGNMENTS

1. Present Hillary Mantel's perceptions and view of the political, social and economic changes that Britain is currently undergoing.
   (*Comprehension*)

2. Examine Hillary Mantel's line of argument throughout the interview. In addition, pay particular attention to the use of historical references and how these intensify Mantel's stance on Britain's development.
   (*Analysis*)

3. You have a choice here. Choose **one** of the following tasks:

   3.1 "It seems as though Britain today wants to retreat from the world, as though it has become war-weary, disinterested in global affairs and obsessed with immigration." (ll. 13 f.) Comment on Hillary Mantel's observation and criticism and state whether (or not) you share her view.
   (*Comment/Evaluation*)

   3.2 Imagine you are a British citizen who is concerned about the recent developments around you. Taking Hillary Mantel's observations and criticisms into consideration, write a formal letter to your local political representative, in which you express your concerns and demand changes and improvements.
   ((*Re-*)*Creation of text*)

---

[11] **austerity** [ɔːˈsterɪti] financial hardship and difficult economic conditions, often caused by a government reducing its overall spending – [12] **benefit** welfare; financial help given by the government to people in need – [13] **remedy** a cure for an illness or a successful way of dealing with a problem or difficulty – [14] **disaffection** dissatisfaction, alienation – [15] **electorate** all the people who are allowed to vote – [16] **tie-up** connection

Part B: Listening Comprehension

Sara Firth

Britain's Squeezed Middle Class

In the RT Live news coverage at hand, *Russia Today* journalist Sara Firth interviews three Britons about their perception of the economic problems of Britain's economy in general and the economic struggle of Britain's middle class in particular:

- Liz Hoggard (a freelance journalist struggling to find new contracts)
- Giselle Cory (an analyst from the "Resolution Foundation" think tank)
- Gary Cady (founder of the "Give & Take" store in East Dulwich)

Source: www.youtube.com/watch?v=DGjWro3CN8s, 27 February 2013 (03:55 mins)

Annotations ⟫⟫

to bear the brunt of sth. to be the most strongly affected by sth. unpleasant ■ **tax hike** a sudden, dramatic increase in money that has to be paid to the government ■ **to tap away** here: to type on a computer keyboard over a long period of time ■ **mortgage** ['mɔːɡɪdʒ] *Hypothek* ■ **to thrive** to do very well ■ **perk** (*infml.*) an advantage or bonus, esp. extra money, additional luxuries, or here: greater opportunities ■ **to stoke fear** to make people more afraid ■ **stark** obvious ■ **deposit** here: *Anzahlung auf ein Haus* ■ **trimmings** here: additional possessions and activities that are nice to have or do, but that are not necessary for daily survival ■ **stocks and shares** *Aktien und Anlagen* ■ **root canal surgery** *Zahnwurzeloperation* ■ **to keep up appearances** *das Gesicht wahren* ■ **charity** *Wohltätigkeit* ■ **voucher** *Gutschein*

First read the vocabulary given above and the tasks given below. After a first listening, complete assignments 1 and 2. Then, after a second listening, pay attention to details and do assignment 3. You do not need to write complete sentences; note form will do.

ASSIGNMENT 1 ⟫⟫⟫⟫⟫

Decide whether the statements below are true or false.

	True	False
1. Many middle class households have lost half of their income.	☐	☐
2. Liz Hoggard was not given a new contract because of budget cuts.	☐	☐
3. Giselle Cory predicts another ten years of economic hardship.	☐	☐
4. Sara Firth explains that middle class people cannot afford to buy houses anymore.	☐	☐
5. Holidays abroad or home improvement projects have had to be put on hold.	☐	☐
6. Liz Hoggard has had to sell household items to pay for surgery on her teeth.	☐	☐
7. Liz Hoggard is selling off stocks and shares in order to make a living.	☐	☐
8. "Give & Take" voucher exchange system can help people to keep up appearances.	☐	☐
9. The "Give & Take" sells designer clothes for charity purposes.	☐	☐
10. Britain's economic middle class is at risk of losing its money to the upper class.	☐	☐

(10 points)

ASSIGNMENT 2

Read the following statements and decide how they could be matched.

1 More than half of Britain's middle class people ...	a ... have been put on hold due to financial problems.
2 Ten million adults in middle class income households ...	b ... that the country risks slowly dividing into two halves.
3 People like Liz Hoggard are suffering emotionally ...	c ... have no savings to fall back on.
4 Typical middle class perks ...	d ... face a loss in buying power due to increased prices and higher taxes.
5 The British government has been warned ...	e ... because they need to sell off their possessions to pay for essentials.

(10 points)

ASSIGNMENT 3

Listen to the recording a second time and complete the statements below.

1. Typical middle class trimmings are:

_____

2. Buying a house has become a major problem for middle class people because ...

_____

3. Gary Cady's business idea for his shop "Give & Take" is ...

_____

4. Liz Hoggard has had to sell off her books because ...

_____

5. The reasons for the economic struggles of Britain's middle class are ...

_____

(10 points)

Bewertungsbogen für: _____	Kurs: _____

Part A: Teilaufgabe 1 (Comprehension)

	Anforderungen **Der Schüler/die Schülerin ...**	maximal erreichbare Punktzahl	erreichte Punkte
1	... beschreibt die dargestellten **politischen Veränderungen** und benennt z. B. ● Großbritanniens Rückzug aus und Desinteresse an der Weltpolitik, ● die zunehmende Fokussierung auf Einwanderungspolitik, ● den politischen Rechtstrend (➔ UKIP) und die damit einhergehende Verunglimpfung von Menschen in Armut und sozialen Notlagen durch die britische Regierung.	3	
2	... skizziert die **sozialen Veränderungen** und die damit verbundenen Konsequenzen, z. B. ● die Rückkehr zum statischen Gesellschaftssystem und fehlenden Aufstiegsmöglichkeiten im viktorianischen Zeitalter, ● demgegenüber das fehlende Bewusstsein der Bevölkerung für die (wahren) Ursachen der sozialen Ungerechtigkeit, ● eine Zunahme der „sozialen Hackordnung".	3	
3	... arbeitet die **wirtschaftlichen Veränderungen** in Großbritannien heraus und stellt z. B. dar, dass ● universitäre/akademische Ausbildung für viele Briten finanziell nicht (mehr) leistbar ist, ● der Staat sich zunehmend aus der sozialen Verantwortung für und finanzieller Unterstützung von sozialschwachen Briten zurückzieht, ● es ein gravierendes Missverhältnis gibt zwischen den unverändert niedrigen Löhnen und den zunehmend steigenden Lebenshaltungskosten.	3	
4	... führt die **möglichen Konsequenzen** für Großbritannien und die Briten an und benennt z. B., dass ● die o. g. Veränderungen Großbritannien in die (weltpolitische) Isolation führen, ● das wirtschaftliche und soziale Klima im Lande vergiftet wird und ehemals errungene sozialdemokratische Werte aufgegeben werden, ● sich die Kluft zwischen arm und reich weiten wird und soziale Hackordnungen sich verschärfen werden.	3	
5	... erfüllt ein weiteres aufgabenbezogenes Kriterium. (2) ●	2	
		12	

Part A: Teilaufgabe 2 (Analysis)

	Anforderungen **Der Schüler/die Schülerin ...**	maximal erreichbare Punktzahl	erreichte Punkte
1	... untersucht Hillary Mantels ***line of argument*** und stellt z. B. dar, dass ● sie zunächst vor dem Hintergrund ihrer persönlichen Erfahrungen argumentiert (*I was born into a working class family; I was lucky to get a government grant ...*), ● sie die Rückständigkeit der gegenwärtigen Politik hervorhebt und anprangert, indem sie sie mit Politik aus dem 19. und 16. Jahrhundert vergleicht (*It's a retreat ...; the thinking of the Victorians ...; Even in the 16th century ...*), ● sie den politischen Rechtstrend und die damit verbundene Verunsicherung und Aggressivität in der Bevölkerung hervorhebt (*a big turn to the right; UKIP ... the party ... for people who are angry; ... to make everyone terrified ...*), ● sie auf die Verschärfung der sozialen Kluft hinweist (*a wider gap between rich and poor; freezing and cutting benefits*).	5	
2	... arbeitet **historische Beispiele** heraus, auf die sich Hillary Mantel bezieht, z. B. ● der radikale gesellschaftspolitische Kurs von Margaret Thatcher in den 1980er-Jahren und der Bruch mit sozialdemokratischen Strukturen (*after the war ... a social democratic path ...; Ms. Thatcher ... knocked it down ...*), ● das viktorianische Zeitalter, währenddessen eine strenge getrennte Klassengesellschaft herrschte sowie eine Verelendung der Arbeiterklasse (*The government portrays poor and unfortunate people as being morally defective ... the thinking of the Victorians ...*), ● Thomas Cromwell (*16th century*), der den Staat in Verantwortung gegenüber Arbeitslosen und Armen sah (*Even ... Cromwell ... something must be done by the state ...*).	5	
3	... untersucht und erklärt **rhetorische Stilmittel**, die der Intensivierung der Argumentation dienen, z. B. ● *use of contrast and antithesis (By the time I was a child ↔ Victorians; 16th century; even back then ...*), ● *use of abstractions and generalizations (It seems as though Britain today wants ...; The government portrays poor and unfortunate people as ...; there is certainly a big turn to the right ...; traditionally, working class voters ...*), ● *use of grammatical persons (I was born into ...; I was a child ...; I was lucky ...; we perceive Ms. Thatcher as ...*).	5	

4	... verdeutlicht den **unterschwellig appellativen Charakter** des Textes, indem er/sie z. B. <ul><li>auf die angstschürende und (einseitig) wertende Überschrift hinweist,</li><li>auf Anspielungen auf die potentielle Gefahr (*for people who are angry; make everyone terrified; holding a hand grenade*) verweist,</li><li>die deutliche Kritik an der populistischen UKIP Partei sowie der Regierungspartei hervorhebt (*populist party UKIP ... for people who are angry; The last few years of austerity ... the government is freezing and cutting benefits; It's a question of ideology ...; vote for the Conservatives ... don't see the tie-up*).</li></ul>	5	
5	... erfüllt ein weiteres aufgabenbezogenes Kriterium. (4) <ul><li></li></ul>	4	
		20	

Part A: Teilaufgabe 3.1 (Evaluation/Comment)

	Anforderungen **Der Schüler/die Schülerin ...**	maximal erreichbare Punktzahl	erreichte Punkte
1	... greift die von Mantel vertretene These, dass **Großbritannien sich isoliert**, auf und bezieht sich z. B. auf <ul><li>den seit Jahren von Premierminister Cameron angedrohten „Brexit" (möglicher Austritt Großbritanniens aus der EU),</li><li>die Verstärkung des isolationistischen Trends durch Parteien wie UKIP,</li><li>die zunehmende Abneigung gegen EU-freundliche Parteien wie die Labour Party.</li></ul>	3	
2	... greift die These der **„war-weariness" Großbritanniens** auf und benennt z. B. als mögliche Gründe <ul><li>die enormen Kriegsverluste im Irak-Krieg und den daraus resultierenden Rückzug im Jahre 2009,</li><li>die durch die internationale Finanzkrise (2008) zunehmenden wirtschaftlichen Probleme,</li><li>die innenpolitischen Probleme (z. B. Schottland Referendum, soziale Spannungen), die die Konzentration auf Innenpolitik notwendig machen.</li></ul>	3	
3	... diskutiert, auch unter Rückgriff auf unterrichtliche Ergebnisse, Großbritanniens **„Besessenheit" im Umgang mit dem Thema Einwanderung** und benennt z. B. <ul><li>die in den letzten Jahren zunehmend rigide und streng reglementierte Einwanderungspolitik,</li><li>die in Teilen Großbritanniens vorherrschende *Islamophobia* und damit einhergehende Vorurteile gegen muslimische Mitbürger und Einwanderer,</li><li>die durch den politischen Rechtstrend und wirtschaftliche Probleme verstärkten Ressentiments gegen Einwanderer generell.</li></ul>	5	
4	... kommt zu einer **zusammenfassenden Schlussfolgerung**, die sich aus den zuvor entwickelten Gedanken ergibt, z. B., dass <ul><li>es nicht in Sinne eines (auch historisch) global ausgerichteten Landes wie Großbritanniens sein kann, sich von der Welt zu isolieren, v. a. im Zeitalter der Globalisierung,</li><li>– bei allen Differenzen – Großbritannien mit Europa zusammenarbeiten sollte, um die anstehenden Probleme, z. B. Kriege und Einwanderung, zu bewältigen,</li><li>man, zumal in einer globalisierten Welt, Vorurteile und soziale Hackordnungen überwinden sollte.</li></ul>	4	
5	... erfüllt ein weiteres aufgabenbezogenes Kriterium. (4) <ul><li></li></ul>	4	
		16	

Part A: Teilaufgabe 3.2 ((Re-)Creation of text)

	Anforderungen **Der Schüler/die Schülerin ...**	maximal erreichbare Punktzahl	erreichte Punkte
1	... nimmt durchgängig die vorgegebene **Perspektive des *concerned British citizen*** ein, indem er/sie z. B. <ul><li>die vorherrschende Situation (Armut, soziale Ungleichheit/Ungerechtigkeit) beklagt,</li><li>sein/ihr Unverständnis gegenüber den Entscheidungen der Regierung (*freezing and cutting benefits; loss of public services*) zum Ausdruck bringt,</li><li>seine Sorge über wachsende Einwandererzahlen/den Unmut der britischen Bevölkerung/soziale Spannungen verdeutlicht.</li></ul>	3	
2	... veranschaulicht die **sozialen und wirtschaftlichen Probleme in Großbritannien** und benennt z. B. <ul><li>die ständig steigenden Preise von *transport, gas, electricity, housing* gegenüber von stagnierenden Lohnzahlungen,</li><li>die fehlende finanzielle Unterstützung für Ausbildung und Studium und damit verbundene Überschuldung von Studenten sowie Perspektivlosigkeit für bestimmte soziale Schichten und Einkommensgruppen,</li><li>die Zunahme der Kluft zwischen Arm und Reich und die daraus resultierende gesellschaftliche Polarisierung und Spaltung.</li></ul>	3	

3	... betont dringend **notwendige Verbesserungen und Wandel** und fordert z. B. • die Übernahme sozialer und politischer Verantwortung durch <u>alle</u> Parteien, • einen kritischeren und bewussteren Umgang der Bevölkerung mit politischen Parteien und deren Entscheidungen und Ideologien, • eine Umkehr der Politik im Umgang mit sozialschwachen Bevölkerungsschichten (z. B. keine Verunglimpfung, kein politisches Aufheizen der bestehenden sozialen Spannungen).	5	
4	... verarbeitet die **formal-stilistischen Elemente eines „formal letter"**, z. B. • die persönliche Anrede und Grußformel zum Abschluss des Briefes, • die persönliche Vorstellung und Benennung des Anliegens/des Anlasses, • die sprachlichen Normen/Formal English/Höflichkeitsfloskeln.	4	
5	... erfüllt ein weiteres aufgabenbezogenes Kriterium. (4) •	4	
		16	

Part B: Listening Comprehension

	Anforderungen	maximal erreichbare Punktzahl	erreichte Punkte
1	**Listening Comprehension 1** – je richtiger *true-false* Antwort 1 Punkt (10 x 1)	10	
2	**Listening Comprehension 2** – je richtigem *matching* 2 Punkte (5 x 2)	10	
3	**Listening Comprehension 3** – je richtiger *sentence completion* 2 Punkte (5 x 2)	10	
		30	

Part B: Listening Comprehension – Solutions

ASSIGNMENT 1

1, 4, 7, 9, 10: false
2, 3, 5, 6, 8: right

ASSIGNMENT 2

1 c, 2 d, 3 e, 4 a, 5 b

ASSIGNMENT 3

1. Typical middle class trimmings are:
   foreign holidays, restaurant meals/eating out, home improvement projects.

2. Buying a house has become a major problem for middle class people because
   a first time buyer now has to save for about 22 years to have enough money for a deposit (compared to 4 years in the past).

3. Gary Cady's business idea for his store "Give & Take" is
   exchanging designer clothes for credit to be used in his store; an exchange voucher system.

4. Liz Hoggard has had to sell off her books in order to
   pay for the newspaper bill; pay for root canal surgery (the dentist).

5. The reasons for Britain's middle class's economic struggles are
   Britain's economic struggles as a consequence of the global economic crisis of 2008; tax hikes; budget cuts; lack of financial reserves, living on credit, stagnating wages.

Part B: Listening Comprehension – Transcript

Sara Firth

Britain's Squeezed Middle Class

Britain's squeezed middle classes are bearing the brunt* of the country's struggles to revive the economy. A study shows tax hikes* are leaving them £280 a year worse off – and more than half of them have no savings to fall back on. It means major lifestyle changes for many, as Sara Firth now explains.

5 **Sara Firth:** For a large part of her life, Liz Hoggard has been tapping away* at building a life for herself. As a freelance journalist, she's been part of Britain's middle class. They own credit cards, pay their mortgages* on time, and they thrive* during boom time. But then came the bust, and with it, the decline of opportunities that were for so long a middle class perk*.

Liz Hoggard: I didn't get a contract renewed because budgets were being cut, and so all those little
10 things you have in place – you always live slightly on credit, you know. You're in anticipation that you'll get paid quite soon. That got much tougher.

Sara Firth: Low incomes coupled with high living costs are stoking fears* of a shrinking middle in Britain. Fears backed up in a report by the "Resolution Foundation" think tank. It looked into what the future holds for the 10 million adults in low to middle income households, and it forecast an-
15 other decade of hardship.

Giselle Cory (policy analyst, "Resolution Foundation"): Well, unfortunately it's a bit of a grim prospect. Prices have risen faster than earnings for some time now. And what that means is that people are earning a similar amount, perhaps a little more – but they can't buy as much with it.

Sara Firth: A stark* example of this is housing.
20 **Giselle Cory:** A couple of decades ago you'd have to save for a couple of years, maybe three or four years to get a deposit* on a house if you were a low to middle income first-time buyer. At the moment you're looking at about 22 years.

Sara Firth: So, middle class trimmings* like foreign holidays, meals out and home improvement are on hold for the time being – as Liz has found out. She's having to sell off possessions to pay for
25 essentials like dental treatment.

Liz, how does it feel packing up these books that you've acquired, sort of throughout your lifetime and having to sell them off?

Liz Hoggard: It's quite emotional at times, and you have a rush of memory. And then you think 'Actually I haven't read them for 10 years. And probably if it's something really important, I can find it
30 online now.' That has revolutionized it. But I also think, you know, these books are my investment in a way. It's really interesting, the exhibition catalogues that I bought back, you know, for not much money, just the normal price. And then of course they've become rarer as the years go by. So, in some ways, my stocks and shares* have been sitting on my shelves, which I haven't known about. So you know, when you look online at Amazon and think 'Oh, my goodness, that book's going for
35 £100 now'. So there is a sense of 'Oh well, at least I can pay for my newspaper bill or my root canal surgery* doing that.' You know, you have to not be a snob.

Sara Firth: In tough economic times, it can be hard to keep up appearances*. That's why schemes like the one run by this store here in East Dulwich are proving so popular. You bring along your designer clothes and you can exchange it for credit, which can be reused in the store.
40 **Gary Cady** (founder "Give & Take"): I think this is a bit of a first actually. I think we're the first persons to actually combine the dress exchange element with the charity* element and introducing the exchange voucher* system rather than buying stock in. That's the kind of "Give & Take" element.

Sara Firth: As more and more families look for ways to make their money go further, the government's being warned that, without shared growth, Britain risks becoming a country of two halves.
45 The rich getting richer and the middle classes increasingly losing out.

Meanwhile, Liz and a generation like her are facing up to the reality that, for Britain's middle classes, the next chapter is looking pretty bleak. (*728 words*)

www.youtube.com/watch?v=DGjWro3CN8s, 27 February 2013 [11.05.2015], transcribed by Iris Edelbrock

*vocab given along with the assignments

> **Topic:** The UK – Between Tradition and Modernity
>
> **Skills:** Analysis of a non-fictional text (magazine article); writing an interview (*Zieltextformat*); listening comprehension
>
> **Texts:** **Part A:** Ethnic Minorities: Breaking Out, The Economist, 2015 (468 words)
> **Part B:** Multicultural Society – UK Whites & Ethnics Choose to Live Apart, TV news coverage (02:47 mins)

Part A: Reading/Writing

Ethnic Minorities: Breaking Out

In Britain, Bangladeshis have overtaken Pakistanis. Credit[1] the poor job market when they arrived and the magical effect of London.

Fatima Patel, the editor of *Asian Sunday*, a local newspaper, says Bradford's leaders look ruefully[2] at Tower Hamlets, a poor borough[3] of London 200 miles to the south. And that comparison has an
5 ethnic tinge[4], because Bradford is heavily Pakistani, whereas Tower Hamlets is the heart of Bangladeshi Britain.

In many people's minds, and often in official statistics, the 447,201 people who called themselves Bangladeshi in the 2011 census and the 1,124,511 who identified themselves as Pakistani are lumped[5] together. And the two groups have much in common. Mass immigration for both began
10 in the 1950s. Both are largely working-class and Muslim. Both tend to vote Labour. Both are concentrated in one business – restaurants in the case of Bangladeshis, taxi-driving among Pakistanis. But their fortunes[6] are now diverging[7]. And that says something about what it takes to succeed as an immigrant in Britain. [...]

Bangladeshis born in Britain are also more likely than their Pakistani counterparts to socialise with
15 people of a different ethnicity, according to another study. Both still overwhelmingly wed[8] within their own ethnic group. But among young men, for whom marrying out[9] is easier, 26 % of Bangladeshis now do so compared with 17 % of Pakistani youths. [...]

The growing success of Bangladeshis appears odd because their living conditions are often so dismal[10]. More than one-third live in social housing, compared with a national average of 18 %. Near
20 Morpeth School, a fence outside grotty[11] flats is topped[12] with upturned nails to deter[13] intruders. Pakistanis are more likely to own houses. But, since those houses are often in the wrong place, that has not helped them much. Those living in decayed[14] northern towns are tied to[15] properties whose value is hardly rising, stopping them moving to more dynamic spots. "It is a stake[16] that only allows you to move around the corner to equally bleak[17] economies," says Mr Saggar.
25 Cultural conservatism, which has deepened among many British Pakistanis, makes things worse. Cousin marriage is more common among Pakistanis than among Bangladeshis, as is the bringing over of partners from the subcontinent, argues Parveen Akhtar, a sociologist at the University of Bradford. Nuzhat Ali, a campaigner in the city, reckons[18] such marriages are actually more common among recent[19] Pakistani migrants than among their grandparents. The practice[20] means that
30 more Pakistanis in a city like Bradford are first-generation migrants than might be expected by now. It might also mean that young men are less driven to succeed – the desire to find a marriage partner being an unstated[21] reason for going to university among people of all races.

The experience of Bangladeshis suggests that it is foolish to judge the success of immigrants after just a few years in Britain. (*468 words*)

The Economist, 21 February, 2015, pp. 29 f.

---

[1] **to credit sth. to sb./sth.** *jdm./etw. gutschreiben* – [2] **rueful** ['ruːfəl] (*lit.*) feeling sorry and full of regret – [3] **borough** ['bʌrə] part of a city with its own local government – [4] **tinge** [tɪndʒ] *ein Hauch von etw.* – [5] **to lump sb./sth. together** (*phr. v.*) *etw./jdn. über einen Kamm scheren* – [6] **fortune** *Schicksal* – [7] **to diverge** [ˌdaɪˈvɜːdʒ] to become different or follow a different direction – [8] **to wed** to marry sb. – [9] **to marry out** to marry sb. from a different culture – [10] **dismal** miserable, gloomy – [11] **grotty** (*infml.*) dirty, run-down – [12] **to top sth.** *etw. überragen* – [13] **to deter** [dɪˈtɜːr] *abschrecken* – [14] **decayed** *heruntergekommen* – [15] **to be tied to sth.** *an etw. gebunden sein* – [16] **stake** a wooden or metal post that is pushed into the ground and that sb./sth. is tied to – [17] **bleak** sad and without hope – [18] **to reckon** to think that sth. is probably true – [19] **recent** here: newly-arrived – [20] **practice** *Brauch* – [21] **unstated** *implizit*

© Schöningh Verlag, Best.-Nr. 040158

ASSIGNMENTS

1. Describe the living conditions and cultural background of Pakistani and Bangladeshi immigrants in Britain.
   (*Comprehension*)

2. Compare the situation of Pakistani and Bangladeshi immigrants in Britain and explain why – according to the author – Bangladeshis "have overtaken Pakistanis".
   (*Analysis*)

3. You have a choice here. Choose **one** of the following tasks:

   3.1 In the concluding sentence, the author states that "it is foolish to judge the success of immigrants after just a few years in Britain" (ll. 33 f.).
   Comment on this statement, referring both to aspects mentioned in the text itself, as well as to knowledge you have gained in class.
   (*Comment/Evaluation*)

   3.2 As a reporter for a local radio station, conduct a radio interview with a Bangladeshi and a Pakistani immigrant about their life and experiences in Britain.
   You may include and refer to information given in the text, as well as to aspects you have dealt with in class.
   (*(Re-)Creation of text*)

Part B: Listening Comprehension

Multicultural Society – UK Whites and Ethnics Choose to Live Apart

In the context of an ongoing discussion about the possible failure of multiculturalism in the UK and the need to integrate ethnic minorities, RT News Channel journalist Sara Firth informs viewers about a worrying trend.

Source: www.youtube.com/watch?v=13kOeTojCBI, 28 November, 2013 (02:47 mins)

Annotations »»»

colour-coded here: separated or organized on the basis of skin colour ■ **hostility** *Feindseligkeit* ■ **Sheffield** a city in South Yorkshire in the north of England that was formerly an important centre of steel production, but was badly affected by the collapse of coal mining and steel production in the 1970s and 1980s; about 8% of the population is Asian ■ **Roma** a traditionally itinerant (*umherziehend*) ethnic group living mostly in Europe and the Americas ■ **to play out** *sich abspielen* ■ **to acknowledge sb./sth.** to accept that sth. is true or exists ■ **to opt** to choose ■ **diverse** [daɪˈvɜːs] here: relating to or containing people from many different ethnicities and social backgrounds ■ **to retain** to keep ■ **leafy** full of trees ■ **belt** here: area

ASSIGNMENT 1

Before listening to the news coverage for the first time, read the vocabulary given above and the statements given below. While listening, match the various statements to the correct speaker by ticking the correct box: Sara Firth (RT Times Reporter); Eric Kaufmann (Professor of Politics, University of London) or general information provided by the anchorwoman.

Statement	Sara Firth	Eric Kaufmann	General information
More than 100,000 people from ethnic minority groups have moved out of London.			
You are getting white British people avoiding very diverse areas.			
A new study warns of comfort zone segregation.			
A local Sheffield community has hit the headlines over community tensions between Roma population and other ethnic groups.			
Britain is turning into a colour-coded society.			
In parts of East London, Newham or parts of South London, there are fewer and fewer white British people living there.			
Segregation really needs to be addressed in the U.K.			
Some 600,000 white Britons left London between 2001 and 2011.			

White Britons are driven by the need to stay in the majority.			
We see the same trends in the United States ... and that could be a concern for integration.			

(10 x 2/20 points)

ASSIGNMENT 2

After a second listening, complete the sentence starters below.

1. In the UK, whites and ethnic minorities are choosing to live apart because ...

_____

2. According to the think tank "Demos" and "Birkbeck", University of London, people from ethnic minorities are ...

_____

3. Segregation needs to be addressed and acknowledged because ...

_____

4. White British people are avoiding very diverse areas and ...

_____

5. Similar trends can be seen in the United States because there ...

_____

Bewertungsbogen für: _____	Kurs: _____

Part A: Teilaufgabe 1 (Comprehension)

	Anforderungen Der Schüler/die Schülerin ...	maximal erreichbare Punktzahl	erreichte Punkte
1	... umreißt die **wesentlichen Aspekte**, die in dem Artikel dargestellt werden und benennt z. B. • die seit den 1950er-Jahren bestehende Masseneinwanderung von Emigranten aus Pakistan und Bangladesch, • dass, nach offiziellen Angaben, 447,201 *Bangladeshis* einer fast dreimal so hohen Anzahl von *Pakistanis* gegenüberstehen (1,124,511), • dass beide Einwanderergruppen der britischen *working class* angehören und tendenziell eher die Labour Partei wählen, • beide Einwanderergruppen vorwiegend innerhalb ihrer ethnischen Gemeinschaft Ehen schließen.	3	
2	... beschreibt den **kulturellen Hintergrund und die Lebensbedingungen** von britischen ***Bangladeshis*** und stellt z. B. dar, dass • Tower Hamlets das Zentrum von *Bangladeshi Britain* ist, • *Bangladeshis* vorwiegend im Restaurant-Sektor tätig sind und auch außerhalb ihrer ethnischen Gemeinschaft Freundschaften schließen, • trotz ihrer Geschäftstüchtigkeit ca. 30 % der *Bangladeshis* in Sozialwohnungen leben.	3	
3	... beschreibt den **kulturellen Hintergrund und die Lebensbedingungen** von britischen ***Pakistanis*** und hebt z. B. hervor, dass • sie vorwiegend als Taxifahrer tätig sind, • sie vorwiegend innerhalb ihrer eigenen ethnischen Gemeinschaft Freunde suchen und Ehen schließen, • sie, obwohl sie häufig Hauseigentümer sind, daraus keinen wirtschaftlichen Vorteil ziehen können, denn die Häuser liegen i. d. R. in eher heruntergekommenen Stadtvierteln.	3	
4	... fasst die **Situation für beide Einwanderergruppen** kurz zusammen und nennt z. B. • dass unter Pakistanis verbreiteter *cultural conservatism* ihre Situation eher verschlechtert, • dass v. a. Pakistanis ihre (aus Pakistan stammenden) Cousins/Cousinen heiraten, die dann in das UK einwandern, • als Konsequenz, dass vielen jungen Männern der Ehrgeiz fehlt, „Karriere zu machen", um so ihren Status innerhalb einer multikulturellen Community zu festigen/verbessern.	3	
5	... erfüllt ein weiteres aufgabenbezogenes Kriterium. (2) •	2	
		12	

Part A: Teilaufgabe 2 (Analysis)

	Anforderungen Der Schüler/die Schülerin ...	maximal erreichbare Punktzahl	erreichte Punkte
1	... vergleicht – unter Bezugnahme auf Aufgabe 1 – **die Situation beider Einwanderergruppen** und verweist z. B. auf • die deutlich divergierende Bevölkerungszahl der beiden Gruppen (*447,201 Bangladeshis vs. 1,124,511 Pakistanis*), • berufliche und politische Gemeinsamkeiten (*restaurants ... taxi-driving ... Labour ...*), • demgegenüber deutliche Unterschiede bzgl. ihres Integrationswillens (*Bangladeshis socialise with people of a different ethnicity ...; 26% of Bangladeshis marry out vs. 17% of Pakistanis ...*), • ähnliche wirtschaftliche Rahmenbedingungen (*Bangladeshis ... their living conditions are often ... dismal ... more than one-third live in social housing; Pakistanis are more likely to own houses ... in decayed northern towns ...*).	5	
2	... arbeitet weitere Rahmenbedingungen mit Fokus auf den **kulturellen Hintergrund der beiden Bevölkerungsgruppen** heraus, z. B. dass • *cultural conservatism* ein zunehmender Trend unter britischen Pakistanis ist (ll. 25 f.), • junge Pakistanis – im Gegensatz zu ihren *first-generation grandparents* – eher dazu neigen, ihre(n) Cousine/Cousin aus Pakistan zu heiraten und sich damit die Zahl der *first-generation* Pakistanis (wieder) erhöht, • im Gegensatz dazu britische Bangladeschis zwar auch meistens innerhalb ihrer ethnischen Community heiraten, dies dann jedoch Ehen zwischen *second-* oder *third-generation immigrants* sind, die sich dem britischen *way of life* bereits angepasst haben, bzw. die dort geboren sind.	5	

3	... arbeitet **mögliche Gründe für den Erfolg der Bangladeschis** heraus und belegt das z. B. durch • deren größere Bereitwilligkeit, sich mit Briten und anderen Bevölkerungsgruppen anzufreunden (ll. 14 f.), • den Ansporn und Ehrgeiz, Karriere zu machen und damit verbunden auch dem Wunsch/der Notwendigkeit, eine höhere Schulbildung zu erzielen (ll. 17 f.), • ihre geringere Anzahl (im Vergleich zu den Pakistanis), die es ihnen eher ermöglicht, aus bestehenden Strukturen herauszukommen (ll. 16 f.).	5	
4	... deutet und interpretiert die im **Text genannten Hintergründe und Trends** und erwähnt z. B., dass • Bangladeschis zwar bestimmte kulturelle Traditionen gewahrt haben (*wed within their ethnic group, cousin marriage*), aber insgesamt der britischen Kultur gegenüber offener gegenüberstehen als Pakistanis (*socialise ...; 26 % marrying out ...; going to university among people of all races ...*), • junge Pakistanis zunehmend konservativ sind und eher unwillig sich zu integrieren (*cultural conservatism ... has deepened ...; more common among recent Pakistani migrants than among their grandparents ...*), • der fehlende Wille zur Integration junge pakistanische Männer damit auch gesellschaftlich und wirtschaftlich zurückwirft (*young men are less driven to succeed ...*).	5	
5	... erfüllt ein weiteres aufgabenbezogenes Kriterium. (4) •	4	
		20	

Part A: Teilaufgabe 3.1 (Evaluation/Comment)

	Anforderungen **Der Schüler/die Schülerin ...**	maximal erreichbare Punktzahl	erreichte Punkte
1	... nimmt Bezug auf die **im Text gegebenen Informationen** und verweist z. B. auf • die (gesellschaftliche, wirtschaftliche) Notwendigkeit, sich den Gegebenheiten des Einwanderungslandes anzupassen (ohne jedoch die eigene Identität vollständig aufzugeben), • die Gefahr, sich gesellschaftlich und wirtschaftlich zu isolieren, wenn man (ausschließlich) auf konservativ-kulturellen Werten und Traditionen beharrt, • das große Durchhaltevermögen, das Einwanderer haben müssen (*... began in the 1950s ...; working class ...; the growing success appears odd ...; living conditions are ... dismal; social housing; grotty flats ...*).	3	
2	... greift die im Text genannten **Aspekte des „Erfolgs"** auf und bewertet sie kritisch, z. B. • die vergleichsweise große Zahl der pakistanischen Einwohner, die jedoch gesellschaftlich eher isoliert sind, • die Tätigkeit im Service-Sektor (Restaurant, Taxi), in dem jedoch die Einkommensmöglichkeiten zunehmend schlecht sind, • der Besitz eines Eigenheims, der jedoch aufgrund der schlechten Lage der Häuser eher zur Belastung wird.	3	
3	... kommt unter Rückgriff auf unterrichtliche Ergebnisse sowie seines/ihres Weltwissens zu einer **kommentierenden Bewertung** und erläutert z. B., dass • aufgrund der politischen Radikalisierung verschiedener Gruppen in Pakistan Einwanderer (z. B. im UK) zunehmend mit Angst oder Misstrauen konfrontiert sind, • der zunehmend einwanderungskritische Kurs der britischen Regierung in den vergangenen Jahren zu einer weiteren Verschärfung und Aufheizung der Situation geführt hat, • die globale politische Situation (*Al Qaida, ISIS* etc.) das generelle Misstrauen gegenüber dem Islam verstärkt hat, nicht nur im UK.	5	
4	... kommt in Abwägung der verschiedenen Aspekte zu einer **Schlussfolgerung**, z. B., dass • es weiterer Anstrengungen auf beiden Seiten (UK und Einwanderer) bedarf, um die Situation zu entschärfen und zu verbessern, • in einer globalen Welt nur durch kulturellen Austausch und Kennenlernen der anderen Traditionen etc. Hass, Isolation und Krieg/Terror überwunden werden können, • Städte, Länder und Regierungen sich zunehmend Konzepte überlegen müssen, um Ghettoisierungen vorzubeugen bzw. sie abzubauen.	5	
5	... erfüllt ein weiteres aufgabenbezogenes Kriterium. (4) •	4	
		16	

Part A: Teilaufgabe 3.2 ((Re-)Creation of text)

	Anforderungen Der Schüler/die Schülerin ...	maximal erreichbare Punktzahl	erreichte Punkte
1	... versetzt sich durchgängig in die **Perspektive des Journalisten** und berücksichtigt dabei z. B. • eine neutrale, wertungsfreie und unemotionale Haltung gegenüber den Interviewpartnern bzw. der Thematik, • eine klare Strukturierung des Interviews (Einleitung (Thema, Gesprächspartner) – strukturierte Fragesequenz – Abschluss), • eine strategisch geschickte Fragestellung sowie Antworten und (Re-)Agieren auf die Interviewpartner.	3	
2	... berücksichtigt – unter Bezug auf Informationen des Textes sowie unterrichtlicher Ergebnisse – die **Bangladeshi perspective** und stellt z. B. dar, dass • sie vorrangig als Briten/britische Bürger und nicht als *„immigrant"* wahrgenommen werden wollen, • sie sich als vollwertige, hart arbeitende Mitglieder der britischen Gesellschaft sehen, die es nicht verdient haben, in *social housing* und *dilapidated* oder *decayed towns or areas* zu leben/leben zu müssen, • Bangladeschis einen großen Teil des britischen Service-Sektors bewerkstelligen und organisieren, der ohne sie nicht funktionieren würde.	3	
3	... greift in entsprechender Weise rollen- und kontextgemäß die Perspektive und Belange der **Pakistani community** auf und benennt z. B., dass • sich viele Pakistanis zu Unrecht unter Generalverdacht sehen, gefährlich zu sein oder der Terrorszene anzugehören, • sie nicht dafür verurteilt werden wollen, ihre Traditionen und Werte hochzuhalten, • sie als britische Bürger, die arbeiten und zum Einkommen des Landes beitragen, auch erwarten, respektiert zu werden.	5	
4	... kommt zu einem kontextgemäßen und abwägenden Abschluss des Interviews und formuliert z. B., dass • im Sinne einer *„win-win"*-Situation für alle Beteiligten man stärker auf Gemeinsamkeiten als auf Unterschiede fokussieren sollte, • sowohl Politiker als auch die Bürger selbst gefordert sind, sich an einen „runden Tisch" zu setzen und gemeinsam Lösungen zu finden.	5	
5	... erfüllt ein weiteres aufgabenbezogenes Kriterium. (4) •	4	
		16	

Part B: Listening Comprehension

	Anforderungen	maximal erreichbare Punktzahl	erreichte Punkte
1	**Listening Comprehension 1** – je richtigem *statement* 2 Punkte (= 10 x 2)	20	
2	**Listening Comprehension 2** – je richtiger *sentence completion* 2 Punkte (= 5 x 2)	10	
		30	

Part B: Listening Comprehension – Solutions

ASSIGNMENT 1

Statement	Sara Firth	Eric Kaufmann	General information
More than 100,000 people from ethnic minority groups have moved out of London.	X		
You are getting white British people avoiding very diverse areas.		X	
A new study warns of comfort zone segregation.			X
A local Sheffield community has hit the headlines over community tensions between Roma population and other ethnic groups.	X		
Britain is turning into a colour-coded society.			X
In parts of East London, Newham or in parts of South London, … there are fewer and fewer white British people there.		X	
Segregation really needs to be addressed in the UK	X		
Some 600,000 white Britons left London between 2001 and 2011.			X
White Britons are driven by the need to stay in the majority.		X	
We see the same trends in the United States … and that could be a concern for integration.		X	

(20 points)

ASSIGNMENT 2

1. In the UK, whites and ethnic minorities are choosing to live apart because …
   they feel more comfortable within established minority communities or communities where they are the majority.

2. According to the think tank "Demos" and "Birkbeck", University of London, people from ethnic minority groups are …
   moving out of London to mixed areas with established minority groups.

3. Segregation needs to be addressed and acknowledged because …
   it could lead to hostility and division between communities; it has serious implications for community relations.

4. White British people are avoiding very diverse areas and …

moving to areas where they are in a comfortable majority.

5. Similar trends can be seen in the United States because there …

are diverse cities like Houston or Los Angeles where there are very few white people living there.

(10 points)

Part B: Listening Comprehension – Transcript

Multicultural Society – UK Whites and Ethnics Choose to Live Apart

Anchorwoman: Britain is turning into a colour-coded* society with the UK's whites and ethnic minorities choosing to live apart. That's according to a new study that warns of comfort zone segregation, which could lead to division and hostility* between the communities. RT Sara Firth has more on the worrying trend:

5   **Sara Firth:** Well, that warning that Britain could be drifting towards becoming a colour-coded society coming from the former head of the "Equalities and Human Rights Commission", Trevor Phillips.

Now, Mr Phillips has been leading some research with think tank "Demos" and "Birkbeck", University of London.

10 And what they've done is: analysed data from the 2001 census and the 2011 census and what they found is: During that time, more than 100,000 people from ethnic minority groups have moved out of London. But instead of moving to areas considered predominantly white, have preferred instead to move to so-called "mixed areas", where there are already established minority groups.

Now, here in Sheffield* a local community has hit the headlines over recent weeks for concerns

15 raised over community tensions between the Roma* population and other ethnic groups in that community.

What this research is saying is that this could be a pattern that we see played out* across the UK that segregation really needs to be addressed and acknowledged* because of course it does have very serious implications for community relations across the UK.

20 **Anchorwoman:** It's estimated that some 600,000 white Britons left London between 2001 and 2011 – opting* to move to areas with a high white population. Eric Kaufmann, Professor of Politics at the University of London, says they're driven by the need to stay in the majority.

Eric Kaufmann (Professor of Politics, University of London): One of the negative consequences is that you are getting white British people avoiding very diverse* areas. So, it's not because they dis-

25 like any one group but they just want to be in a comfortable majority. So, you can get a situation where, like in parts of East London, Newham or in parts of South London, each census there are fewer and fewer white British there and it is possible that there will be areas that have very few to no, not no, but very few white British people living there. We see the same trends in the United States: there are sections of the diverse cities like Houston or Los Angeles, where there are very

30 few white people living there and that could be a concern for integration. So, it's just that inability to attract or retain* white British population in some of these areas that are maybe not so close to Central London, but are not far enough away to be sort of leafy* and green. So, it's that belt* where you might get this effect.

(462 words)

www.youtube.com/watch?v=13kOeTojCBI, 28 November 2013 [11.05.2015], transcribed by Iris Edelbrock

*vocab given along with the assignments

Topic: The American Dream – Reveries and Realities

Skills: Analysis of a non-fictional text (magazine article); writing a speech script (*Zieltextformat*); listening comprehension

Texts: **Part A:** Rana Foroohar: Starbucks for America, New York, 2015 (599 words)
Part B: The Young Turks (TYT): Starbucks End Controversial "Race Together" Campaign, TV discussion (04:14 mins)

Part A: Reading/Writing

Rana Foroohar

Starbucks for America

The 61-year-old Starbucks CEO[1] doesn't mind tears or hugs[2] or displays of emotion of any kind. This is front and center[3] on an icy January afternoon in New York City, where Schultz is leading a forum on race. Shocked by recent police shootings and unrest in Ferguson, Mo., New York City and Oakland, Calif., he decided to hold open meetings in five cities where Starbucks employees from
5 top managers to entry-level baristas could speak frankly about their experiences with racism.
A little more than 40 % of the company's baristas are minorities, and the audience of 400 or so at Cooper Union's auditorium reflects that. Schultz has just come from a meeting with New York City police commissioner William Bratton in which the two discussed ways the company could help ease[4] tensions. Like a candidate holding forth[5] during a televised town hall[6], Schultz is speaking
10 from a spot on the floor near the crowd. "People have told me we shouldn't touch this issue, that we might stir things up, upset the shareholders[7]. I don't agree with that," he says. "Conversations are being ignored because people are afraid to touch this issue. But if I ignore this and just keep ringing the register[8], then I become part of the problem. So here we are. Let's talk."
Pretty soon, the floodgates are open[9]. The microphone is passed around, and dozens of partners, as
15 Starbucks employees are called, begin sharing their stories. Some are crying, others angry. [...]
Starbucks – whose baristas, at Schultz's suggestion, wrote COME TOGETHER on coffee cups in protest over the shutdown[10] – already had a reputation at that point as a progressive company, having been one of the first retailers in the country to offer affordable, comprehensive health care to full-time and eligible[11] part-time employees and their families, as well as a stock-grant program[12]
20 (Bean Stock) for all. And there have also been big pushes in areas like workforce training (the company and the Schultz Family Foundation together have trained nearly 700 disadvantaged young people for jobs in retail[13] or customer service), hiring and training of returning veterans (Starbucks has pledged[14] to employ 10,000), student debt and access to education (the company has promised to help pay for employees to get their bachelor's degree, an investment that will likely cost Star-
25 bucks tens of millions of dollars).
Schultz says he is deeply invested in[15] these ideas not only because making the company a preferred employer helps keep turnover[16] costs lower and service quality higher than the industry average but also because he believes corporations have a duty to help people realize the American Dream. "I think the private sector simply has to take a larger role than they have in the past. Our
30 responsibility goes beyond the P&L[17] and our stock price. We have to take care of people in the communities that we serve. If half the country or at least a third of the country doesn't have the same

---

[1] **CEO** [ˌsiː iː ˈou] (*abbr.*) Chief Executive Officer; the president of a large company – [2] **hug** *Umarmung* – [3] **front and center** (*infml.*) important and worthy of attention – [4] **to ease sth.** to make sth. less severe – [5] **to hold forth** (*phr. v.*) to speak at great length about sth. – [6] **town hall** *Rathaus* – [7] **shareholder** *Aktionär(in)* – [8] **to ring the register** *die Kasse klingeln lassen* – [9] **to open the floodgates** (*infml.*) to allow many people to do sth. that was previously not allowed; here: to show emotions openly – [10] **the shutdown** here: period from Oct 1st to 16th, 2013, when the Republican-controlled House of Representatives caused a shutdown of most government agencies by refusing to grant funding for the budget in protest at Obama's Healthcare legislation – [11] **eligible** [ˈelidʒəbl] entitled, meeting certain criteria – [12] **stock-grant program** *Gratis-Aktien* – [13] **retail** *Einzelhandel* – [14] **to pledge** to officially promise – [15] **to be invested in sth.** to be deeply committed to sth. – [16] **(staff) turnover** *Mitarbeiterfluktuation* – [17] **P&L** (*abbr.*) Profit and Loss (statement)

opportunities as the rest going forward, then the country won't survive. That's not socialism," says Schultz, it's practical reality. [...]

On the policy front, the company is planning to dramatically ramp up[18] the number of out-of-work
35 younger people, veterans and other struggling groups that get workforce training through Starbucks. On Feb. 9 [2015] in L.A., Schultz is holding the company's first open forum on racism with non-Starbucks participants. Meanwhile, the early-morning emails with the next big idea – to staffers[19], friends, his wife, other CEOs – are unlikely to stop coming anytime soon. "I like to take big swings," says Schultz, smiling and chugging[20] yet another Sumatra[21]. "Maybe it's all the coffee."

(*599 words*)

Time, 16 February 2015, pp. 16 ff.

ASSIGNMENTS

1. Give an outline of Foroohar's article about Starbucks' political and social commitment, paying attention to what she points out about:
   – Starbucks CEO Howard Schultz's reaction to the police shootings and racial tensions in the USA,
   – Starbucks' understanding of social responsibility,
   – Schultz's understanding of how to realize the American Dream.
   (*Comprehension*)

2. Analyse the stylistic devices employed in the article and explain their function in presenting the Starbucks company, its CEO Howard Schultz and his policies.
   (*Analysis*)

3. You have a choice here. Choose **one** of the following tasks:

   3.1 Keeping in mind your knowledge of aspects and issues in connection with the so-called "American Dream", critically comment on Howard Schultz's view that "corporations have a duty to help people realize the American Dream" (ll. 28 f.).
   (*Comment/Evaluation*)

   3.2 You are a stockholder of the Starbucks company and have watched the various political and social campaigns that CEO Howard Schultz has suggested and promoted over time.
   Prepare a short speech to be delivered at an open meeting, in which you state whether (or not) you share Schultz's ideas and express your views.
   ((*Re-*) *Creation of text*)

---

[18] **to ramp sth. up** (*phr. v.*) to dramatically increase sth. – [19] **staffer** (*AE*) employee – [20] **to chug sth.** *etw. auf ex trinken* – [21] **Sumatra** a dark roast coffee

Part B: Listening Comprehension

The Young Turks

Starbucks Ends Controversial "Race Together" Campaign

The Young Turks (TYT) is an American liberal/progressive political and social online news and talk show that offers Internet-only information and commentary via their YouTube channel. The show is hosted by Cenk Uygur and Ana Kasparian.

Source: www.youtube.com/watch?v=ilSU9ENNRZQ, 28 March, 2015 [04.04.2015] (04:14 mins)

Annotations ⟫⟫

kerfuffle commotion or fuss, esp. caused by conflicting views ▪ **to put sb. on notice** here: to warn or make sb. aware of sth. ▪ **inclusive** here: not excluding any particular groups of people ▪ **backlash** a strong, negative reaction to a new trend, change, suggestion, etc. ▪ **praise** *Lob* ▪ **to bring sth. up** (*phr. v.*) to introduce a topic ▪ **to push an agenda** to aggressively promote a cause or idea ▪ **conventional wisdom** the generally-accepted belief or opinion about sth. ▪ **flop** (*infml.*) a failure ▪ **camp** here: a group with the same ideas and beliefs ▪ **goofy** (*US: infml.*) silly, uncool ▪ **awkward** uncomfortable, *heikel* ▪ **to tackle sth.** to deal with sth. difficult ▪ **to push past sth.** to overcome a problem or difficulty ▪ **to fall short of sth.** to be not (good) enough ▪ **to spark sth.** *etw. entfachen* ▪ **to capitalize on sth.** (*phr. v.*) *aus einer Situation Kapital schlagen* ▪ **valid** true ▪ **opportunistic** using a situation to your own advantage ▪ **to polarize** *polarisieren* ▪ **on the heels of sth.** following shortly after sth., esp. an event ▪ **insane** crazy ▪ **to be on that side of the ledger** ['lɛdʒə] here: following that line of argumentation or set of ideals

ASSIGNMENT 1 ⟫⟫⟫⟫⟫

Before the recording is presented, read the vocabulary above and the statements given below. Make sure you understand them. While listening, match the statements to the correct speaker by ticking the correct box.

Statements	Cenk Uygur	Ana Kasparian	Howard Schultz	Starbucks customers	General information
Starbucks want to start a dialogue about race.					
They're not here to push their political agenda.					
A lot of people actually hated this campaign.					
Look at the bravery of a corporation to do that.					
We didn't expect universal praise.					
It actually cost them some customers.					
Race is an uncomfortable thing to bring up.					

Statements	Cenk Uygur	Ana Kasparian	Howard Schultz	Starbucks customers	General information
Starbucks is deciding to end a portion of their race awareness campaign.					
I applaud them for wanting to hire more minorities.					
Baristas are putting the hashtag "Race Together" on coffee cups.					
They shouldn't have done that in the first place.					
They could have publicized it in a more effective way.					

(24 points)

ASSIGNMENT 2

After a second listening, complete the sentence starters given below.

1. The Starbucks "Race Together" campaign was about …

_____

_____

2. The Starbucks customers' reaction to the campaign was …

_____

_____

3. People come to Starbucks because …

_____

_____

(6 points)

Bewertungsbogen für: _____ Kurs: _____

Part A: Teilaufgabe 1 (Comprehension)

	Anforderungen Der Schüler/die Schülerin ...	maximal erreichbare Punktzahl	erreichte Punkte
1	... stellt heraus, dass Howard Schultz den **Starbucks Mitarbeitern ein Forum zur Aussprache bietet** und benennt z. B. ● die *five open meetings*, die der offenen Aussprache und einem Erfahrungsaustausch dienten, ● die Starbucks *baristas*, die selbst zu ca. 40 % Migrationshintergrund haben, ● dass die Starbucks *meetings* sehr emotional waren und viele Mitarbeiter die Möglichkeit zu einem offenen Gespräch nutzten.	3	
2	... beschreibt **Schultz' Umgang mit den Rassenunruhen** in Ferguson und weiteren Städten und stellt z. B. dar, dass ● Schultz schockiert war von der Polizeigewalt und den Unruhen, ● Schultz das Gespräch mit der New Yorker Polizei gesucht hat, um über Lösungen zu diskutieren, ● Schultz keine Angst hat, durch die „Race Together" Kampagne seine Aktionäre zu verärgern, sondern die Probleme durch einen offensiven Umgang damit zu lösen versucht, damit Starbucks nicht selbst Teil dieses Rassenproblems wird.	3	
3	... legt **Starbucks Personalpolitik** und *social responsibility* dar und erwähnt z. B., dass ● das Unternehmen als eines der ersten in den USA *affordable, comprehensive health care* für seine Mitarbeiter angeboten hat, ● Starbucks sowohl (700) sozial benachteiligte junge Leute ausgebildet als auch Kriegsveteranen eingestellt und ausgebildet hat, ● Starbucks die Angestellten beim Studium finanziell unterstützt.	3	
4	... skizziert Schultz' Vorstellungen bzgl. der **Umsetzung des *American Dream*** und nennt z. B. ● die Verpflichtung von Unternehmen, den Menschen bei der Realisierung des *American Dream* zu helfen, ● die zunehmende Verantwortung des privaten Sektors, ● die Notwendigkeit, *opportunities* für die Menschen zu schaffen, um wirtschaftliches Vorankommen und soziale Stabilität zu schaffen.	3	
5	... erfüllt ein weiteres aufgabenbezogenes Kriterium. (2) ●	2	
		12	

Part A: Teilaufgabe 2 (Analysis)

	Anforderungen Der Schüler/die Schülerin ...	maximal erreichbare Punktzahl	erreichte Punkte
1	... untersucht **sprachliche Stilmittel und deren Funktion** und verweist z. B. auf ● den durchgängigen Gebrauch der *word fields* zu den Themen *politics* und *economy* und deren z. T. kontrastiven Gebrauch (*CEO ↔ tears, hugs, emotions; shareholders; ringing the register ↔ sharing, crying ... angry; shutdown ↔ progressive company; stock-grant program; work force training*, etc.), ● den durchgängigen Gebrauch von *word fields* in Zusammenhang mit *social life, social responsibility* und *serving* (*speaking frankly about ...; people are afraid to touch this issue ... Let's talk; affordable, comprehensive health care; work force training; the Schultz Family Foundation*, etc.), ● die Darstellung von Howard Schultz als jemanden, der besorgt ist, sich um die Belange der Menschen kümmert und Verantwortung übernimmt (*Starbucks CEO doesn't mind tears or hugs ...; Schultz is leading ...; shocked by ... he decided to ...; Schultz is speaking from a spot on the floor ...*, etc.).	5	
2	... zeigt auf, wie durch den **Einsatz von *allusions* und *references* auf aktuelle Probleme** in der amerikanischen Gesellschaft hingewiesen und Starbucks als „Problemlöser" dargestellt wird, z. B. ● die Polizeigewalt und Rassenunruhen in Ferguson, New York City und Oakland (*police shootings and unrest in ... → accumulation*) → *he decided to hold open meetings ... top managers to entry-level baristas → unity, communication*), ● Schultz' Hilfsangebot und die New Yorker Polizei (*meeting NYC police commissioner ... the two discussed ways the company could help ease tensions ...*), ● Schultz als Kommunikator und praktisch-zupackender Problemlöser (*conversations are being ignored → Let's talk; we have to take care of people ...; it's practical reality; people have told me ...; the early morning emails with the next big idea ...*).	5	

3	... untersucht **weitere Stilmittel** und verdeutlicht, wie sie Stil und Ton des Artikels sowie die Darstellung Howard Schultz' verstärken. Er/sie benennt z. B. • den Gebrauch von Zahlen und Fakten zur Verstärkung der Darstellung des Engagements von Starbucks (*40% of the company's baristas ...; the audience of 400 or so ...; 700 disadvantaged young people ...; employ 10,000*), • den durchgängigen, aber einseitigen, Gebrauch von Zitaten (➜ Fokus auf Schultz), • die z. T. an *human interest* grenzende Art der Darstellung (*tears or hugs or displays of emotions ...; Starbucks employees could speak frankly ...; sharing their stories ... crying ... angry ...*).	5	
4	... interpretiert die im Text genannten **Anspielungen auf den American Dream**, indem er/sie darstellt, dass in dem entsprechenden Textabschnitt (ll. 24–33) • wiederholt das Nomen „*country*" zur Verstärkung des Solidaritätsgefühls vorkommt, • „Starbucks' *American Dream*" (wie Schultz ihn sieht) als Gegenentwurf zu bzw. Weiterentwicklung des *American Dream* der Vergangenheit verstanden wird (*a larger role ... than in the past: the same opportunities ... going forward ... practical reality*), • Schultz im Sinne einer *grass roots democracy* die bestehenden Probleme angehen und lösen will.	5	
5	... erfüllt ein weiteres aufgabenbezogenes Kriterium. (4) •	4	
		20	

Part A: Teilaufgabe 3.1 (Evaluation/Comment)

	Anforderungen **Der Schüler/die Schülerin ...**	maximal erreichbare Punktzahl	erreichte Punkte
1	... stellt vor dem Hintergrund unterrichtlicher Ergebnisse die **Kerngedanken des *American Dream*** dar und benennt z. B. • die bereits in der *Declaration of Independence* verankerten Grundrechte wie *equality* und *the pursuit of happiness*, • das Vertrauen in den *protestant work ethic* (➜ *hard work will finally pay off*), • die von James Truslow Adams benannten Kriterien des *American Dream*, z. B. *opportunity for each according to ability or achievement; the ability to grow; the fullest development of man and woman; possibility to achieve the American Dream for citizens of every rank*, etc.).	3	
2	... nimmt konkreten Bezug auf im Text von **Howard Schultz genannte Aspekte des *American Dream***, z. B. • die Verantwortung des privaten Sektors, • die Notwendigkeit der Chancengleichheit für alle, • die Einbeziehung aller sozialen Schichten (*disadvantaged, young people, veterans ...*), • die offene Diskussion und den Gedankenaustausch (*open meetings, open forum* ➜ *grass roots democracy*).	3	
3	... gibt Beispiele für **die (indirekte) Verknüpfung von wirtschaftlichen Interessen und den Idealen des *American Dream***, z. B., dass • sich Ehrgeiz und Ansporn der Menschen, den *American Dream* zu realisieren, für Unternehmen (wie Starbucks) finanziell auszahlen (*making the company a preferred employer helps keep turnover costs lower ...*), • sich soziales Engagement und Investitionen in die Ausbildung letztendlich auch für das Unternehmen auszahlen.	5	
4	... kommt zu einer **Stellungnahme, die sich plausibel aus den Ausführungen ergibt**, und kommt zu einem begründeten Resümee. Er/sie stellt z. B. dar, dass • er/sie Anstrengungen eines so einflussreichen Unternehmens wie Starbucks unterstützt, weil dadurch politisch und wirtschaftlich Einfluss genommen werden kann, • er/sie die Ausführungen von Howard Schultz für strategische Augenwischerei und reine Unternehmenspolitik aus wirtschaftlichen Interessen hält, • er/sie unterstützt, dass Howard Schultz in seinem Unternehmen soziale Verantwortung zeigt und auf „Augenhöhe" mit seinen Angestellten diskutiert.	5	
5	... erfüllt ein weiteres aufgabenbezogenes Kriterium. (4) •	4	
		16	

Part A: Teilaufgabe 3.2 ((Re-)Creation of text)

	Anforderungen **Der Schüler/die Schülerin ...**	maximal erreichbare Punktzahl	erreichte Punkte
1	... ist in der Lage, **sich in die Position eines Starbucks Aktionärs zu versetzen**, und stellt seine grundlegenden Erwartungen an das Unternehmen dar, z. B. ● dass Starbucks auch weiterhin so erfolgreich arbeiten soll (und die Aktien weiterhin an Wert gewinnen), ● den Wunsch nach der Weiterführung der bisherigen Unternehmenspolitik und -philosophie (exklusive, kosmopolitische Atmosphäre, gehobene Preise ➔ gehobenes Publikum), ● die Forderung nach der Schaffung einer „Wohlfühlatmosphäre" für Angestellte und Kunden.	3	
2	... befürwortet das **politische und soziale Engagement des Unternehmens** und seines Geschäftsführers und benennt z. B. ● das umfangreiche Sozialpaket für Starbucks-Angestellte, ● das Ernstnehmen von sozialen Missständen als auch von Belangen der Angestellten, ● Schultz' Besinnung auf amerikanische Grundwerte und die Darstellung der Notwendigkeit zur Übernahme von sozialer Verantwortung.	3	
3	... **kritisiert demgegenüber**, dass Schultz die bestehenden sozialen Unruhen für seine Zwecke ausnutzt und verweist z. B. auf ● Starbucks kompromisslose Geschäftspolitik, wenn es z. B. um das Zahlen von Steuern an Städte und Gemeinden oder die Bezahlung von Bauern in den Produktionsländern des Kaffees geht, ● die Mitarbeiter von Starbucks, die mehrheitlich aus Teilzeit-Jobbern bestehen und daher nur sehr begrenzt auf die angepriesenen Sozialleistungen Anspruch haben, ● den Widerspruch, sich für soziale Randgruppen oder sozial benachteiligte Menschen einsetzen zu wollen und das Starbucks Geschäftsmodell, das auf gehobenes Ambiente und zahlungskräftige Kundschaft setzt.	5	
4	... formuliert eine **sach- und adressatengerechte Rede**, indem er/sie z. B. ● durch eine knappe Selbstdarstellung sowie Nennung des Redeanlasses und der Intention einleitet, ● die Rede klar strukturiert (Einleitung – Hauptteil (Fakten, Beispiele, Wertungen ...) – Abschluss (Fazit, Appell)), ● eine gewisse Rhetorisierung vornimmt (rhetorische Mittel, *informal vs. formal* English, etc.).	5	
5	... erfüllt ein weiteres aufgabenbezogenes Kriterium. (4) ●	4	
		16	

Part B: Listening Comprehension

	Anforderungen	maximal erreichbare Punktzahl	erreichte Punkte
1	**Listening Comprehension 1** – je richtigem *matching* 2 points (= 12 x 2 = 24 points)	24	
2	**Listening Comprehension 2** – je richtiger *sentence completion* 2 points (= 3 x 2 = 6 points)	6	
		30	

Part B: Listening Comprehension – Solutions

ASSIGNMENT 1

Statements	Cenk Uygur	Ana Kasparian	Howard Schultz	Starbucks customers	General information
Starbucks wanted to start a dialogue about race.					X
They're not here to push their political agenda.				X	
A lot of people actually hated this campaign.					X
Look at the bravery of a corporation to do that.	X				
We didn't expect universal praise.			X		
It actually cost them some customers.	X				
Race is an uncomfortable thing to bring up.				X	
Starbucks is deciding to end a portion of their race awareness campaign.					X
I applaud them for wanting to hire more minorities.		X			
Baristas are putting the hashtag "Race Together" on coffee cups.					X
They shouldn't have done that in the first place.	X				
They could have publicized it in a more effective way.		X			

(24 points)

ASSIGNMENT 2

1. The Starbucks "Race Together" campaign was about ...
   ... raising awareness about race relations in the USA; ... informing people that Starbucks intends to hire more people from different minorities.

2. The Starbucks customers' reaction to the campaign was …
   … critical and negative; … that it made people feel uncomfortable; … that it made people hate Starbucks and want to avoid spending time there; … that it was inappropriate/goofy/strange.

3. People come to Starbucks because …
   … they want to study, read, write or relax; … they just want to have some coffee.

(6 points)

Part B: Listening Comprehension – Transcript

The Young Turks

Starbucks Ends Controversial "Race Together" Campaign

Ana Kasparian: Starbucks is deciding to end a portion of their race awareness campaign where they are putting the hashtag "Race Together" on coffee cups.

Now, there is a lot of controversy, there's huge kerfuffle* over this issue. They wanted to not only raise awareness about race relations here in the United States, but they also wanted to basically put
5   people on notice* and let them know that Starbucks as a company is going to be much more inclusive* in their hiring process; they want to start a dialogue about race in the country.

Now, people did not take kindly to this campaign. They thought that it was strange for baristas to get involved; they thought it was strange for baristas to use that hashtag on coffee cups. A lot of people go to Starbucks with the intention of studying or writing or just relaxing and so they felt like this
10 wasn't the proper forum in order to have this conversation.

Now, Howard Schultz, who is the CEO of Starbucks, did speak to the press about this and some of the backlash* and here's what he had to say:

"While there has been criticism of the initiative – and I know this hasn't been easy for any of you [speaking to his employees] – let me assure you that we didn't expect universal praise*."
15 Well, it's good that he didn't expect that because a lot of people absolutely hated this campaign.

One person said the following:

"Most people come to Starbucks for coffee. Race is an uncomfortable thing to bring up*, especially in a Starbucks." (Ninette Musili)

Another person said:
20 "They're here for coffee. They're not here to push their political agenda*. I even contemplated not coming here because of it. There are other ways you can go about doing things to stimulate interest in what you're doing. They must be doing so well they don't have to worry about losing customers over that." (Shane Mulholland)

Cenk Uygur: Okay, so conventional wisdom* is – this was a flop; it was a bad idea and they
25 shouldn't have done that in the first place – and they realized now that they shouldn't have – that's why they are stopping. So, Starbucks says, 'It's not true, we had already planned to stop on March 22nd [2015], we just didn't announce that earlier.'

That part of the story I don't really care about, if you know they decided to stop now or earlier, so what, right? …
30 Here's what I do care about:

I actually really applaud them for doing it. I'm not in the camp* that thinks it was stupid and goofy*. Don't get me wrong. Like Howard Schultz said, it's really hard, and it might have actually cost them some customers, and it is uncomfortable. But – look at the bravery of a corporation to do that and to do it with good intent, right? Knowing that they might lose customers, knowing that
35 they're gonna get blown apart.

You think they didn't know, when they put the hashtag "Race Together", that people were gonna make fun of them – and like they … it didn't occur to them that having a conversation with your barista about race is a little awkward*. Like, they knew that was coming. And they tackled* it anyway. Even if this isn't a shining success, at this moment, when you look at it in a short-term way, it's at

40 least them trying to do the right thing by getting people to push past* that uncomfortableness to have that conversation. I think it's phenomenal.

Ana Kasparian: I applaud them for wanting to hire more minorities, I applaud them for wanting to open up stores in areas that have more minorities living there. But at the same time, I think that this kind of falls short of* sparking* an important dialogue, right? So, what has happened so far –
45 from them using this hashtag on coffee cups? Absolutely nothing.

No one's had a discussion. If anything, people have just criticized Starbucks and that's it.

And so, I think that this was the initial phase of them publicizing something good that they're gonna do, but they could have publicized it in a more effective way.

And also, you know, because of the timing, people are criticizing them because of the Ferguson pro-
50 test and they think that they're kind of exploiting that or capitalizing on* that. I can understand that criticism and it could be a valid criticism*. But nonetheless, I ... if they used what happened in Ferguson to spark a dialogue about race, then I'm in favour of it. I just don't think that this component of their campaign was really successful.

Cenk Uygur: Yeah, I don't believe that it was opportunistic* at all. If anything, it's gonna polarize*
55 people and cost them customers and they did it anyway because they thought it was the right thing to do. To criticize them on the heels* of Ferguson is insane* if you are on the issue of civil rights and on that side of the ledger*. You want people to talk about it and this is a perfect time to talk about it.

(*841 words*)

www.youtube.com/watch?v=ilSU9ENNRZQ, 28 March 2015 [04.04.2015], transcribed by Iris Edelbrock

*vocab given along with the assignments

Topic: The UK – Between Tradition and Modernity – Multicultural Britain

Skills: Analysis of a fictional text (short story); continuation of a fictional text (*Zieltextformat*); listening comprehension

Texts: **Part A:** Antoinette Moses: Frozen Pizza, London, 2004 (526 words)
Part B: Vox Pops International: What Does "Being British" Mean to Millennials?, TV interviews (02:40 mins)

Part A: Reading/Writing

Antoinette Moses

Frozen Pizza

The young man looked around the room and wondered whether he had made a mistake. Perhaps he should have stayed at the university and not chosen to have a room in the town. But he thought that living in a family would help him to improve his English. It was already quite good. Good enough, in fact, for him to have won a place at the university to study science. He had a degree[1] in
5 his own country, but he wanted to carry out some additional research in England. [...]
'The poor boy,' thought Mrs Stonehouse. 'I suppose that in his country they don't have very much. I suppose that the women stay at home and cook simple food like they did in England before I was born. I expect that he feels that he's very lucky to be able to stay in a house like this.'
'Oh, I don't cook.' She laughed. 'We're a very modern family. We don't waste our time on things like
10 that and I've never been one for the cookery. I love reading cookery books, of course,' she added. 'But that's different.' [...]
The young man was now very confused. Mrs Stonehouse opened the freezer. 'Here,' she said. 'Everything you could want.'
The freezer was taller than the young man. Inside were boxes and boxes of frozen pizzas and ready-
15 cooked meals. They filled all the shelves.
'You can help yourself to any of the packets. You just open the packet and put it into the microwave,' said Mrs Stonehouse. 'Nothing can be easier.' [...]
'But when do you have dinner? He asked.
'We don't have dinner,' she said. 'As I said, we all just help ourselves. I eat when I get back from
20 my aerobics class and the kids grab something to eat when they get back from school before they go out. Though sometimes, like today, they go straight from school to their friends' houses. And Harry, that's my husband, he eats at different times. It depends whether he's working late or at the pub. We're a very independent family.'
'I was right,' she thought. 'In his country it must be very different. He's never been in a home like
25 this.' She felt sorry for him.
'Her husband works late and goes by himself to the pub and the children go to their friends' houses. She must be very lonely,' thought the young man. 'That is why she doesn't cook proper meals.' He felt sorry for her. [...]
The next morning the young man moved out. He went to a café and had some breakfast, and then
30 he went to the university housing office. The woman there listened to him and immediately found him another place to stay.
She also rang Mrs Stonehouse and told her that the young man had moved out.
'Was it the rabbits?' Mrs Stonehouse asked. 'I offered to put him in another room, but he said that he wanted a desk. He even had his own television. Really,' she continued, getting more and more
35 angry. 'Compared with what he must have come from in his own country, you would have thought that he'd be grateful.' (*526 words*)

Antoinette Moses: Frozen Pizza and other Slices of Life. Cambridge University Press, Cambridge 2004, pp. 39 ff.

---

[1] **degree** a qualification that proves you have completed a course of study at a college or university

ASSIGNMENTS

1. Describe what the young foreign student learns about the Stonehouse family's way of life.
   (*Comprehension*)

2. Analyse the narrative and stylistic devices the author employs to emphasize the cultural clash that the young man and Mrs Stonehouse experience.
   (*Analysis*)

3. You have a choice here. Choose **one** of the following tasks:

   3.1 Comment on the young man's reaction. Was he right to leave the Stonehouse's home without any comment or should he have explained to Mrs Stonehouse why he did not want to stay?
   (*Comment/Evaluation*)

   3.2 As can be seen, several parts of the original short story have been omitted. Imagine which further observations both characters might have made and which cultural clashes they might have experienced and write an additional part to the short story.
   (*(Re-)Creation of text*)

Part B: Listening Comprehension

Vox Pops International

What Does "Britain" and "Being British" Mean to Millennials?

Vox Pops International (VPI) is a British market research company, focusing on so-called "consumer insight" videos, which are aimed at communicating and providing information about consumer messages, marketing insights and data. In March 2015, VPI spoke to Millennials in Birmingham, Leeds and London about what "Britain" and "Being British" means to them.

Source: www.youtube.com/watch?v=wWGMvmAlIvA, 4 March, 2015 [04.04.2015] (02:40 mins)

Annotations 》》》

millennial person born between 1980 and 2000 ■ **collective** of or shared by every member of a group of people ■ **to embrace sth.** to welcome and accept willingly, to include as an integral part of sth. larger

ASSIGNMENT 1 》》》》

Before listening to the interviews, read the vocabulary above and the statements below. After listening, decide whether each one is true, false or not given in the text. Tick off the appropriate box and make corrections to the false statements.

	True	False	Not given
1. Britons are strong and independent people.	☐	☐	☐
2. Britain consists of a collective of countries which are dependent on each other.	☐	☐	☐
3. Being British means being patriotic and being Scottish, Irish and English.	☐	☐	☐
4. Being British means being cosmopolitan and having a collective identity.	☐	☐	☐
5. The British are tolerant and embracing.	☐	☐	☐
6. The British are patriotic and respect their own people.	☐	☐	☐
7. Britons love international food and ethnic diversity.	☐	☐	☐

	True	False	Not given
8. Britishness means keeping production and manufacturing in England and not outsourcing it to foreign countries.	☐	☐	☐
9. London is Britain's most popular attraction.	☐	☐	☐
10. Tourists love the British countryside and the famous cup of tea.	☐	☐	☐
11. Britain has a certain kind of national pride and a very strict class system.	☐	☐	☐
12. Britons love a nice cup of tea, going out for a dog walk and fish and chips.	☐	☐	☐
13. Britons have black humour and are sarcastic.	☐	☐	☐
14. Britain has a strict legislature and fights discrimination.	☐	☐	☐
15. Britons are freedom-loving and inventive people.	☐	☐	☐

(15 x 2 = 30 points)

| Bewertungsbogen für: _____ | Kurs: _____ |

Part A: Teilaufgabe 1 (Comprehension)

	Anforderungen Der Schüler/die Schülerin ...	maximal erreichbare Punktzahl	erreichte Punkte
1	... skizziert **die Rahmenbedingungen** der dargestellten Situation und benennt z. B., dass • der „junge Mann" in seinem Heimatland ein Auslandsstipendium für *„Science"* gewonnen hat und nun weitere Studien in England durchführen möchte, • der junge Mann in einer englischen Familie leben möchte, um seine Sprachkenntnisse zu verbessern, • die Vermieterin, Mrs Stonehouse, sich selbst und ihre Familie als modern und selbstständig darstellt.	3	
2	... umreißt die Perspektive des jungen **Mannes** und stellt z. B. dar, dass • er nicht versteht, wie man eine so moderne und gut ausgestattete Küche haben kann, aber überhaupt nicht kochen möchte, • der junge Mann die vielfältigen außerhäuslichen Aktivitäten der Familienmitglieder als Grund für die mögliche Einsamkeit der Frau bewertet sowie ihren Unwillen, für die Familie zu kochen, • der junge Mann die von Mrs Stonehouse angepriesenen Qualitäten des Haushalts nicht wertschätzt (*frozen pizzas, ready-cooked meals, desk, television*, etc.) und sie sogar bemitleidet.	3	
3	... beschreibt **das Leben der Familie Stonehouse**, z. B., dass • alle Familienmitglieder ihren individuellen Tagesablauf haben und offenbar wenige Aktivitäten gemeinsam unternehmen, • sie sich als moderne und unabhängige Familie verstehen, • es zwar ein umfangreich ausgestattetes Haus beinhaltet, das jedoch von den Mitgliedern der Familie kaum genutzt wird, weil sie ständig unterwegs sind.	3	
4	... arbeitet **Mrs Stonehouses Perspektive** heraus und benennt z. B., dass • sie Kochen für Zeitverschwendung und unmodern hält, • sie die Lebensweise im Heimatland des jungen Mannes für rückständig hält und annimmt, er müsse froh sein, in einem Haus wie dem ihren zu leben, • sie den jungen Mann bemitleidet und nicht verstehen kann, warum er ausgezogen ist, anstatt dankbar zu sein.	3	
5	... erfüllt ein weiteres aufgabenbezogenes Kriterium. (2) •	2	
		12	

Part A: Teilaufgabe 2 (Analysis)

	Anforderungen Der Schüler/die Schülerin ...	maximal erreichbare Punktzahl	erreichte Punkte
1	... arbeitet die **charakteristischen Merkmale einer *Short Story*** heraus und weist sie am Text nach. Er/sie verweist z. B. auf • den unmittelbaren Anfang und das offene Ende der Geschichte, • die Figuren, die entweder namenlos sind (*young man*) oder „Allerweltsnamen" haben (*Stonehouse*) und damit die Funktion von Repräsentanten von (anoynmen) Durchschnittsmenschen, • den Ausschnittcharakter der Situation(en) (*snapshots of life*); eine konkrete Handlung wird nicht entwickelt.	5	
2	... analysiert, wie durch die ***narrative devices*** die Thematik des *„cultural clash"* verdeutlicht wird. Er/sie belegt das z. B. mit • dem Einsatz von *interior monologue*, der die Gedanken der Figuren wiedergibt (*The poor boy ... they don't have very much, I suppose ...; Her husband works late ... She must be very lonely.*), • den Kommentaren des *third-person narrators* (*The young man ... wondered whether he had made a mistake ... he should have stayed ...; ... was now confused ...; the freezer was taller than the young man, etc.*), • die parallele und gleichzeitig kontrastive Dialog- und Erzählstruktur im Aufbau des Textes, die den *"clash"* verstärkt (*... when do you have dinner?* → *We don't have dinner; she felt sorry for him* → *he felt sorry for her*).	5	

3	... untersucht den **Gebrauch von *contrast* und *irony*** und weist sie am Text nach. Er/sie verdeutlicht z. B.	5	
	• den Gegensatz zwischen der Unsicherheit des jungen Mannes (*wondered whether ...; perhaps he should ...; But he thought ...; very confused ...; But when do you ...?*) mit dem Selbstbewusstsein und dem insgesamt sicheren Auftreten von Mrs Stonehouse (*We're a modern family. We don't waste our time ...; We're a very independent family, ... etc.*),		
	• den Gebrauch von *irony* und *hyperbole* als Verstärkung der Gegensätzlichkeit der Kulturen (*... living in a family ...; the women stay at home and cook simple food ...; Everything you want ...; The freezer is taller than the young man; He's never been in a home like this, ... etc.*),		
	• den Gegensatz zwischen der Erwartungshaltung der beiden Figuren und der Realität (*old-fashioned vs. modern; poor vs. rich*, etc.).		
4	... analysiert weitere **Stilmittel**, wie z. B. die sprachlichen Mittel und verweist z. B. auf	5	
	• den Gebrauch von *everyday spoken English*, das den Alltagscharakter der Situation unterstreicht,		
	• den verstärkten Gebrauch von Pronomen, der die Atmosphäre der Anonymität und Isolation unterstreicht.		
5	... erfüllt ein weiteres aufgabenbezogenes Kriterium. (4)	4	
	•		
		20	

Part A: Teilaufgabe 3.1 (Evaluation/Comment)

	Anforderungen	maximal erreichbare Punktzahl	erreichte Punkte
	Der Schüler/die Schülerin ...		
1	... greift die **thematischen Ansätze des Textes** auf und stellt z. B. dar, dass	3	
	• der junge Mann von Anfang an unsicher und vermutlich auch schüchtern war (*wondered whether ...; perhaps ...*),		
	• demgegenüber Mrs Stonehouse Selbstbewusstsein und z. T. auch Überheblichkeit ausstrahlt (*The poor boy ... in his country they don't have very much ... he feels that he is very lucky to be able to stay ...*),		
	• sich beide Figuren von Anfang an gegenseitig bemitleiden.		
2	... erörtert die **Position und Rolle des jungen Mannes** und verweist z. B. auf	3	
	• seinen akademischen Hintergrund (*a place at the university to study science; He had a degree in his own country ...*),		
	• die durchgängige Skepsis des jungen Mannes der Situation der Frau und ihrer Familie gegenüber (*looked around the room ... wondered whether he had made a mistake ...; very confused; he felt sorry for her*),		
	• seine Sichtweise der englischen Familie (*Her husband works late ... goes by himself to the pub ... the children go to their friends ... she must be very lonely ...*).		
3	... nimmt im Umkehrschluss Bezug auf **das mögliche Leben des jungen Mannes in seiner Heimat** und stellt z. B. dar, dass	5	
	• er ein ambitionierter, intelligenter und fleißiger junger Mann ist (*won a place at the university; ... English ... quite good ...*),		
	• das gemeinsame Familienleben und Miteinander offensichtlich eine wichtige Rolle spielt,		
	• das Kochen und gemeinsame Essen in der Familie bedeutsam sind.		
4	... kommt vor dem Hintergrund seiner persönlichen Meinungsbildung in Abwägung der Analyseergebnisse zu einer **begründeten Einschätzung**. Er/sie stellt z. B. dar, dass	5	
	• der Mann aus Höflichkeit der Frau seine Entscheidung hätte mitteilen/erklären sollen, um sie nicht zu verärgern und evt. weitere Vorurteile zu provozieren,		
	• es andererseits vermutlich sinnlos gewesen wäre, der Frau die Gründe für seinen Auszug zu erklären, da sie ihn nicht verstanden hätte,		
	• der junge Mann z. B. hätte anbieten können, etwas für die Familie zu kochen und gemeinsam zu essen.		
5	... erfüllt ein weiteres aufgabenbezogenes Kriterium. (4)	4	
	•		
		16	

Part A: Teilaufgabe 3.2 ((Re-)Creation of text)

	Anforderungen **Der Schüler/die Schülerin ...**	maximal erreichbare Punktzahl	erreichte Punkte
1	... ist in der Lage, sich in **die in der *Short Story* vorgegebene Situation** zu versetzen und berücksichtigt z. B. ● „typisch" britische Klischees wie *tea-time, fish and chips, pub*, etc., ● die tendenzielle Überheblichkeit der Frau, ● die auf beiden Seiten grundsätzlich unterschiedliche Erwartungshaltung und (falsche) Vorstellung von der Lebensweise des anderen.	3	
2	... fügt seinen/ihren Text an der entsprechenden Stelle ein und **berücksichtigt den Kontext**, z. B. ● den Hinweis auf den akademischen Grad des jungen Mannes und seinen Wunsch, einen gewissen Familienanschluss zu finden (ll. 2 ff.), ● die grundsätzliche Ablehnung der Frau von jeder Art von Kochen (*I've never been one for the cookery* ...), ● dass der junge Mann offenbar in dieser Familie auf sich selbst gestellt ist (*you can help yourself ...; We don't have dinner.; I eat when ... the kids grab something to eat ...; Harry eats at different times ...*).	3	
3	... berücksichtigt evtl. unter Einbeziehung unterrichtlicher Ergebnisse (*western values; Britishness*) **weitere mögliche *observations* des jungen Mannes** sowie *cultural clashes*. Er/sie benennt z. B. ● die Auswahl/Qualität der *frozen pizzas* und *ready-cooked meals*, fehlende Gewürze etc., ● die mögliche Innenausstattung und Dekoration des Hauses/des Zimmers des jungen Mannes (Blumentapete; Fotos der Royal Family; kitschige Deko-Artikel etc.), ● fehlendes Familienleben und fehlende Kommunikation, stattdessen Fernsehen, Videospiele etc.	5	
4	... berücksichtigt die **stilistischen Charakteristika einer Short Story** und greift z. B. zurück auf ● (ironisch-wertende) Erzählerkommentare, ● eher spärliche Dialoge im Gegensatz zu umfangreicheren *interior dialogues*, ● Alltagssprache.	5	
5	... erfüllt ein weiteres aufgabenbezogenes Kriterium. (4) ●	4	
		16	

Part B: Listening Comprehension

	Anforderungen	maximal erreichbare Punktzahl	erreichte Punkte
1	**Assignment 1** – 15 richtige *true – false – not given tasks* (15 x 2 points)	30	
		30	

Part B: Listening Comprehension – Solutions

ASSIGNMENT 1

True: No. 1, 2, 5, 7, 8, 9, 12, 15

Not given: No. 4, 10, 14

False:

No. 3
Being British involves both a collective identity as well as being individuals within the UK.

No. 6
The British are not particularly patriotic and are respectful to foreigners and people living outside the country.

No. 11
Being British means having a certain kind of nationality and a culture Britons are proud of, e. g. certain standards and particular class standards.

No. 13
Britons understand irony and sarcasm.

(15 x 2 = 30 points)

Part B: Listening Comprehension – Transcript

Vox Pops International

What Does "Britain" and "Being British" Mean to Millennials*?

VPI spoke to Millennials in three UK cities; Birmingham, Leeds and London to find out what 'Britain' and 'Being British' means to them (16 interviews).

1) **Dana, 30, civil servant**

I'm quite proud to be British, to be honest. I think we're a good group of people and are quite strong and quite independent in a lot of ways.

2) **Matthew, 26, market trader**

A collective* of countries working together, which I like. Obviously, we're independent as countries, but we sort of, we work well together.

3) **Hannah, 27, banking**

It's the place I live. I am British. It's part of my identity. I don't think … I wouldn't say I'm particularly patriotic. I'm kind of a bit Irish, I'm a bit Scottish and English.

4) **Georgie, 21, student**

Well, for me, because I'm Welsh, so, British for me is like a collective identity. It's nice that like all of us being part of the United Kingdom are able to feel something together as well as individuals. So, that's what British is for me.

5) **Jessica, 25, social development**

There's like other cultures living here, so I think British embraces* all that as well.

6) **Faisal, 19, student**

Unity. I feel like the British are very accepting of people living outside of uh like their countries compared to like other areas of the world.

7) **Zina, 19, student**

When I also listen to that word, I know that most of you have a great respect towards other people.

8) **Stacy, 17, retail manager**

Multicultural. A lot of different food.

9) **Brandon, 32, engineer**

British to me means trying to keep all of our manufacturing, trying to keep business within England. Everything's going abroad and we don't seem to do anything in this country anymore. We need to get it back.

10) **Saffron, 24, beauty consultant**

I just say London. It's what we're known for. That's what everyone comes over here to see. They all want to go and see London Eye, Big Ben and Tower of London and all that sort of thing.

11) **Anthony, 24, barista**

I would say out of the town and more in the countryside. British things like going out for a dog walk and going out and getting a cup of tea, things like that.

12) **Sushma, 20, student**

Really smart people, where there's like rights for people, and there's no discrimination. You can trust people here.

13) **Max, 19, student**

British is like the stereotypical kind of nationality, you want to give like class. Like every country has culture they can be proud of, but I think if somebody says British, you think of class, certain standards.

14) **Matthew, 26, market trader**

A nice cup of tea, fish and chips, understanding irony, understanding sarcasm ...

15) **Anurag, 32, IT**

If I was to sum up what British means to me in one word, it would be freedom. And new ideas.

16) **Samal, 26, entertainer**

I'm proud to be British; it means that I wouldn't want to be anything else.

(*480 words*)

www.youtube.com/watch?v=wWGMvmAllvA, 4 March 2015 [04.04.2015], transcribed by Iris Edelbrock

*vocab given along with the assignments

Topic: Science (Fiction) and Technology – Towards a Better World?!

Skills: Analysis of a fictional text (novel); continuation of a fictional text (*Zieltextformat*); listening comprehension

Texts: **Part A:** Ira Levin: This Perfect Day, London, 1970 (651 words)
Part B: Frank Appel: The World in 2050, online promotional documentary (04:58 mins)

Part A: Reading/Writing

Ira Levin

This Perfect Day

Chip's mother said, 'One of the children told Chip about the incurables[1].'
'Hate,' his father said.
'I'm calling Bob,' his mother said, going to the phone. [...]
He was the youngest adviser they had ever had – twenty-one, and barely a year out of the Academy.
5 There was nothing different or unsure about him though; on the contrary, he was more relaxed and confident than advisers of fifty or fifty-five. They were pleased with him.
He went to Chip's room and looked in. Chip was in bed, lying on an elbow with his head in his hand, a comic book spread open before him.
'Hi, Li,' Bob said.
10 Chip said, 'Hi. Bob.'
Bob went in and sat down on the side of the bed. He put his telecomp on the floor between his feet, felt Chip's forehead and ruffled his hair. 'Whatcha readin'?' he said.
'*Wood's Struggle*,' Chip said, showing Bob the cover of the comic book. He let it drop closed on the bed and, with his forefinger, began tracing the wide yellow W of 'Wood's'.
15 Bob said, 'I hear somebody's has been giving you some cloth[2] about incurables.'
'Is that what it is?' Chip asked, not looking up from his moving finger.
'That's what it is, Li,' Bob said. 'It used to be true, a long, long time ago, but not any more; now it's just cloth.'
Chip was silent, retracing the W.
20 'We didn't always know as much about medicine and chemistry as we do today.' Bob said, watching him, 'and until fifty years or so after the Unification[3], members used to get sick sometimes, a very few of them, and feel that they *weren't* members. Some of them ran away and lived by themselves in places the Family wasn't using, barren[4] islands and mountain peaks and so forth.'
'And they took off their bracelets?'
25 'I suppose they did,' Bob said. 'Bracelets wouldn't have been much of use to them in places like that, would they, with no scanners to put them to?'
'Jesus said they did something called "fighting".'
Bob looked away and then back again. '"Acting aggressively" is a nicer way of putting it,' he said. 'Yes, they did that.'
30 Chip looked up at him. 'But they're dead now?' he said.
'Yes, all dead,' Bob said. 'Every last one of them.' He smoothed[5] Chip's hair. 'It was a long, long time ago,' he said. 'Nobody gets that way today.'
Chip said, 'We know more about medicine and chemistry today. Treatments work.'
'Right you are,' Bob said. 'And don't forget there were separate computers in those days. Once one
35 of those sick members had left his home continent, he was completely unconnected.'
'My grandfather helped build UniComp.'
'I know, he did, Li. So next time anyone tells you about the incurables, you remember two things: one, treatments are much more effective today than they were a long time ago; and two, we've got

---

[1] **incurable** unable to be healed; here: used to describe a personality type that cannot be changed or does not want to change – [2] **cloth** (*infml.*) nonsense – [3] **unification** the act of bringing different parts together to create a single entity – [4] **barren** *kahl, unfruchtbar* – [5] **to smooth sth.** *etw. glattstreichen*

UniComp looking out for us everywhere on Earth. Okay?'

40 'Okay,' Chip said and smiled.

'Let's see what it says about you,' Bob said, picking up his telecomp and opening it on his knees. Chip sat up and moved close, pushing his pyjama sleeve clear of[6] his bracelet. 'Do you think I'll get an extra treatment?' he asked.

'If you need one,' Bob said. [...]

45 Chip touched his bracelet to the scanner plate, and the blue light inside turned red.

Bob tapped the input keys[7]. Chip watched his quickly moving fingers. Bob kept tapping and then pressed the answer button; a line of green symbols glowed on the screen, and then a second line beneath the first. Bob studied the symbols. Chip watched him.

Bob looked at Chip, from the corners of his eyes, smiling.

50 'Tomorrow at 12.25,' he said.

'Good!' Chip said. 'Thank you!'

'Thank Uni,' Bob said, switching off the telecomp and closing the cover. 'Who told you about the incurables?' he asked. (*651 words*)

Ira Levin: This Perfect Day. Corsair Books, London 1970, pp. 5 ff.

Note: *This Perfect Day* is a science fiction novel and technocratic dystopia and describes the life of people, called "Family members", who are permanently controlled by a central computer called UniComp.

Each "Family member" is identified by means of a bracelet, which is scanned regularly. In order to prevent and eliminate opposition, people get monthly treatments (= "cures"), during which they are drugged and made emotionless. Additionally, everyone is assigned an adviser or confessor, who serves as a "mentor" and reports possible violations against "sisters" or "brothers" at a weekly confession.

The protagonist of the novel is Li RM35M4419, who is nicknamed "Chip".

ASSIGNMENTS

1. Give an outline of the conversation between Chip and Bob, paying particular attention to what is revealed about:
   – the incurables   – UniComp   – the importance of medicine and chemistry. (*Comprehension*)

2. Examine the conversation between Chip and Bob and
   a) illustrate Bob's qualities as an adviser and Chip's mentor and
   b) explain what the conversation reveals about the dystopian character of the novel. (*Analysis*)

3. You have a choice here. Choose **one** of the following tasks:

   3.1 Relate the author's description of the function of "bracelets", as well as "medicine and chemistry" in the novel, to the rising popularity of so-called "connected bracelets" like *Jawbone Up, iWatch* or *smartwatches*, along with the increasing consumption of sedatives and tranquilizers by many people in today's society.
   Against this background, assess whether (or not) the author's depiction of a dystopian and nightmarish society has finally come true.
   (*Comment/Evaluation*)

   3.2 During one of the so-called "weekly confessions", Bob has to report his "counseling conversation" with Chip to UniComp.
   Imagine what Bob might say in this interview and write a text that reflects the dystopian atmosphere, as well as Bob's character as depicted in the excerpt.
   ((*Re-*)*Creation of text*)

---

[6] **to push sth. clear of sth.** to move sth. away from sth. – [7] **key** button you press on a computer keyboard to produce letters and numbers

Part B: Listening Comprehension

Frank Appel

The World in 2050

In 2012, the Deutsche Post DHL Group commissioned the compilation of a study imagining the state of the world in 2050 in five scenarios that depict possible challenges and risks as well as opportunities and options for people and companies.

Source: www.youtube.com/watch?v=VE0lPTfsBoI, 24.02.2012 [04.04.2015] (04:58 mins)

Annotations ⟫⟫

renowned well-known and respected ■ **to ponder** (*fml.*) to think long and carefully about sth. ■ **to emerge** to come into being ■ **impending** about to happen, esp. sth. unpleasant or unwanted ■ **to accelerate** to start to move or happen faster ■ **to set the pace for sth.** to establish the speed that a group needs to move at in order to succeed, for example, in a race or competition ■ **to run hot** to overheat or break down due to overuse ■ **sustainable** *nachhaltig* ■ **pillar** *Säule* ■ **rural** of or related to the countryside ■ **to customize sth.** to tailor-make sth. according to a particular buyer's or user's needs ■ **ethos** set of beliefs, ideas, etc. about social behaviour and the relationships of a person or group ■ **to facilitate** (*fml.*) to make sth. possible or easier ■ **uniform** identical, standardized ■ **to vanish** to disappear ■ **supply chain** *Versorgungskette; Zulieferkette* ■ **diversity** [daɪˈvɜːsɪti] difference and variety ■ **to paralyze** to make sb./sth. unable to move ■ **protectionism** government policies designed to help a country's trade or industry by taxing goods bought from other countries ■ **to impose sth.** to officially enforce a rule, tax, punishment, etc. ■ **mutual** *gegenseitig* ■ **customs** *Zoll* ■ **occurrence** sth. that happens; *Ereignis*

ASSIGNMENT 1 ⟫⟫⟫⟫

Listen to the recording and tick off the right statement (a, b, c, d). You will hear the recording twice. Only one answer is correct each time.

1. Three factors noted by Deutsche Post DHL as impacting their business are ...

   ☐ a) ... imagination, innovation, ideas.

   ☐ b) ... technology, the environment, changing social circumstances.

   ☐ c) ... revolutions, science, climate change.

   ☐ d) ... robotics, science, innovation.

2. Logistics 2050 emerged because Deutsche Post DHL ...

   ☐ a) ... aims to become the world's leading logistics company by 2050.

   ☐ b) ... wanted renowned experts to help them to change the future.

   ☐ c) ... hopes to organize journeys around the world by 2050.

   ☐ d) ... needs to be prepared for the future in order to make the right decisions.

3. Scenario 1 is about ...

   ☐ a) ... the threat posed by global mass consumption and accelerating climate change.

   ☐ b) ... a lack of economic growth leading to the breakdown of world trade and the global economy.

   ☐ c) ... the need to exploit global resources more systematically to prevent world hunger.

   ☐ d) ... the need for faster transport networks to match the rising demand for goods.

4. The reasons for a possible collapse are ...

☐ a) ... too many goods are being transported by ever faster networks.

☐ b) ... natural resources are being strained by overpopulation, mass consumption and continual growth.

☐ c) ... too many countries are competing for too few resources.

☐ d) ... the planet is running hot due to global warming and the greenhouse effect.

5. Scenario 2 considers the future development of mega-cities to be ...

☐ a) ... entirely positive.

☐ b) ... difficult to sustain.

☐ c) ... full of downsides.

☐ d) ... mega-efficient.

6. It is claimed that rapid global urbanization would lead to ...

☐ a) ... the growth of social tensions.

☐ b) ... greater progress and global cooperation.

☐ c) ... the destruction of rural areas.

☐ d) ... the unlimited growth of transport networks.

7. Customized lifestyles ...

☐ a) ... are only possible because of 3D-printing.

☐ b) ... require new commercials and different types of advertising.

☐ c) ... are only suitable for people who like Do-It-Yourself projects.

☐ d) ... facilitate a world of colour and diversity.

8. 3D-printing ...

☐ a) ... turns local consumers into mass producers.

☐ b) ... helps people to produce self-made and individually-tailored items.

☐ c) ... makes uniform and mass-produced items unnecessary.

☐ d) ... increases awareness about the need for recycling.

9. New production processes ...

☐ a) ... revolutionize supply chains and make individual lifestyles possible.

☐ b) ... help to make locally-produced goods more uniform.

☐ c) ... make display windows unnecessary.

☐ d) ... increase awareness about the need for recycling.

10. Protectionism ...

☐ a) ... restricts trade to regional blocs.

☐ b) ... means that natural resources cannot be exchanged between nations.

☐ c) ... reduces conflicts by establishing clear borders between countries.

☐ d) ... helps to protect local markets from stagnation.

11. When international exchange comes to a standstill, ...

☐ a) ... nationalism becomes a thing of the past.

☐ b) ... countries re-impose their borders by putting up high barriers.

☐ c) ... mutual mistrust and stagnation are the norm.

☐ d) ... there are fewer conflicts over resources.

(11 x 2 = 22 points)

ASSIGNMENT 2

Listen to the recording again, and based on the information given, match the numbers and the letters to form correct statements. Be aware that there are two more letters than you need.

1.	The rapid growth of world trade ...	a)	... have vanished from display windows.
2.	Global urbanization ...	b)	... leads to customs barriers and stagnation.
3.	Innovation and efficient technology ...	c)	... has come to a standstill.
4.	The systematic exploitation of natural resources ...	d)	... sets the pace for business and the economy.
5.	International exchange ...	f)	... turns consumers into producers.
6.	The consequence of customized lifestyles ...	g)	... cannot satisfy the appetite for growth.
7.	Mass-produced items ...	h)	... is a more colourful, diverse and local world.
8.	Protectionism ...	i)	... is restricted to global trade blocs.
		j)	... has its downsides.
		k)	... make transport more sustainable and much faster.

(8 x 1 = 8 points)

Bewertungsbogen für: _____ Kurs: _____

Part A: Teilaufgabe 1 (Comprehension)

	Anforderungen Der Schüler/die Schülerin ...	maximal erreichbare Punktzahl	erreichte Punkte
1	... skizziert **den groben Verlauf des Gesprächs** zwischen Chip und Bob und erwähnt z. B., dass • Bob als sehr junger, aber auch entspannter und selbstsicherer *adviser* vorgestellt wird, der schnell das Vertrauen von Chip gewinnen kann, • Chip zunächst einen verängstigten und verstörten Eindruck macht, dann aber bei Bob Sicherheit, Zuversicht und Hilfe sucht und findet, • Bob es geschickt anstellt, Chip zu beruhigen, indem er in sachlicher, aber kindgerechter Weise mit ihm spricht und ihm dadurch ein Gefühl der Sicherheit vermittelt.	3	
2	... stellt die im Text gegebenen **Hinweise auf die *incurables*** heraus und führt z. B. aus, dass • sie von Bob als Relikt der Vergangenheit dargestellt werden, • es sich um aufrührerische, aggressive und kämpfende „*members*" handelt(e), die von der *Family* getrennt und auf isolierte Inseln, Berggipfel etc. verdammt wurden, • Bob eine (indirekte) Parallele herstellt zwischen den *incurables* und „*sick members*", die eigentlich gar keine *members* waren, sondern gesellschaftliche Außenseiter.	3	
3	... arbeitet die im Text gegebenen **Aspekte bzgl. UniComp** heraus und benennt z. B., dass • Chips Großvater geholfen hat, UniComp zu bauen (l. 36), • UniComp dazu dient, nach allen Menschen weltweit Ausschau zu halten (l. 38 f.), • die über die Scanner aus den *bracelets* eingelesenen Daten an UniComp weitergeleitet und ausgewertet werden, der dann wiederum über eine mögliche „Behandlung" entscheidet (ll. 42 ff.), • in früherer Zeit nicht alle Computer verlinkt waren (ll. 38 ff.).	3	
4	... hebt die im Text von Bob **dargestellte *importance of medicine and chemistry*** hervor, und weist z. B. darauf hin, dass • ca. 50 Jahre nach der sogenannten *Unification* die Gesellschaft noch nicht viele Kenntnisse über *medicine and chemistry* hatte und es daher manchmal auch *sick members* gab (von denen wiederum einige „weggelaufen" sind), • nach Bobs Darstellung gegenwärtig niemand mehr derartig „erkrankt", weil die *treatments* funktionieren, • Chip sich darauf zu freuen scheint, ein *extra treatment* zu bekommen, dies also etwas Positives zu sein scheint.	3	
5	... erfüllt ein weiteres aufgabenbezogenes Kriterium. (2) •	2	
		12	

Part A: Teilaufgabe 2 (Analysis)

	Anforderungen Der Schüler/die Schülerin ...	maximal erreichbare Punktzahl	erreichte Punkte
1	... untersucht **Bobs Qualitäten als *adviser* und Mentor** und belegt dies z. B. mit • seinem Arzt-ähnlichen Auftreten (*put his telecomp on the floor; felt Chip's forehead ... ruffled his hair ...*, etc.), • seinem freundschaftlichen, fast kumpelhaften Auftreten, um Chips Vertrauen zu erlangen (*Hi, Li; Whatcha readin'?: some cloth ... → informal language*), • Bobs Auftreten als „Märchenonkel", der Chip „Geschichten aus der Vergangenheit" erzählt, die jedoch in der Gegenwart keine Bedeutung mehr haben und keine Gefahr beinhalten (*It used to be true, a long, long time ago, but not anymore ...; we didn't always know ...; Yes, all dead ...*, etc.).	5	
2	... analysiert **Bobs Strategie**, Chip einerseits zu beruhigen und ihn andererseits unter Kontrolle zu bringen, z. B. • zunächst „die Technik" beiseite zu lassen (*put the telecomp on the floor ...*) und Chip auf „menschlicher" Ebene zu begegnen, • schließlich – nachdem er Chip beruhigt hat – den *telecomp*, sein Kontrollinstrument, einzusetzen (*picking up his telecomp and opening it on his knees*) – worauf Chip sofort in konditionierter Weise reagiert (*sat up, moved close ... pushing his pyjama sleeve clear ... touched his bracelet to the scanner plate ...*), • abschließend, „*smiling*", quasi als Belohnung, Chip ein *treatment* anzubieten (*Thank Uni ...*) – um schließlich, fast beiläufig, Chip die eigentliche Frage zu stellen (*Who told you about the incurables?*).	5	

3	... benennt die für eine **Dystopie charakteristischen Elemente** und weist sie am Text nach, z. B. • *manipulation through drugs* (→ *treatments; medicine and chemistry*), • *lack of freedom/total control/repressive state* (→ *Unification; some ran away; all dead; Unicomp looking out for us everywhere ...*), • *elements of technology* (→ *bracelets; telecomp; UniComp*, etc.).	5	
4	... arbeitet **erzählerische Stilmittel** heraus und benennt z. B. • die Erzählperspektive (*third-person narrator, limited point of view*), • die Darstellungsart: *scenic presentation*, • der insgesamt chronologische Ablauf mit einzelnen eingestreuten Verweisen und Anspielungen auf die Vergangenheit (*fifty years or so after ... long ago ... my grandfather ...*).	5	
5	... erfüllt ein weiteres aufgabenbezogenes Kriterium. (4) •	4	
		20	

Part A: Teilaufgabe 3.1 (Evaluation/Comment)

	Anforderungen	maximal erreichbare Punktzahl	erreichte Punkte
	Der Schüler/die Schülerin ...		
1	... nimmt Bezug auf und erläutert die **Funktion der *bracelets*** im Roman und benennt z. B., dass • *sick members* als *completely unconnected* beschrieben werden, die auf *barren islands* oder *mountain peaks* gesellschaftlich ausgeschlossen waren, • das Abnehmen der *bracelets* als offenbar negative oder gefährliche Handlung gilt, die nur von „Aussteigern" gewagt wurde, • *bracelets* als Kontrollinstrument dienen, aus denen Daten ausgelesen, an den Zentralcomputer übermittelt werden und dann als Grundlage für weitere Kontrolle oder Sanktionen dienen.	3	
2	... arbeitet die **Funktion von *medicine and chemistry***, wie im Text dargestellt, heraus und führt z. B. an, dass • sie zur Behandlung und Gesundung von *sick members* eingesetzt werden/wurden (ll. 33 f.), • sie der Ruhigstellung und zur Besänftigung dienen (l. 32), • sie von Chip mit Dank und offensichtlicher Freude betrachtet werden (ll. 51 f.).	3	
3	... betrachtet demgegenüber die **Bedeutung und den Einsatz von „modernen" *bracelets*** und den übermäßig gestiegenen **Konsum von Sedativa und Tranquilizern** und führt z. B. aus, dass • moderne *bracelets* wie *Jawbone Up* oder *iWatch* als positive, den Menschen unterstützende Fitnesstracker vermarktet werden, • demgegenüber moderne *bracelets* auch als Kontrollinstrumente des täglichen Lebens ihrer Nutzer dienen (können) und ebenfalls zentral ausgelesen und ausgewertet werden (können), • eine zunehmende Zahl von Menschen weltweit in die Einnahme von Medikamenten „flüchtet", um mit Problemen, Stress etc. fertig zu werden.	5	
4	... kommt zu einer **begründeten Einschätzung der Situation**, die sich schlüssig aus den Ausführungen ergibt, z. B. • wertet er/sie den Text und die darin beschriebene Situation als reine Fiktion, die mit der heutigen Zeit wenig zu tun hat, • wertet er/sie den Text als realitätsnahe Vorschau auf die heutige Situation, in der Menschen sich durch Marketing Tricks manipulieren und kontrollieren lassen, • stellt er/sie moderne Technologie als Chance dar, die man nicht einseitig als negativ bewerten und ablehnen sollte, sondern mit der man lernen sollte, umzugehen und sie sinnvoll zu nutzen.	5	
5	... erfüllt ein weiteres aufgabenbezogenes Kriterium. (4) •	4	
		16	

Part A: Teilaufgabe 3.2 ((Re-)Creation of text)

	Anforderungen Der Schüler/die Schülerin ...	maximal erreichbare Punktzahl	erreichte Punkte
1	... versetzt sich in die **Rolle und Situation von Bob** und berücksichtigt dabei z. B. ● dass er noch sehr jung ist, aber sehr sicher und selbstbewusst, ● die Notwendigkeit, dass er von Chip den Namen desjenigen erfährt, der von den *incurables* erzählt hatte, ● dass Bob möglicherweise unter besonderem Druck steht, da er sich als sehr junger Mentor noch beweisen muss.	3	
2	... greift auf **technische Besonderheiten** zurück, indem er/sie Bob darstellen lässt, dass ● er noch die *telecomp*-Daten auswerten muss, ● er auf die Auswertung von *UniComp* verweist, ● er auf die positive Wirkung des *treatment* bei Chip hinweist.	3	
3	... nutzt die **Charakteristika einer dystopischen Atmosphäre**, z. B., dass ● Bobs Report von verschiedenen Kameras aufgezeichnet wird, ● Bobs *bracelet* auch zur Kontrolle ausgelesen und ausgewertet wird, ● Bob selbst auch einem *treatment* unterzogen und/oder unter Drogen gesetzt wird.	5	
4	... verarbeitet die Elemente des **Zieltextformats „Interview"**, z. B. ● benutzt der *spoken English*, ● lässt er die Interviewpartner strategisch geschickt fragen und antworten und auch rollengemäß interagieren, ● gibt dem Interview eine dem Kontext entsprechende Struktur und Atmosphäre (angespannt, (un-)emotional, insistierend, ausweichend etc.).	5	
5	... erfüllt ein weiteres aufgabenbezogenes Kriterium. (4) ●	4	
		16	

Part B: Listening Comprehension

	Anforderungen	maximal erreichbare Punktzahl	erreichte Punkte
1	**Listening Comprehension 1** – *multiple choice*: 11 x 2 points	22	
2	**Listening Comprehension 2** – je richtigem *matching*: 1 point (8 x 1)	8	
		30	

Part B: Listening Comprehension – Solutions

ASSIGNMENT 1

1b, 2d, 3a, 4b, 5d, 6b, 7d, 8b, 9a, 10a, 11c

ASSIGNMENT 2

1 – d; 2 – j; 3 – k; 4 – g; 5 – c; 6 – h; 7 – a; 8 – b

Not correct: i, f

Part B: Listening Comprehension – Transcript

Frank Appel

The World in 2050

We can sense that the world is changing every day.
As the leading logistics company worldwide, Deutsche Post DHL is a driver of change. At the same time, numerous factors impact our business, including technology, the environment and changing social circumstances. Together with renowned* experts, we pondered* what the future may hold.
5 This is how "Logistics 2050" emerged*.
Join us on our journey into the year 2050. What will influence everyday reality then? To be prepared for the future and make the right decisions, we have to think in alternatives. Let's stretch our imaginations and look ahead.

Scenario 1: Untamed Economy – Impending* Collapse

10 2050. Simply breathtaking. Over nine billion people. Global mass consumption. Climate change is accelerating*. The rapid growth of world trade sets the pace* for business and the economy. Fast transport networks supply the world with more and more goods. The planet is running hot*. Even the systematic exploitation of natural resources cannot satisfy the appetite for growth. Competition for natural resources puts our eco-systems at risk. Are there alternatives?

15 Scenario 2: Mega-Efficiency in Mega-Cities

2050. A long green period for sustainable* thinking and actions. Mega-metropolises are centres of progress and pillars* of global cooperation. But: global urbanization has its downsides. Rural* areas are left behind. Thanks to innovative and more efficient technologies transport is more sustainable and much faster – for humans and for goods.

20 The world has reinvented itself. We enjoy unlimited interaction and global cooperation.
But could things turn out differently?

Scenario 3: Customized* Lifestyles

2050. Our world is much more colourful, diverse and local. Technical progress, especially in 3D-printing turns consumers into producers. Self-made and individually tailored become the new
25 ethos* for society. New types of production processes facilitate* a world with a multitude of individual lifestyles. Uniform* goods and mass-produced items have vanished from display windows and apartments. The consequence of this development is not only a revolution in supply chains*, awareness about the need for recycling is growing, creating new commercial perspectives. It is a world characterized by diversity*.
30 But: are more possibilities out there?

Scenario 4: Paralyzing* Protectionism*

2050. Gloomy prospects. Nationalism dominates and globalization is a thing of the past. Everywhere borders are re-imposed*. Trade is restricted to regional blocs. Mutual* mistrust leads to high customs* barriers. Stagnation is the norm. International exchange has come to a standstill. Con-
35 flicts over natural resources are a daily occurrence*. Will the future take us back to the past? Or are there different worlds?

(409 words)

www.youtube.com/watch?v=VE0lPTfsBol, 24.02.2012 [04.04.2015], transcribed by Iris Edelbrock

*vocab given along with the assignments

Topic: Economy, Energy, Efficiency – The World Going Global

Skills: Analysis of a non-fictional text (magazine article, interview); writing a letter to the editor (*Zieltextformat*); listening comprehension

Texts: **Part A:** Naomi Klein: The Economic System We Have Created Global Warming, 2015 (515 words)

Part B: Barack Obama: 2014 UN Climate Summit Speech, political speech (04:40 mins)

Part A: Reading/Writing

Naomi Klein

The Economic System We Have Created Global Warming

SPIEGEL: Ms. Klein, why aren't people able to stop climate change?

Klein: Bad luck. Bad timing. Many unfortunate coincidences[1].

SPIEGEL: The wrong catastrophe at the wrong moment?

Klein: The worst possible moment. The connection between greenhouse gases[2] and global warm-
5 ing has been a mainstream political issue for humanity since 1988. It was precisely the time that the
Berlin Wall fell and Francis Fukuyama[3] declared the "End of History," the victory of Western capitalism. Canada and the US signed the first free-trade agreement, which became the prototype for the
rest of the world.

SPIEGEL: So you're saying that a new era of consumption and energy use began precisely at the
10 moment when sustainability and restraint[4] would have been more appropriate?

Klein: Exactly. And it was at precisely this moment that we were also being told that there was no
longer any such thing as social responsibility and collective action, that we should leave everything
to the market. We privatized our railways and the energy grid[5], the WTO[6] and the IMF[7] locked in[8]
an unregulated capitalism. Unfortunately, this led to an explosion in emissions.

15 **SPIEGEL:** You're an activist, and you've blamed capitalism for all kinds of things over the years.
Now you're blaming it for climate change too?

Klein: That's no reason for irony. The numbers tell the story. During the 1990s, emissions went up
by 1 percent per year. Starting in 2000, they started to go up by an average of 3.4 percent. The American Dream was exported globally and consumer goods that we thought of as essential to meet our
20 needs expanded rapidly. We started seeing ourselves exclusively as consumers. When shopping as a
way of life is exported to every corner of the globe, that requires energy. A lot of energy.

SPIEGEL: Let's go back to our first question: Why have people been unable to stop this development?

Klein: We have systematically given away the tools. Regulations of any kind are now scorned[9]. Gov-
25 ernments no longer create tough rules that limit oil companies and other corporations. This crisis
fell into our laps[10] in a disastrous way at the worst possible moment. Now we're out of time. Where
we are right now is a do-or-die moment[11]. If we don't act as a species, our future is in peril[12]. We
need to cut emissions radically. [...]

SPIEGEL: Your son Toma is two-and-a-half years old. What kind of world will he be living in when
30 he graduates from high school in 2030?

---

[1] **unfortunate coincidence** *unglücklicher Zufall* – [2] **greenhouse gas** *Treibhausgas (z. B. CO$_2$)* – [3] **Francis Fukuyama**
(*1952) American political scientist and economist – [4] **restraint** *Zurückhaltung* – [5] **energy grid** *Energieversorgung* –
[6] **WTO** (*abbr.*) World Trade Organisation – [7] **IMF** (*abbr.*) International Monetary Fund – [8] **to lock in** here: to fix into place, to firmly establish – [9] **to scorn sth.** *etw. verachten* – [10] **to fall into sb.'s lap** to happen quickly and unex-
pectedly – [11] **do-or-die moment** *Jetzt-oder-nie-Moment* – [12] **peril** great danger

Klein: That is what is being decided right now. I see signs that it could be a radically different world from the one we have today – and that change could either be quite positive or extremely negative. In any case, it's already certain that it will at least in part be a worse world. We're going to experience global warming and far more natural disasters, that much is certain. But we still have time to
35 prevent truly catastrophic warming. We also have time to change our economic system so that it does not become more brutal and merciless[13] as it deals with climate change. (*515 words*)

www.spiegel.de/international/world/global-warming-interview-with-naomi-klein-a-1020007.html, interview by Klaus Brinkbäumer, 25 February 2015 [02.04.2015]

ASSIGNMENTS

1. Present Naomi Klein's view of the state of the planet, as well as the reasons she considers to be responsible for climate change and global warming.
   (*Comprehension*)

2. Examine the style of the interview and explain how the use of rhetorical devices underlines Naomi Klein's intention and the message of the text.
   (*Analysis*)

3. You have a choice here. Choose **one** of the following tasks:

   3.1 In the interview, Naomi Klein blames the "export of the American Dream globally" (ll. 18 f.) for having started an "unregulated capitalism", which finally has led to the current deplorable ecological problems.
   Discuss Naomi Klein's thesis, taking into consideration aspects of the American Dream, as well as the components and impacts of globalization that you have dealt with in class.
   (*Comment/Evaluation*)

   3.2 After reading this interview, you – as a young reader and consumer – are given the opportunity to comment on Naomi Klein's view and warnings.
   Write a "Letter to the Editor", in which you state your opinion on the matter and express whether (or not) you share Naomi Klein's opinion that "now is a do-or-die moment"
   (ll. 26 f.).
   ((*Re-*)*Creation of text*)

---

[13]**merciless** *gnadenlos*

Part B: Listening Comprehension

Barack Obama

2014 UN Climate Summit Speech

In September 2014, international leaders of governments, the private sector and the general public gathered in New York City to discuss concrete actions towards creating a "low-carbon world" in order to tackle climate change. The guests and speakers attended the summit at the invitation of UN Secretary-General Ban Ki-Moon.

Source: www.youtube.com/watch?v=oWrzXp2uJRM, 23.09.2014 [04.04.2015] (04:40 mins)

Annotations ⟫

to address sth. to deal with sth., esp. a problem or challenge ▪ **contour** the shape, outline or complex characteristics of sth. ▪ **sting** here: sth. that causes pain ▪ **to flood** to become covered with water ▪ **high tide** *Flut* ▪ **to parch sth.** to cause sth. to dry out, *ausdörren* ▪ **drought** [draʊt] *Dürre* ▪ **to drench** to make sb./sth. extremely wet ▪ **hurricane** here: reference to Hurricane Sandy, the most destructive and deadliest hurricane of the 2012 hurricane season ▪ **irreparable** unable to be fixed or repaired ▪ **to condemn** *verdammen* ▪ **emitter** sb./sth. that sends out pollutants, gases, etc. ▪ **to harness** to control sth., usually in order to make use of its power ▪ **unprecedented** never having happened or existed in the past ▪ **appliance** *Haushaltsgerät* ▪ **climate-resilient infrastructure** infrastructure that can withstand extreme climactic conditions ▪ **sound** here: secure and stable

ASSIGNMENT 1 ⟫⟫⟫⟫

The following phrases are taken from President Obama's speech. Before listening to the recording, read the phrases, as well as the vocabulary above, and then, while listening, put the phrases into the correct order.

☐ A. ... we are the first generation to feel the impact of climate change ...

☐ B. ... the past decade has been our hottest on record ...

☐ C. Climate change is faster than our efforts to address it.

☐ D. Advances have helped create jobs and grow our economy.

☐ E. ... all the immediate challenges ... terrorism, instability, inequality, disease ...

☐ F. We have the technological innovation and scientific imagination to begin the work now.

☐ G. A hurricane left parts of this great city dark and underwater.

☐ H. ... our understanding of climate change has advanced ...

☐ I. We have to work together as a global community.

☐ J. We've made unprecedented investments.

(10 x 1 = 10 points)

ASSIGNMENT 2

Listen to the recording a second time and decide whether the statements below are true, false or not given in the speech. Make corrections to the false statements.

	True	False	Not given
1. Climate change will define the contours of the 21st century most dramatically.	☐	☐	☐
2. This distant threat has to be overcome.	☐	☐	☐
3. Along the southern coast, the city of Miami now floods at high tide.	☐	☐	☐
4. In the Midwest, farms have had to deal with the worst drought and the wettest spring.	☐	☐	☐
5. The summer of 2014 was the hottest on record worldwide.	☐	☐	☐
6. Each country has to tackle the threat of global warming on its own.	☐	☐	☐
7. We are condemning our grandchildren to cut carbon emissions.	☐	☐	☐
8. The U.S. is the world's largest emitter of carbon dioxide.	☐	☐	☐
9. U.S. consumers are cutting the energy needed for their homes, buildings and appliances.	☐	☐	☐
10. There will always be a strong conflict between a sound environment and economic growth.	☐	☐	☐

(10 x 2 = 20 points)

Bewertungsbogen für: _____ Kurs: _____

Part A: Teilaufgabe 1 (Comprehension)

	Anforderungen Der Schüler/die Schülerin ...	maximal erreichbare Punktzahl	erreichte Punkte
1	... stellt die **gegenwärtige Situation** und den ***state of the planet*** heraus und benennt z. B. • den immer noch ungeminderten und auch weiterhin ansteigenden CO_2-Ausstoß, • die nach wie vor rücksichtslose Verschwendung von Energie und *resources* weltweit, • die Ohnmacht der Regierungen gegenüber globalen Korporationen.	3	
2	... arbeitet **die in der Vergangenheit liegenden Gründe** für die derzeitige Situation heraus, z. B. • das am Ende der 1990er-Jahre abgeschlossene Freihandelsabkommen zwischen den USA und Kanada, • die darauffolgende Privatisierung der Bahnunternehmen und Energieversorgung, die einen ungehinderten Kapitalismus auslöste, der auch die WTO und den IMF unter Druck setzte, • ein ausschließlich den Gesetzen des Marktes und uneingeschränkten Handels folgendes Handeln, das keine Rücksichten auf ökologische Notwendigkeiten nimmt.	3	
3	... umreißt die durch **Globalisierung und Konsum verursachten Probleme** und nennt z. B. • den dramatischen Anstieg der CO2-Emissionen von 1 % auf 3.4 % seit 2000, der Hochzeit der *new economy* und in Verbindung damit einer explosionsartigen Globalisierung der Märkte, • das Konsumverhalten der Menschen seit dieser Zeit, das Konsum als Lebensinhalt definiert, • die explosive Zunahme des Energieverbrauchs, bedingt durch weltweiten Handel und Transport.	3	
4	... beschreibt den **Export des *American Dream*** als den Hauptverursacher der Klima-Problematik und verweist z. B. auf • die Zunahme von Egoismen und Rücksichtslosigkeit auf Kosten von *social responsibility* und *collective action*, • die neue Definition des *shopping as a way of life* und die damit verbundene Reduzierung der Menschen auf Konsumenten, • der mit der Fokussierung auf Konsum einhergehende Machtverlust der Gesellschaft und der Machtzuwachs auf Seiten der Konzerne.	3	
5	... erfüllt ein weiteres aufgabenbezogenes Kriterium. (2) •	2	
		12	

Part A: Teilaufgabe 2 (Analysis)

	Anforderungen Der Schüler/die Schülerin ...	maximal erreichbare Punktzahl	erreichte Punkte
1	... arbeitet den **appellativen und latent aggressiven Ton** des Artikels heraus und belegt dies z. B. mit • dem Hinweis des Interviewers darauf, dass Naomi Klein Aktivistin ist (l. 15) und wiederholt den Kapitalismus für „alles Mögliche" verantwortlich gemacht hat (*you've blamed capitalism for all kinds of things over the years ... Now ...?*), • Naomi Kleins Darstellung eines „Weltuntergangs-Szenarios" (*worst possible moment; "End of History"; do-or-die moment*), • Naomi Kleins direkte und unvermittelte Art auf Fragen zu antworten (*Bad luck. Bad timing. That's no reason for irony.*).	5	
2	... zeigt auf, wie der Einsatz von **rhetorischen Stilmitteln** den Inhalt der Darstellung verstärkt und verweist z. B. auf • den Einsatz von **contrast/antithesis** (*consumption* vs. *sustainability and constraint; consumption* vs. *responsibility and collective action*, etc.), • den wiederholten Gebrauch von verstärkenden Adverbien und Adjektiven (*unfortunate; worst possible; precisely; unregulated; essential; rapidly*, etc.), • ein Wortfeld mit *negative emotive words* im Zusammenhang mit dem Thema *climate change* (*bad luck; bad timing; catastrophe; unregulated capitalism; explosion*, etc.).	5	
3	... erläutert die **Kernaussage (message)** des Artikels, indem er/sie z. B. darstellt, dass Naomi Klein • auf die Manipulation der Menschen durch Konzerne aufmerksam macht, • den fatalen Zusammenhang zwischen Klimawandel und der Zerstörung der Erde und dem Konsumwahn der Menschen verdeutlicht und anprangert, • den dringenden Appell an die Menschen richtet, sich ihrer Verantwortung bewusst zu werden und (wieder) zu einer *collective action* zu kommen, die dem rücksichtslosen Kapitalismus entgegentritt und damit auch beginnt, gegen den Klimawandel vorzugehen.	5	

4	... untersucht den **latent ironischen und distanzierten Fragestil des Interviewers** und verdeutlicht das z. B. durch <ul><li>die wiederholten ironisch-provokanten Fragen bzgl. der Inkompetenz und Dummheit der Menschen (*why aren't people able ...?; Why have people been unable ...?*),</li><li>die latente Infragestellung von Naomi Kleins Position und der Berechtigung ihrer Kritik (*you're an activist ... you've blamed capitalism for all kinds of things ... Now ... for climate change, too?; So, you are saying ...*).</li></ul>	5	
5	... erfüllt ein weiteres aufgabenbezogenes Kriterium. (4) <ul><li></li></ul>	4	
		20	

Part A: Teilaufgabe 3.1 (Evaluation/Comment)

	Anforderungen **Der Schüler/die Schülerin ...**	maximal erreichbare Punktzahl	erreichte Punkte
1	... nimmt Bezug auf die **von Naomi Klein vorgenommene Kritik** und benennt z. B. <ul><li>die Darstellung des *American way of life* als Synonym für die weltweite Verfügbarkeit von als essenziell erachteten Konsumgütern (ll. 7 ff.),</li><li>den Export des *American Dream* als Verheißung von uneingeschränktem Konsum in „alle Ecken der Welt" (ll. 18 ff.),</li><li>den enormen Energieaufwand, der weltweit benötigt wird, um *shopping as a way of life* zu ermöglichen.</li></ul>	3	
2	... nimmt Bezug auf den im Text dargestellten **Zusammenhang zwischen *unregulated capitalism* und *global warming/climate change*** und verweist z. B. auf <ul><li>fehlende Kontrolle und/oder Restriktionen durch supra-nationale Institutionen wie WTO oder IMF (l. 13),</li><li>die systematische Entmachtung von Regierungen, die somit den Konzernen und der Klimazerstörung hilflos gegenüberstehen (ll. 24 ff.),</li><li>die gefährlichen Mechanismen, die zu *climate change/global warming* geführt haben und noch weiterhin führen (*instilling needs → consumption → need for transport → privatisation of railways → more energy for production and transport → oil companies/global corporations → free-trade agreements → unrestricted power*).</li></ul>	3	
3	... kommt demgegenüber zu einer Darstellung der **wesentlichen Aspekte des *American Dream***, z. B. <ul><li>*personal and material wealth and success,*</li><li>*individual ways of pursuing one's goals, dreams and realizing one's aims,*</li><li>*a better, richer and fuller life for every man; opportunity for each (J. T. Adams).*</li></ul>	5	
4	... kommt zu einer **Bewertung und Einordnung der Thematik** sowie zu einem **begründeten Resümee**, indem er/sie z. B. <ul><li>vor dem Hintergrund unterrichtlichen Wissens auf Chancen und Risiken der Globalisierung verweist,</li><li>Beschränkungen und Kontrolle der Einflussnahme von globalen Unternehmen fordert,</li><li>einen Appell formuliert und auf die zwingende Notwendigkeit von Maßnahmen und internationaler Kooperation hinweist.</li></ul>	5	
5	... erfüllt ein weiteres aufgabenbezogenes Kriterium. (4) <ul><li></li></ul>	4	
		16	

Part A: Teilaufgabe 3.2 ((Re-)Creation of text)

	Anforderungen **Der Schüler/die Schülerin ...**	maximal erreichbare Punktzahl	erreichte Punkte
1	... reflektiert – auch unter Rückgriff auf unterrichtliche Ergebnisse – **mögliche Ursachen und Folgen des Klimawandels** und benennt z. B. <ul><li>die weltweite Zunahme von extremen klimatischen Veränderungen (Hitzeperioden; Dürre; Überschwemmungen; Stürme etc.),</li><li>den enormen Anstieg von Konsum und Handel z. B. durch das Internet, was ein deutliches Plus an Transport und Energieverbrauch nach sich zieht,</li><li>die immer größer werdenden Anstrengungen und Aufwendungen weltweit, um an Energie zu kommen (z. B. Kontinent-überspannende Gas-/Ölleitungen; Fracking etc.).</li></ul>	3	
2	... bezieht sich auf die **im Interview von Naomi Klein genannten Aspekte** und erwähnt z. B. <ul><li>den rasanten Anstieg von immer mehr und immer preiswerteren Konsumgütern, die global produziert, transportiert und konsumiert werden,</li><li>die auch durch verstärktes Outsourcing zunehmende Notwendigkeit von weltweitem Transport von Gütern,</li><li>den zunehmenden rücksichtslose Umgang mit Ressourcen weltweit (Wälder; fossile Rohstoffe etc.).</li></ul>	3	

3	... kommt zu einer **Stellungnahme**, die sich plausibel aus seinen/ihren Ausführungen ergibt. Er/sie stellt z. B. dar, dass er/sie <ul><li>den Darstellungen und Forderungen von Naomi Klein zustimmt,</li><li>die von Naomi Klein dargestellte „Endzeit-Stimmung" für übertrieben und kontraproduktiv hält und verweist z. B. auf die vielen Bestrebungen und Innovationen in Bezug auf erneuerbare Energien, umweltschonende Verfahren und Produkte etc.,</li><li>die globalen Konzerne in der (Mit-)Verantwortung sieht und appelliert, sie (stärker) zu verändertem Handeln zu zwingen.</li></ul>	5	
4	... formuliert einen **sach- und adressatengerecht formulierten und gestalteten Brief**, indem er/sie z. B. <ul><li>durch eine knappe Selbstvorstellung einleitet,</li><li>seine/ihre Motivation zum Schreiben verdeutlicht,</li><li>die formalen Aspekte (Anrede, Gliederung in thematische Abschnitte, Abschluss/Grußformel) des „*Letter to the Editor*" berücksichtigt.</li></ul>	5	
5	... erfüllt ein weiteres aufgabenbezogenes Kriterium. (4) <ul><li></li></ul>	4	
		16	

Part B: Listening Comprehension

	Anforderungen	maximal erreichbare Punktzahl	erreichte Punkte
1	**Listening Comprehension 1** – *sequencing*: 10 x 1 point	10	
2	**Listening Comprehension 2** – *true – false*: 10 x 2 points	20	
		30	

© Schöningh Verlag, Best.-Nr. 040158

Part B: Listening Comprehension – Solutions

ASSIGNMENT 1

8	A. ... we are the first generation to feel the impact of climate change ...
3	B. ... the past decade has been our hottest on record ...
5	C. Climate change is faster than our efforts to address it.
10	D. Advances have helped create jobs and grow our economy.
1	E. ... all the immediate challenges ... terrorism, instability, inequality, disease ...
7	F. We have the technological innovation and scientific imagination to begin the work now.
4	G. A hurricane left parts of this great city dark and underwater.
2	H. ... our understanding of climate change has advanced ...
6	I. We have to work together as a global community.
9	J. We've made unprecedented investments.

(10 x 1 = 10 points)

ASSIGNMENT 2

True:
No. 1, 4, 5, 9

Not given:
No. 2, 7

False:
No. 3
Along the <u>Eastern</u> coast, the city of Miami now floods at high tide.

No. 6
And we have to <u>work together as a global community</u> to tackle this global threat.

No. 8
The world's <u>second largest</u> emitter.

No. 10
There <u>does not have to be</u> a conflict between a sound environment and strong economic growth.

(10 x 2 = 20 points)

Part B: Listening Comprehension – Transcript

Barack Obama

2014 UN Climate Summit Speech

THE PRESIDENT: Mr. President, Mr. Secretary General, fellow leaders: For all the immediate challenges that we gather to address* this week – terrorism, instability, inequality, disease – there's one issue that will define the contours* of this century more dramatically than any other, and that is the urgent and growing threat of a changing climate.

5 Five years have passed since many of us met in Copenhagen. And since then, our understanding of climate change has advanced – both in the deepening science that says this once-distant threat has moved "firmly into the present," and into the sting* of more frequent extreme weather events that show us exactly what these changes may mean for future generations.

No nation is immune. In America, the past decade has been our hottest on record. Along our east-
10 ern coast, the city of Miami now floods* at high tide*. In our west, wildfire season now stretches most of the year. In our heartland, farms have been parched* by the worst drought* in generations, and drenched* by the wettest spring in our history. A hurricane* left parts of this great city dark and underwater. And some nations already live with far worse. Worldwide, this summer was the hottest ever recorded – with global carbon emissions still on the rise.

15 So the climate is changing faster than our efforts to address it. The alarm bells keep ringing. Our citizens keep marching. We cannot pretend we do not hear them. We have to answer the call. We know what we have to do to avoid irreparable* harm. We have to cut carbon pollution in our own countries to prevent the worst effects of climate change. We have to adapt to the impacts that, unfortunately, we can no longer avoid. And we have to work together as a global community to tackle
20 this global threat before it is too late.

We cannot condemn* our children, and their children, to a future that is beyond their capacity to repair. Not when we have the means – the technological innovation and the scientific imagination – to begin the work of repairing it right now.

As one of America's governors has said, "We are the first generation to feel the impact of climate
25 change and the last generation that can do something about it." So today, I'm here personally, as the leader of the world's largest economy and its second largest emitter*, to say that we have begun to do something about it.

The United States has made ambitious investments in clean energy, and ambitious reductions in our carbon emissions. We now harness* three times as much electricity from the wind and 10
30 times as much from the sun as we did when I came into office. Within a decade, our cars will go twice as far on a gallon of gas, and already, every major automaker offers electric vehicles. We've made unprecedented* investments to cut energy waste in our homes and our buildings and our appliances*, all of which will save consumers billions of dollars. And we are committed to helping communities build climate-resilient infrastructure*.

35 So, all told, these advances have helped create jobs, grow our economy, and drive our carbon pollution to its lowest levels in nearly two decades – proving that there does not have to be a conflict between a sound* environment and strong economic growth. [...] (*558 words*)

www.whitehouse.gov/the-press-office/2014/09/23/remarks-president-un-climate-change-summit, 23 September 2014
[04.04.2015]

*vocab given along with the assignments

> **Topic:** Science (Fiction) and Technology – Towards a Better World?!
>
> **Skills:** Analysis of a non-fictional text (magazine article); writing a letter to the editor (*Zieltextformat*); listening comprehension;
>
> **Texts:** **Part A:** Thomas Schulz: Tomorrowland: How Silicon Valley Shapes Our Future (487 words)
> **Part B:** Amber Case: We Are All Cyborgs Now, TED speech (03:18 mins)

Part A: Reading/Writing

Thomas Schulz

Tomorrowland: How Silicon Valley Shapes Our Future

[...] The technological advances made in the last decade have been breathtaking, but it is likely still just the beginning. The growth of new technologies, after all, has been exponential[1] rather than linear[2], with ever larger advances coming at an increasingly rapid rate. It is like a gigantic avalanche[3] that begins as a tiny snowball at the top of the mountain.

5 The iPhone only made its appearance seven years ago, but most of us no longer remember what the world was like before. Driverless cars were considered to be a crazy fantasy not long ago, but today nobody is particularly amazed by them. All the world's knowledge condensed into a digital map and easily accessible? Normal. The fact that algorithms[4] in the US control some 70 percent of all trading on the stock market? Crazy, to be sure. But normal craziness.

10 Dozens of companies are trying to figure out how to use drones for commercial use, be it for deliveries, data collection or other purposes. Huge armies of engineers are chasing after the holy grail[5] of artificial intelligence. And the advances keep coming. Machines that can learn, intelligent robots: We have begun overtaking science fiction.

The phenomenon is still misunderstood, first and foremost by policymakers. It appears they have 15 not yet decided whether to dive in[6] and create a usable policy framework for the future or to stand aside as others create a global revolution. After all, what we are witnessing is not just the triumph of a particular technology. And it is not just an economic phenomenon. It isn't about "the Internet" or "the social networks," nor is it about intelligence services and Edward Snowden or the question as to what Google is doing with our data. It isn't about the huge numbers of newspapers that are go-20 ing broke[7] nor is it about jobs being replaced by software. It's not about a messaging service[8] being worth €19 billion ($21.1 billion) or the fact that 20-year-olds are launching entire new industries.

We are witnessing nothing less than a societal transformation that ultimately nobody will be able to avoid. It is the kind of sea change[9] that can only be compared with 19th century industrialization, but it is happening much faster this time. Just as the change from hand work to mass production 25 dramatically changed our society over 100 years ago, the digital revolution isn't just altering specific sectors of the economy, it is changing the way we think and live. [...]

The new "masters of the universe", though, are fundamentally different from their predecessors[10]: Their primary focus isn't on money. They don't want to just determine what we consume, but how we consume it and how we live. They aren't trying to capture just one economic sector, but all of 30 them. [...]

Their message seems to be: If societal values such as privacy and data protection stand in the way, then we simply have to develop new values. [...] (*487 words*)

www.spiegel.de/international/germany/spiegel-cover-story-how-silicon-valley-shapes-our-future-a-1021557.html, 4 March 2015
[02.04.2015]

---

[1] **exponential** (*fml.*) *mit multiplizierender Wirkung* – [2] **linear** *gradlinig* – [3] **avalanche** [ˈævəlɑːnʃ] *Lawine* – [4] **algorithm** [ˈælɡərɪðəm] a fixed sequence of arithmetic or programming steps that are used, esp. by computers, to calculate the answer to a mathematical problem – [5] **holy grail** here: a greatly-desired objective or goal – [6] **to dive in** (*phr. v.*) *sich in etw. stürzen* – [7] **to go broke** (*infml.*) to go bankrupt; *Pleite gehen* – [8] **messaging service** a feature that allows a mobile phone to send and receive messages that include special text, pictures, sounds, etc., as well as ordinary text messages – [9] **sea change** a substantial or significant transformation – [10] **predecessor** [ˈpriːdɪˌsesər] *Vorgänger*

ASSIGNMENTS

1. Give an outline of how – according to the author – technological advances and new technologies have created a global digital revolution in every possible way and in all sectors of life.
(*Comprehension*)

2. Examine the author's line of argument, as well as the tone and style of the article, and explain how it emphasizes the author's intention and the overall message of the text.
(*Analysis*)

3. You have a choice here. Choose **one** of the following tasks:

   3.1 Discuss the author's concluding assumption that the "new masters of the universe" want people to radically change the "way [they] think and live" and to "develop new values" concerning data protection and privacy.
   In what way is this kind of revolution different from the industrial revolution in the 19th century and the changes it brought to society?
   (*Comment/Evaluation*)

   3.2 After reading this article, you, as reader, are given the opportunity to comment on the author's assessment that
   a) the digital revolution is changing the way people think and live and
   b) policymakers have not yet created a usable policy framework for the future.
   Write a "Letter to the Editor", stating your opinion on "Tomorrowland".
   ((*Re-*)*Creation of text*)

Part B: Listening Comprehension

Amber Case

We Are All Cyborgs Now

TED (Technology, Entertainment, Design) is a set of global conferences, at which topics, such as technology, science, culture and art are discussed.

Amber Case is an American anthropologist, who studies the interactions between humans and machines/technology. Her thesis is that technology is turning the human being into a screen-staring, button-clicking new version of homo sapiens that relies on "external brains" (e. g. smartphones, computers) to communicate.

Source: www.ted.com/talks/amber_case_we_are_all_cyborgs_now, December 2010 [04.04.2015] (03:18 mins)

Annotations ⟫

cyborg ['saɪbɔːg] in science fiction stories, a creature that is part human and part machine ■ **RoboCop** a 1987 cyberpunk, action film whose protagonist police officer, who is murdered and then later revived as a superhuman, cyborg law-enforcer known as RoboCop ■ **Terminator** a 1984 American, science-fiction, action film whose protagonist is the Terminator – a cyborg assassin ■ **exogenous** [ɪk'sɒdʒɪnəs] coming or produced from outside sth., esp. outside an organism ■ **awkward** [ˈɔːkwəd] difficult and causing problems ■ **anthropology** [ˌænθrəˈpɒlədʒi] the study of human culture and society ■ **modification** a change made to sth., esp. to improve it ■ **Mary Poppins technology** refers to the magical carpet bag carried by the protagonist of a 1964 American musical fantasy film about a nanny with special, magical powers, who visits a dysfunctional family in London and improves their lifestyle ■ **adolescent** [ˌædəl'esənt] a teenager ■ **adolescence** [ˌædəl'esəns] the period in sb.'s life between being a child and an adult

ASSIGNMENT 1 ⟫⟫⟫

In her presentation, Amber Case addresses certain topics that are listed below, but which are not in the correct order. First, read through them, and then, while listening, put them in the correct order according to when they are covered in the presentation. Be careful, however: there are two additional topics listed that are not dealt with by Amber Case.

(10 x 1 = 10 points)

ASSIGNMENT 2 ⟫⟫⟫

During a second listening, take notes on what Amber Case explains in detail about the following topics:

☐ The inside of a computer ... _____

_____

☐ We're a new form of Homo Sapiens because ... _____

_____

☐ People are becoming like the Terminator and RoboCop and ... _____

_____

☐ Maintaining one's second self is about ... _____

_____

☐ A good definition for cyborg: _____

_____

☐ For thousands of years, tool use has been ... _____

_____

☐ The concept of traditional anthropology is ... _____

_____

☐ Having a second self means ... _____

_____

☐ Going through two adolescences like this causes mental problems because ... _____

_____

☐ Humans like to add things to their bodies so ... _____

_____

(10 x 2 = 20 points)

Bewertungsbogen für: _____ Kurs: _____

Part A: Teilaufgabe 1 (Comprehension)

	Anforderungen Der Schüler/die Schülerin ...	maximal erreichbare Punktzahl	erreichte Punkte
1	... skizziert das vom Autor dargestellte **Ausmaß der *technological advances***, z. B. • die exponentiale Zunahme von neuen Technologien und Entwicklungen (ll. 2 ff.), • die lawinenartige und bedrohliche Entwicklung, die nicht aufzuhalten ist (ll. 3 f.), • die Hilflosigkeit und Unfähigkeit z. B. von Politikern im Umgang mit und der Kontrolle von digitalen Medien.	3	
2	... arbeitet vom Autor genannte **Beispiele für die Entwicklung und Einsatzmöglichkeiten digitaler Medien** heraus und benennt z. B. • das erst 2008 auf den Markt gebrachte iPhone, das bereits nach so kurzer Zeit unersetzlich scheint (ll. 5 f.), • die ursprünglichen Phantasien von *driverless cars*, die inzwischen kein Erstaunen mehr auslöst (ll. 6 f.), • die unaufhaltsame Entwicklung und „Verbesserung" von lernfähigen Maschinen und Robotern (l. 12).	3	
3	... umreißt den vom Autor vorgenommenen **Vergleich zwischen der industriellen und digitalen Revolution** und erwähnt z. B. • die Vergleichbarkeit des Ausmaßes der sozialen Umwälzungen, die beide Revolutionen ausgelöst haben (ll. 22 f.), • das noch rasantere Tempo der Veränderungen und Umwälzungen auf allen Gebieten der Gesellschaft und des Lebens (ll. 24 f.), • die noch tiefergreifenden Veränderungen: 19. Jahrhundert ➔ Veränderung der Wirtschaft; 21. Jahrhundert ➔ Veränderung des Denkens/der Werte (ll. 24 ff.).	3	
4	... stellt die **grundsätzlichen Unterschiede zwischen der industriellen und digitalen Revolution** dar, z. B., dass • der Fokus heute nicht ausschließlich auf dem Absatz von Produkten liegt, sondern auf der Beeinflussung des Menschen darin, wie sie konsumieren und leben (ll. 28 ff.), • in der heutigen Zeit alle Wirtschaftsbereiche davon betroffen sind, keiner kann sich dem Einfluss entziehen (ll. 28 f.), • gesellschaftliche Werte wie Privatsphäre und Datensicherheit radikal aus dem Weg geräumt und verändert werden (ll. 31 f.).	3	
5	... erfüllt ein weiteres aufgabenbezogenes Kriterium. (2) •	2	
		12	

Part A: Teilaufgabe 2 (Analysis)

	Anforderungen Der Schüler/die Schülerin ...	maximal erreichbare Punktzahl	erreichte Punkte
1	... verdeutlicht die ***line of argument*** und belegt dies z. B. durch • den klaren und sich inhaltlich steigernden Aufbau des Textes (Einleitung: *tiny snowball* ➔ *gigantic avalanche*; Hauptteil: sich steigernde Beispiele: *iPhone* ➔ *driverless cars/digital maps* ➔ *drones* ➔ *intelligent robots* ➔ *overtaking science fiction; industrial revolution* ➔ *digital revolution; changing production and consumption* ➔ *changing values and way of thinking*), • Science Fiction als Leitmotiv in der Argumentation (*Tomorrowland; overtaking science fiction; kind of sea change; triumph of technology*), • die in einer Art Klimax abschließende Bedrohung: *we simply have to develop new values* (l. 32).	5	
2	... zeigt auf, wie durch den **Einsatz von Antithese** der Inhalt des Textes verstärkt wird, und verweist z. B. auf • kontrastive eingesetzte Satzbaumuster (*The iPhone made ... but ...; Driverless cars were ... but ...; All the world's knowledge ...? Normal.; Crazy ... But normal.*), • den kontrastiven Einsatz von Personalpronomen (*masters of the universe: they, their* ↔ *society: we*), • die Gegenüberstellung von „Wahnsinn" (*craziness*) und atemberaubendem technischem Fortschritt (*breathtaking technological advances – a crazy fantasy; algorithms control – normal craziness*).	5	

3	... untersucht **weitere Stilmittel** und verdeutlicht, wie sie den Ton und Stil des Artikels verstärken. Er/sie benennt z. B. <ul><li>den durchgängigen Gebrauch von einschränkenden Konjunktionen und Phrasen (*but it is likely ...; but most of us ...; but today ...; it is not ...; it isn't about ...*),</li><li>die elaborierte Wortwahl (*exponential; knowledge condensed into ...; algorithms*, etc.) und die häufig verwendete Hypotaxe, die den Autor als wortgewandt und gebildet ausweisen,</li><li>die aus dem Wortfeld *science/robotics* entnommenen Fachbegriffe, die den Autor als Kenner der Thematik ausweisen,</li><li>den Gebrauch von *hyperbole* und *irony* sowie metaphorischer Formulierungen zur Verstärkung der kritischen Sichtweise (*exponential rather than ...; increasingly rapid ...; huge armies ...; much faster ...; dramatically; armies of engineers are chasing the holy grail ...; the kind of sea change; the new masters of the universe*, etc.).</li></ul>	5	
4	... erläutert die **Kernaussage** des Artikels, indem er/sie darstellt, dass <ul><li>der Autor durch Parallelismen und Negationen das Ausmaß der Beeinflussung hervorhebt (*And it is not ...; It isn't about ...; nor is it about ...; It isn't about ...; Their focus isn't ...; They don't ...; They aren't ...*),</li><li>der Autor über das unvorstellbare und nicht zu verhindernde Ausmaß der Umwälzungen durch die *digital revolution* informieren und davor warnen will,</li><li>Politiker das „Phänomen" *digital revolution* falsch oder gar nicht verstehen und nicht in der Lage sind, die dramatischen Auswirkungen durch Regeln, Gesetze, Vereinbarungen etc. einzugrenzen oder zu kontrollieren.</li></ul>	5	
5	... erfüllt ein weiteres aufgabenbezogenes Kriterium. (4) <ul><li></li></ul>	4	
		20	

Part A: Teilaufgabe 3.1 (Evaluation/Comment)

	Anforderungen **Der Schüler/die Schülerin ...**	maximal erreichbare Punktzahl	erreichte Punkte
1	... nimmt **konkreten Bezug auf das Zitat** und stellt z. B. dar, dass <ul><li>die neuen *masters of the universe* primär nicht an Geld oder nur dem Absatz von Produkten interessiert sind,</li><li>die Art und Weise des Konsums und der Lebensweise durch digitale Mechanismen bestimmt und kontrolliert werden soll,</li><li>sämtliche Wirtschaftsbereiche „übernommen" und damit kontrolliert werden sollen.</li></ul>	3	
2	... arbeitet die durch die **industrielle Revolution im 19. Jahrhundert** ausgelösten Veränderungen heraus, z. B. <ul><li>die Veränderung von manueller Produktion zur maschinellen Massenfertigung von Produkten,</li><li>die dramatischen sozialen Veränderungen (z. B. Urbanisierung, Landflucht, neue soziale Schichten (z. B. Proletariat), neue soziale Abhängigkeiten, Verelendung etc.),</li><li>die Entstehung der industriellen Konsumgesellschaft.</li></ul>	3	
3	... benennt demgegenüber **den weiterreichenden Einfluss der *digital revolution*,** z. B. <ul><li>der immer schnelleren Taktung der Veränderungen und technischen Entwicklungen,</li><li>das größere (und unkontrollierbarere) Ausmaß der negativen Konsequenzen (*economic exploitation; Internet/ social networks* ➜ *loss of privacy; intelligence services/Edward Snowden* ➜ *spying; Google* ➜ *data abuse*, etc.),</li><li>die Radikalität und der Gehirnwäsche gleichenden Herangehensweise der neuen „*masters*" ➜ grundlegende Werteveränderung.</li></ul>	5	
4	... kommt zu einer **Bewertung und Einordnung der Situation**, indem er/sie z. B. <ul><li>auf den zunehmenden Kontrollverlust hinweist (*policymakers; intelligence services; newspapers; loss of jobs; messaging services, ...* etc.),</li><li>die an dystopische Gesellschaftsformen erinnernden Merkmale der Machtausübung einerseits und des Kontrollsystems andererseits darstellt,</li><li>die wirtschaftliche (und politische) Dominanz und Kontrolle während der industriellen Revolution der „Gedankenkontrolle" in der digitalen Revolution gegenüberstellt.</li></ul>	5	
5	... erfüllt ein weiteres aufgabenbezogenes Kriterium. (4) <ul><li></li></ul>	4	
		16	

Part A: Teilaufgabe 3.2 ((Re-)Creation of text)

	Anforderungen Der Schüler/die Schülerin ...	maximal erreichbare Punktzahl	erreichte Punkte
1	... bezieht sich konkret auf **die im Text genannten Informationen**, z. B. auf • die Verletzung der Privatsphäre im Internet oder sozialen Netzwerken (ll. 28 f.) sowie das Ausspionieren von sensiblen (politischen) Daten, • die Kontrolle über Informationen und deren Herausgabe (z. B. Übernahme und Schließung von Zeitungen), • die Kontrolle über wirtschaftliche Transaktionen (z. B. *U.S. stock market*, ll. 19 f.).	3	
2	... hinterfragt und kommentiert die **Einschätzungen des Autors**, z. B. durch den Verweis auf • die Existenz von bereits bestehenden Kontrollgremien (z. B. Datenschutz, Verbraucherschutz, Kartellamt etc.), • die gesellschaftlichen Werteveränderungen z. B. im oder seit dem 19. Jahrhundert (Entstehung von Gewerkschaften, Verbesserung der Chancengleichheit, Emanzipation, bessere Bildung/Ausbildung für breitere Gesellschaftschichten etc.).	3	
3	... formuliert einen **sach- und adressatengerecht gestalteten Brief**, indem er/sie z. B. • durch eine knappe Selbstvorstellung einleitet, • seine/ihre Motivation zum Schreiben verdeutlicht, • die formalen Aspekte (Anrede, Gliederung in thematische Abschnitte, Abschluss/Grußformel) des „*Letter to the Editor*" berücksichtigt.	5	
4	... formuliert ein **abschließendes, zusammenfassendes Fazit** und berücksichtigt dabei z. B., dass • die Schaffung/Erhaltung von unabhängigen Informations- und Kontrolleinrichtungen (Medien, Datenschutz, Politik) wichtiger denn je ist, • jeder einzelne Mensch Verantwortung übernehmen muss und dies nicht anderen überlassen darf, • die heutige Gesellschaft bereits dystopische Merkmale hat, wie z. B. die Machtnahme durch Technologien; Kontrollverlust über Daten und Informationen; Gehirnwäsche durch (digitale) Medien etc.	5	
5	... erfüllt ein weiteres aufgabenbezogenes Kriterium. (4) •	4	
		16	

Part B: Listening Comprehension

	Anforderungen	maximal erreichbare Punktzahl	erreichte Punkte
1	**Assignment 1** – *sequencing* (10 items)	10	
2	**Assignment 2** – *note-taking* (10 topics)	20	
		30	

Part B: Listening Comprehension – Solutions

6 The inside of a computer ...

is like a thousand pounds of material that you're carrying around all the time.

4 We're a new form of Homo sapiens because ...

we have curious rituals around this technology; ... we're clicking on things and staring at screens.

-- People are becoming like the Terminator and RoboCop and ...

→ not mentioned in the text

8 Maintaining one's second self is about ...

presenting yourself in digital life in a similar way to how you would in your analog life.

1 A good definition for cyborg:

an organism to which exogenous components have been added for the purpose of adapting to new environments.

5 For thousands of years, tool use has been ...

a physical modification of self in order to extend our physical selves, to go faster and hit things harder.

3 The concept of traditional anthropology is ...

somebody goes to another country, says, "How fascinating these people are, how interesting their tools are, how curious their culture is."

7 Having a second self means ...

that you are starting to show up online and that people are interacting with your second self when you're not there; an extension of the mental self.

-- Going through two adolescences like this causes mental problems because ...

→ not mentioned in the text

2 Humans like to add things to their bodies so ...

they can go to the Alps one day and then become a fish in the sea the next.

Assignment 1: 10 points
Assignment 2: 20 points

Part B: Listening Comprehension – Transcript

Amber Case

We Are All Cyborgs* Now

00:00 – 03:18: I would like to tell you all that you are all actually cyborgs, but not the cyborgs that you think. You're not RoboCop*, and you're not Terminator*, but you're cyborgs every time you look at a computer screen or use one of your cell phone devices. So what's a good definition for cyborg? Well, traditional definition is "an organism to which exogenous* components have been added for the purpose of adapting to new environments." That came from a 1960 paper on space travel, because, if you think about it, space is pretty awkward*. People aren't supposed to be there. But humans are curious, and they like to add things to their bodies so they can go to the Alps one day and then become a fish in the sea the next.

So let's look at the concept of traditional anthropology*. Somebody goes to another country, says, "How fascinating these people are, how interesting their tools are, how curious their culture is." And then they write a paper, and maybe a few other anthropologists read it, and we think it's very exotic. Well, what's happening is that we've suddenly found a new species. I, as a cyborg anthropologist, have suddenly said, "Oh, wow. Now suddenly we're a new form of Homo sapiens, and look at these fascinating cultures, and look at these curious rituals that everybody's doing around this technology. They're clicking on things and staring at screens."

Now there's a reason why I study this, versus traditional anthropology. And the reason is that tool use, in the beginning – for thousands and thousands of years, everything has been a physical modification* of self. It has helped us to extend our physical selves, go faster, hit things harder, and there's been a limit on that. But now what we're looking at is not an extension of the physical self, but an extension of the mental self, and because of that, we're able to travel faster, communicate differently. And the other thing that happens is that we're all carrying around little Mary Poppins technology*. We can put anything we want into it, and it doesn't get heavier, and then we can take anything out. What does the inside of your computer actually look like? Well, if you print it out, it looks like a thousand pounds of material that you're carrying around all the time. And if you actually lose that information, it means that you suddenly have this loss in your mind, that you suddenly feel like something's missing, except you aren't able to see it, so it feels like a very strange emotion.

The other thing that happens is that you have a second self. Whether you like it or not, you're starting to show up online, and people are interacting with your second self when you're not there. And so you have to be careful about leaving your front lawn open, which is basically your Facebook wall, so that people don't write on it in the middle of the night – because it's very much the equivalent. And suddenly we have to start to maintain our second self. You have to present yourself in digital life in a similar way that you would in your analog life. So, in the same way that you wake up, take a shower and get dressed, you have to learn to do that for your digital self. And the problem is that a lot of people now, especially adolescents*, have to go through two adolescences*. They have to go through their primary one, that's already awkward, and then they go through their second self's adolescence, and that's even more awkward because there's an actual history of what they've gone through online. And anybody coming in new to technology is an adolescent online right now, and so it's very awkward, and it's very difficult for them to do those things. (*646 words*)

03:19 – 07:38 So when I was little, my dad would sit me down at night and he would say, "I'm going to teach you about time and space in the future." And I said, "Great." And he said one day, "What's the shortest distance between two points?" And I said, "Well, that's a straight line. You told me that yesterday." I thought I was very clever. He said, "No, no, no. Here's a better way." He took a piece of paper, drew A and B on one side and the other and folded them together so where A and B touched. And he said, "That is the shortest distance between two points." And I said, "Dad, dad, dad, how do you do that?" He said, "Well, you just bend time and space, it takes an awful lot of energy, and that's just how you do it." And I said, "I want to do that." And he said, "Well, okay." And so, when I went to sleep for the next 10 or 20 years, I was thinking at night, "I want to be the first person to create a wormhole, to make things accelerate faster. And I want to make a time machine." I was always sending messages to my future self using tape recorders.

50 But then what I realized when I went to college is that technology doesn't just get adopted because it works. It gets adopted because people use it and it's made for humans. So I started studying anthropology. And when I was writing my thesis on cell phones, I realized that everyone was carrying around wormholes in their pockets. They weren't physically transporting themselves; they were mentally transporting themselves. They would click on a button, and they would be connected as A

55 to B immediately. And I thought, "Oh, wow. I found it. This is great."

So over time, time and space have compressed because of this. You can stand on one side of the world, whisper something and be heard on the other. One of the other ideas that comes around is that you have a different type of time on every single device that you use. Every single browser tab gives you a different type of time. And because of that, you start to dig around for your external

60 memories – where did you leave them? So now we're all these paleontologists that are digging for things that we've lost on our external brains that we're carrying around in our pockets. And that incites a sort of panic architecture – "Oh no, where's this thing?" We're all "I Love Lucy" on a great assembly line of information, and we can't keep up.

And so what happens is, when we bring all that into the social space, we end up checking our

65 phones all the time. So we have this thing called ambient intimacy. It's not that we're always connected to everybody, but at anytime we can connect to anyone we want. And if you were able to print out everybody in your cell phone, the room would be very crowded. These are the people that you have access to right now, in general – all of these people, all of your friends and family that you can connect to.

70 And so there are some psychological effects that happen with this. One I'm really worried about is that people aren't taking time for mental reflection anymore, and that they aren't slowing down and stopping, being around all those people in the room all the time that are trying to compete for their attention on the simultaneous time interfaces, paleontology and panic architecture. They're not just sitting there. And really, when you have no external input, that is a time when there is a cre-

75 ation of self, when you can do long-term planning, when you can try and figure out who you really are. And then, once you do that, you can figure out how to present your second self in a legitimate way, instead of just dealing with everything as it comes in – and oh, I have to do this, and I have to do this, and I have to do this. And so this is very important. I'm really worried that, especially kids today, they're not going to be dealing with this down-time, that they have an instantaneous button-

80 clicking culture, and that everything comes to them, and that they become very excited about it and very addicted to it.

So if you think about it, the world hasn't stopped either. It has its own external prosthetic devices, and these devices are helping us all to communicate and interact with each other. But when you actually visualize it, all the connections that we're doing right now – this is an image of the mapping

85 of the Internet – it doesn't look technological. It actually looks very organic. This is the first time in the entire history of humanity that we've connected in this way. And it's not that machines are taking over. It's that they're helping us to be more human, helping us to connect with each other.

The most successful technology gets out of the way and helps us live our lives. And really, it ends up being more human than technology, because we're co-creating each other all the time. And so this

90 is the important point that I like to study: that things are beautiful, that it's still a human connection – it's just done in a different way. We're just increasing our humanness and our ability to connect with each other, regardless of geography. So that's why I study cyborg anthropology.

Thank you.

(940 words)

www.ted.com/talks/amber_case_we_are_all_cyborgs_now/transcript?language=en [03.04.2015]

Note: The first part of the transcript (00:00–03:18) matches the recording used for the listening examination. The second part (03:19–07:50) is given for copyright reasons.

⁎vocab given along with the assignments

> **Topic:** American Dream – Reveries and Realities
>
> **Skills:** Analysis of a fictional text (screenplay); continuation of a fictional text (*Zieltextformat*); mediation
>
> **Texts:** **Part A:** Danny Strong: The Butler, 2013 (574 words)
> **Part B:** Frank Herrmann: Die wütenden Staaten von Amerika, 2014, newspaper article (370 words)

Part A: Reading/Writing

Danny Strong

The Butler

EXT. WHITE HOUSE – GATE – DAY – 1968

HIPPIE PROTESTERS are outside the White House protesting the Vietnam War[1]. We hear their enraged chants:

5 HIPPIE PROTESTERS
HEY HEY LBJ[2], HOW MANY KIDS DID YOU KILL TODAY?! HEY HEY LBJ, HOW MANY KIDS DID YOU KILL TODAY?!

INT. WHITE HOUSE – RED ROOM – DAY – 10 1968

A maid cleans a mirror as she hears the chanting:

HIPPIE PROTESTERS V.O.
HEY HEY, LBJ, HOW MANY KIDS DID YOU 15 KILL TODAY?!

MAID
I wish you'd shut up.

CUT TO – FULL SCREEN ARCHIVAL FOOTAGE – VIETNAM

20 American bombs drop on the JUNGLES of Vietnam.

INT. LORRAINE MOTEL[3] – MEMPHIS – DAY – 1968

MARTIN LUTHER KING, 38, wise, but weary[4], 25 stands in the doorway, various AIDES and STUDENTS fill the hotel room. Louis sits across from him. They are watching footage[5] of the Vietnam War on television.

NEWSCAST
30 "US casualties[6] are on the rise in Vietnam, giving fuel to critics who say there is no end in sight for what has become a bloody war."

Martin Luther King shakes his hand, frustrated.

MARTIN LUTHER KING
35 President Johnson is making a tragic error in Vietnam.

LOUIS
Why shouldn't we fight in Vietnam?

MARTIN LUTHER KING
40 The Vietcong[7] don't call us niggers, for one.

Louis and a few aides laugh.

MARTIN LUTHER KING (CONT'D)
Seriously, how many of your parents support this war?

45 Almost all raise their hands.

MARTIN LUTHER KING (CONT'D)
Well my Lord … (to Louis) Why do your parents support this?

LOUIS
50 We haven't spoken about it specifically, I just know they do.

MARTIN LUTHER KING
What do your daddy do?
Louis looks at him embarrassed.

55 LOUIS
He's a butler.

---

[1] **Vietnam War** (1955–1975) a cold-war era proxy-war (*Stellvertreterkrieg*) that took place in Vietnam, Laos and Cambodia and claimed the lives of more than one million people – [2] **LBJ** (*abbr.*) Lyndon B. Johnson, 36th President of the United States (1963–1969) – [3] **Lorraine Motel** name of the motel where Martin Luther King was assassinated on 4 April 1968 – [4] **weary** ['wɪəri] tired – [5] **footage** a piece of film, esp. showing a news event – [6] **casualty** a person injured or killed in a war – [7] **Vietcong** a South Vietnamese Communist front that fought a guerilla war against anti-communist forces

MARTIN LUTHER KING
The black domestic[8] plays an important role in our history.

60 **LOUIS**
I didn't tell you that to make fun of me.

MARTIN LUTHER KING
Young brother, the black domestic defies[9] racial stereotypes by being hardworking and trust-
65 worthy.
He slowly breaks down racial hatred with the example of his strong work ethic and dignified character.
(Then)
70 Now while we perceive the butler or the maid as being subservient[10], in many ways they are sub-versive[11] without even knowing it.

Louis stares at him, never thought about his dad in this way.

75 **INT. BLAIR HOUSE[12] – R. D. WARNER'S OF-FICE – DAY – 1968**

Cecil sits across from the Chief Usher[13], R. D. Warner. Cecil is nervous, gripping his sweaty palms.

80 **R. D. WARNER**
Come in, Cecil.

CECIL
Good afternoon, Mr Warner. Thank you for see-ing me.

85 **R. D. WARNER**
What do you want?

CECIL
Since the colored ... the black staff ... does just as much work as the white staff, I believe that
90 our salary should reflect our service, sir.

R. D. WARNER
'Black' staff?

CECIL
I also feel that we should have opportunities of
95 advancement[14]. No black houseman have ever been promoted to the engineer's office.

R. D. Warner stares at Cecil for a long beat. Then –

R. D. WARNER
You're very well liked here, Cecil, but if you're
100 unhappy with your salary or position, then I suggest you seek employment elsewhere.

CECIL
With all due respect sir ...

105 **R. D. WARNER**
Don't let that Martin Luther King shit fill your britches[15] out. Just remember where I found you.

CECIL
110 Yes sir.

Long beat.

CECIL
Excuse me.

He walks out of the room, humiliated[16].

115 **EXT. LORRAINE MOTEL – MEMPHIS**
Martin Luther King stands on the balcony of the Lorraine Motel smoking a cigarette. We hear a newscast in V.O.[17]:

TV NEWSCAST V.O.
120 Martin Luther King was shot and killed in Memphis today ...
(*574 words*)

www.pages.drexel.edu/~ina22/splaylib/Screenplay-Butler.pdf, pp. 71 ff. [04.04.2015]

Note: The 2013 historical drama film *The Butler* is based on the real-life experiences of Eugene Allen (1926 – 2010), an African-American born on a cotton plantation in Georgia, who worked his way up from being a hotel servant to serving as a White House butler from 1952 to 1986.
In the film version, the butler, Cecil Gaines, has a wife (Gloria) and two sons (Louis and Charlie). Louis, the older son, is a student who is actively involved in the Civil Rights Movement.

---

[8] **domestic** household servant – [9] **to defy** [dɪ'faɪ] to refuse to obey sb./sth. – [10] **subservient** [səb'sɜːviənt] *unter-würfig* – [11] **subversive** (*fml.*) *zersetzerisch* – [12] **Blair House** in Washington D. C. is the official state guest house for the President of the United States – [13] **Chief Usher** sb. who manages the entire service staff in the White House – [14] **advancement** the development or improvement of sth.; here: better job opportunities – [15] **britches** (*infml.*) trousers, esp. those not covering the whole of your leg; *Kniehose* – [16] **humiliated** *erniedrigt* – [17] **V.O.** (*abbr.*) voice-over

ASSIGNMENTS

1. Give an outline of the sequence of different scenes from the screenplay, which intertwines the protest against the Vietnam War, Martin Luther King's stay at the famous Lorraine Motel in Memphis and Cecil Gaines' conversation with R. D. Warner.
    (Comprehension)

2. Illustrate how the excerpt from the screenplay juxtaposes and portrays the different leitmotifs and views taken on
    – the war in Vietnam,
    – the position and function of "black domestics",
    – Martin Luther King and the Civil Rights Movement.
    (Analysis)

3. You have a choice here. Choose **one** of the following tasks:

    3.1 Contrast Martin Luther King's observations about the "black domestic" (ll. 58 ff.) with Cecil's request for a pay raise and R. D. Warner's reaction to it.
    Evaluate whether Cecil is being "subservient" or "subversive".
    (Comment/Evaluation)

    3.2 When Cecil returns home that night, he tells his family about the humiliating and frustrating conversation with Mr Warner.
    Imagine what his son Louis, who is a member of the Civil Rights Movement, might answer. Write an additional scene to the screenplay, in which father and son express their views in a dialogue.
    ((Re-)Creation of text)

Part B: Mediation

Frank Herrmann

Die wütenden Staaten von Amerika

Washington. Schießwütig* und rassistisch: So denken nicht nur Schwarze über Amerikas Polizisten. Die Entscheidungen in New York und Missouri, Beamte* nicht für ihr tödliches Handeln zu bestrafen, untergraben* das Vertrauen in den Rechtsstaat. Im ganzen Land demonstrieren Tausende.

5 Es ist ein Sit-in im Neonlichtermeer, zwischen den häuserwandgroßen Reklametafeln am Times Square. „I can't breathe, I can't breathe", skandieren die Demonstranten, während sie tapfer ausharren in der Nachtkälte. „Ich kriege keine Luft mehr": Das waren die letzten aufgezeichneten Worte von Eric Garner. Der schwarze New Yorker starb im Juli auf dem Weg ins Krankenhaus, nachdem ihn Polizisten in den Schwitzkasten* genommen und seinen Kopf rabiat aufs Pflaster
10 eines Bürgersteigs gedrückt hatten.

Garner war 43 Jahre alt und Vater von sechs Kindern. Er hatte vor einem Laden auf Staten Island Zigaretten verkauft; lose, nicht in Packungen, woraufhin ihn eine Streife* wegen illegaler Geschäfte festnehmen wollte. Er litt an Asthma und einem schwachen Herzen. Während er den Beamten, die ihn umzingelten, im Ton der Verzweiflung zurief, sie sollten ihn endlich in Ruhe lassen, wurde
15 er von hinten zu Boden gerissen. Auf dem Video einer Handykamera, aufgezeichnet von einem Freund Garners, kann man die Szene lückenlos sehen. Die Aufnahmen* lassen keinen Zweifel daran, dass es die Polizisten waren, die einen Mann angriffen, der keinerlei Bedrohung darstellte. Schon das unterscheidet den Tod Eric Garners vom Tod Michael Browns, des Jugendlichen, der in der US-Kleinstadt Ferguson erschossenen wurde. Während Brown den Ordnungshüter, der ihn
20 nach einem Ladendiebstahl anzuhalten versuchte, wütend mit Fausthieben attackierte, flehte Garner nur, dass man ihn nicht anrühren solle. Doch genau wie im Fall Browns entschied eine Grand Jury, besetzt mit 14 weißen und neun nichtweißen Geschworenen, niemanden vor einen Richter zu stellen. Auch nicht Daniel Pantaleo, der Garner in den Schwitzkasten nahm, obwohl solche Griffe nach den Bestimmungen des New York Police Department verboten sind.
25 Wie klar oder knapp die Jury eine Anklage* am Mittwoch ablehnte, bleibt vorläufig unter Verschluss*. Das Gremium tagte im Geheimen, so wie im November in Ferguson auch. Doch im Unterschied zu der heruntergekommenen Kleinstadt in Missouri, wo nach dem Urteil reihenweise Geschäfte in Flammen aufgingen, scheinen die Weltbürger der Millionenmetropole gerade jetzt ihre Toleranz unter Beweis stellen zu wollen: die Demonstranten zeigten ihre Wut, blieben aber
30 friedlich. (*370 words*)

www.rp-online.de/politik/ausland/new-york-city-die-wuetenden-staaten-von-amerika-aid-1.4717605, 5 December 2014 [02.04.2015]

Annotations »»»

schießwütig trigger happy ■ **Beamter** civil servant ■ **untergraben** to undermine ■ **jdn. in den Schwitzkasten nehmen** to get/hold sb. in a headlock ■ **Streife** police patrol ■ **Aufnahme** recording ■ **Anklage (erheben)** (to press) charges against sb. ■ **unter Verschluss bleiben** to remain classified

ASSIGNMENT »»»»»

You are planning to do an internship in the USA, and the agency that is organizing it has suggested an African-American family for you to stay with. Against the background of the ongoing unrest and racial tensions in various U.S. cities, however, you are concerned about the situation. At the same time, you are also indignant about the obvious injustice and racism involved. In an e-mail, tell your host family about your worries and concerns, referring to relevant aspects mentioned in the newspaper article, and ask them for their advice and assessment of the situation.

© Schöningh Verlag, Best.-Nr. 040158

Bewertungsbogen für: _____ Kurs: _____

Part A: Teilaufgabe 1 (Comprehension)

	Anforderungen Der Schüler/die Schülerin ...	maximal erreichbare Punktzahl	erreichte Punkte
1	... umreißt die **jeweilige Situation der dargestellten Szenen** und benennt z. B. • den Einsatz von amerikanischen Soldaten und die damit verbundenen hohen Verluste im Vietnamkrieg sowie der Protest von Hippies gegen den Krieg (ll. 5 ff.), • die Gespräche von Civil Rights Aktivisten mit Martin Luther King in dem durch das Attentat auf King berühmt gewordenen Lorraine Motel in Memphis (ll. 24 ff.), • Cecils Forderung nach einer Lohnerhöhung und Beförderungsmöglichkeiten für afro-amerikanische Bedienstete im Weißen Haus mit seinem Chef R. D. Warner (ll. 77 ff.).	2	
2	... arbeitet heraus, wie **Martin Luther King die Situation von afro-amerikanischen *domestics*** charakterisiert und verweist z. B. auf • die Bedeutung ihres Arbeitswillens und ihres starken Charakters für den Abbau von Hass auf Afro-Amerikaner, • den Abbau von Vorurteilen und Stereotypen bedingt durch den Fleiß und die Vertrauenswürdigkeit von Afro-Amerikanern, • ihre nach außen getragene Unterwürfigkeit, die jedoch das Ansehen von Afro-Amerikaners verbessert und daher subversiv ist.	2	
3	... skizziert **das Scheitern von Cecils Verhandlungsversuch** mit R. D. Warner und erwähnt z. B. • seine nach außen getragene Unterwürfigkeit gegenüber seinem Vorgesetzten, • Cecils klar, aber höflich formulierte Forderung nach einer Gleichbehandlung von weißen und schwarzen Bediensteten im Weißen Haus, • das zunächst freundlich-distanzierte Auftreten von R. D. Warner, das schließlich mit einer deutlichen Drohung gegen Cecil sowie einer abfälligen Bemerkung gegen M. L. King endet.	3	
4	... zeigt die inhaltliche **Verknüpfung der Filmszenen** auf und verweist z. B. auf • das durchgängige Thema der *civil rights* (*soldiers* ➜ *Vietnam; M. L. King* ➜ *African-American servants in the USA; Cecil* ➜ *raise/promotion/equal treatment and opportunities*), • das ablehnende Verhalten der *Maid* in Korrespondenz mit M. L. Kings Bemerkungen sowie R. D. Warners Reaktion auf Cecil (*shut up* ➜ *subversive; M. L. King shit ...* ➜ *humiliation*), • das Scheitern und die Demütigung Cecils in Kombination mit dem Attentat auf M. L. King.	3	
5	... erfüllt ein weiteres aufgabenbezogenes Kriterium. (2) •	2	
		10	

Part A: Teilaufgabe 2 (Analysis)

	Anforderungen Der Schüler/die Schülerin ...	maximal erreichbare Punktzahl	erreichte Punkte
1	... erläutert die durch die *juxtaposition* der Szenen hervorgehobene **Darstellung von vielen sozialen und politischen Problemen**, mit denen die USA im Jahr 1968 konfrontiert waren und benennt z. B. • die gesellschaftliche Protest- und Umbruchsituation insgesamt (*Hippies; demonstrations, protests; Civil Rights Movement*, etc.), • den Krieg in Vietnam mit vielen Todesopfern (*how many kids did you kill ...*) sowie konkrete Proteste der jungen Generation (Hippies) gegen die Politik und den Präsidenten, • die Bürgerrechtsbewegung unter Leitung von M. L. King als Folge der Rassentrennung und der ungerechten Behandlung von Afro-Amerikanern (*call us niggers ...; the black domestic ... defies stereotypes ... ; that Martin Luther King shit ...*).	4	
2	... analysiert die sich durch alle Szenen ziehenden **zentralen Leitmotive** und verweist z. B. auf • das Motiv der Unterdrückung in Kombination mit Protest (*Hippie protesters ... enraged chants; call us niggers ...; subversive ...; we should have opportunities ...;* etc.), • das Motive des Scheiterns und Sterbens (*how many kids did you kill ...?; American bombs drop ...; don't let that ... shit fill your britches ...*), • den Kampf für und das Einfordern von Rechten und Gleichbehandlung (*Hippie protesters; in many ways, they are subversive; we should have opportunities and advancement ...*).	4	

3	... untersucht und erklärt **sprachliche Stilmittel**, die den Charakter der Szenen verstärken, z. B. • die rhythmischen Protestgesänge der Hippies, die sie als „typische" Protester und Demonstranten kennzeichnen (ll. 5 f.; 14 f.), • den z. T. umgangssprachlichen Sprachgebrauch von M. L. King als Ausdruck der Solidarisierung (*... don't call us niggers ...; what do your daddy do?; Young brother ...*), • den kontrastiven Sprachgebrauch von Cecil und Warner (*I believe a salary should reflect ...* → polite, Standard English vs. *What do you want?; Don't let ... M. L. King shit ... Just remember* → colloquial language; offensive; threatening).	5	
4	... benennt **weitere Stilmittel**, z. B. • das Einfügen historischer Fernsehnachrichten zur Veranschaulichung des historischen Hintergrundes (ll. 27 f.; 19 f.), • die erläuternden und z. T. die Atmosphäre verstärkenden Regieanweisungen (*M. L. King ... wise but weary; frustrated; Cecil is nervous, gripping his sweaty palms; R. D. Warner stares at Cecil ... he walks out ... humiliated*), • die Auswahl von symbolträchtigen Orten (*White House; jungles of Vietnam; Lorraine Motel*).	5	
5	... erfüllt ein weiteres aufgabenbezogenes Kriterium. (4) •	4	
		18	

Part A: Teilaufgabe 3.1 (Evaluation/Comment)

	Anforderungen Der Schüler/die Schülerin ...	maximal erreichbare Punktzahl	erreichte Punkte
1	... nimmt **konkreten Bezug auf das Zitat von M. L. King** und stellt z. B. dar, dass • während sich Louis für das „Dienen" seines Vaters schämt, demgegenüber M. L. King die damit verbundenen Vorteile hervorhebt (*defies racial stereotypes; breaks down racial hatred*), • M. L. King den *black domestic* ausschließlich positiv charakterisiert (*hardworking; trustworthy; strong work ethic; dignified*), • M. L. King den Unterschied zwischen (falscher) Wahrnehmung und Realität hervorhebt (*we perceive ... as being subservient, they are subversive ...*).	3	
2	... beschreibt **Cecils unterwürfiges Auftreten** vor seinem Vorgesetzten und erwähnt z. B. • seine betonte Höflichkeit (*Thank you for seeing me; I believe that ... sir; I also feel ...*), • seine Unterwürfigkeit als Reaktion auf R. D. Warners Drohungen (*With all due respect, sir ...; Yes sir.; Excuse me.*), • Cecils Nervosität und Angespanntheit (*Cecil is nervous, gripping his sweaty palms*).	3	
3	... beschreibt demgegenüber **Cecils klare Sprache und Bestimmtheit** und verweist z. B. • auf sein bescheidenes, aber bestimmtes Auftreten, • auf seine hypotaktischen Satzkonstruktionen und höflich-bestimmte Argumentationsweise (*Since the black staff ... does just as much work as the white staff ... our salary should reflect our service; we should have opportunities of advancement ...*), • darauf, dass Cecil der Situation Stand hält und Haltung bewahrt, obwohl R. D. Warner ihn bedroht und beleidigt).	4	
4	... kommt in Abwägung der verschiedenen Aspekte zu einer **begründeten und logischen Schlussfolgerung** und führt z. B. an, dass • M. L. Kings Beobachtung genau auf Cecils Verhalten passt, da er sowohl unterwürfig ist als auch Mut beweist und für gleiche Rechte von afro-amerikanischen Bediensteten eintritt, • Cecil wegen seiner Qualitäten und guten Arbeitsleistung anerkannt ist, wie es M. L. King ausführte (*You're well-liked here ...*), • man Cecil vermutlich nicht als „typischen" *black domestic* bezeichnen kann, da er als Butler im Weißen Haus und mit unmittelbarem Kontakt zum US-Präsidenten eine besondere Stellung hat.	4	
5	... erfüllt ein weiteres aufgabenbezogenes Kriterium. (4) •	4	
		14	

Part A: Teilaufgabe 3.2 ((Re-)Creation of text)

	Anforderungen Der Schüler/die Schülerin ...	maximal erreichbare Punktzahl	erreichte Punkte
1	... nimmt durchgängig die **vorgegebene(n) Perspektive(n)** ein, indem er/sie z. B. • aus Cecils Sicht argumentiert, der zwar frustriert ist, aber Angst davor hat, seinen Job zu verlieren, • aus Louis' Sicht argumentiert, der die Gleichbehandlung von Schwarzen fordert und das ungerechte gesellschaftliche System anprangert, • aus sehr konträren Perspektiven heraus argumentieren lässt.	3	

© Schöningh Verlag, Best.-Nr. 040158

2	... greift zur Verdeutlichung von **Louis' Argumentation** auf im Text genannte Aspekte als auch auf unterrichtliche Kenntnisse zurück und verweist z. B. auf • die Ausbeutung und Ungleichbehandlung der Afro-Amerikaner in den USA (Rassentrennung etc.), • die vielen Qualitäten, die Schwarze immer wieder unter Beweis gestellt haben, • die veränderte Situation in der Gegenwart (*Civil Rights Movement, M. L. King* etc.).	3	
3	... lässt demgegenüber **Cecil argumentieren**, dass • er sich durch seine Arbeit und sein (devotes) Verhalten „hochgearbeitet" und Kariere gemacht hat (*plantation → White House*), • er seinen guten Ruf nicht riskieren will (*you are well-liked*), • er Angst hat, seine Arbeit zu verlieren und damit seine Existenz aufs Spiel zu setzen, • derartige Politik im Weißen Haus nichts zu suchen habe.	4	
4	... integriert die formal-stilistischen Elemente eines *Screenplays*, z. B. • Regieanweisungen, *slug lines*, • Dialoge und Interaktion der Charaktere, • die Einbeziehung von *props, music, camera positions*.	4	
5	... erfüllt ein weiteres aufgabenbezogenes Kriterium. (4) •	4	
		14	

Part B: Mediation – Inhalt

	Anforderungen Der Schüler/die Schülerin ...	maximal erreichbare Punktzahl	erreichte Punkte
1	... fasst die Informationen situations- und adressatenbezogen sinngemäß zusammen, auch unter Berücksichtigung impliziter Aussageabsichten.	4	
2	... konzentriert sich dabei – bezogen auf den situativen Kontext – auf wesentliche Inhalte und wichtige Details.	4	
3	... antizipiert ggf. unter Berücksichtigung des Welt- und Kulturwissens mögliche Missverständnisse und fügt ggf. für das Verstehen erforderliche Erläuterungen hinzu.	5	
4	... greift den in der Aufgabenstellung vorgegebenen situativen und thematischen Kontext auf und stellt eine inhaltlichen Bezug zwischen den soziokulturellen Gegebenheiten in Deutschland und den USA her.	5	
5	... erfüllt ein weiteres aufgabenbezogenes Kriterium. (2) •	2	
		18	

Part B: Mediation – Sprache

Sprache (60 %)	Der Schüler/die Schülerin ...	Lösungsqualität	
		maximal erreichbare Punktzahl	erreichte Punkte
Kommunikative Textgestaltung	• richtet seinen/ihren Text konsequent und explizit auf die **Intention** und den **Adressaten** im Sinne der **Aufgabenstellung** aus. • berücksichtigt den **situativen Kontext**. • beachtet die Textsortenmerkmale des geforderten **Zieltextformats**. • erstellt einen sachgerecht **strukturierten** Text. • gestaltet seinen/ihren Text hinreichend ausführlich, aber ohne unnötige Wiederholungen und Umständlichkeiten.	9	
Ausdrucksvermögen/ Verfügbarkeit sprachlicher Mittel	• löst sich vom Wortlaut des Ausgangstextes und formuliert **eigenständig**, ggf. unter Verwendung von Kompensationsstrategien. • verwendet funktional einen sachlich wie stilistisch angemessenen und differenzierten allgemeinen und thematischen **Wortschatz** sowie **Funktionswortschatz**. • verwendet einen variablen und dem jeweiligen Zieltextformat angemessenen **Satzbau**.	9	
Sprachrichtigkeit	• beachtet die Normen der sprachlichen Korrektheit im Sinne einer **gelingenden Kommunikation** in den Bereichen **Wortschatz**, **Grammatik** und **Orthographie**.	9	
	Summe Sprache	27	
	Summe Klausurteil B: Aufgabe 3	45	

Part B: Mediation – Possible Solution

Dear …,

I'm really happy that my dream of completing an internship in the United States is finally about to come true and that I will be staying with your family. The information that the agency has given me about you and your family's background has totally convinced me that we have a lot of things in common, so I am sure that we will have a great time together and I am really looking forward to it! ☺

However, I must admit that, only recently, I read an article in a German newspaper that worried me a lot. It was about a sit-in on Times Square where people were demonstrating against the killing of Eric Garner, an African-American, who was killed by police officers who were trying to arrest him for illegally selling cigarettes in front of a store on Long Island. Although he had told the police officers that he couldn't breathe, they kept him in a headlock – which eventually led to his death.

The newspaper reported that, even though there was a mobile phone recording of the incident, a Grand Jury decided not to press any charges against the police officers. Although the reactions of the New Yorkers to the verdict weren't as violent and aggressive as in Ferguson, I am nevertheless worried and concerned about what the situation in the U.S. is actually like right now.

Most importantly, how am I supposed to behave? I am sure you and your family have already discussed the issue as well … Can you give me some information about what I can expect – and some advice about how to act appropriately and what (not) to say?

As you probably know, here in Germany, there are also areas where people are prejudiced and threaten or even attack immigrants or non-white people. However, just like the protestors in New York, activists and local citizens over here have also organized demonstrations and marches where people can express their solidarity with the immigrants and protest strongly against racism. Fortunately, it seems that most people have learned from the past and are open-minded and against racism, so perhaps the same is also true in America.

Hope to hear from you soon ☺

Warmest regards

XXX

(373 words)

121

Topic: India: Democracy, Diversity, Determination

Skills: Analysis of a non-fictional text (magazine article); mediation

Texts: Part A: India's Economy: A Chance to Fly, 2015 (467 words)
Part B: Willi Germund, Spiegelbild einer kranken Gesellschaft, newspaper article (290 words)

Part A: Reading/Writing

India's Economy: A Chance to Fly

India has a rare opportunity to become the world's most dynamic big economy

Emerging markets[1] used to be a beacon[2] of hope in the world economy, but now they are more often a source of gloom[3]. China's economy is slowing. Brazil is mired[4] in stagflation[5]. Russia is in recession, battered[6] by Western sanctions and the slump in the oil price; South Africa is plagued by inef-
5 ficiency and corruption. Amid the disappointment one big emerging market stands out: India. [...]
India possesses untold promise[7]. Its people are entrepreneurial and roughly half of the 1.25 billion population is under 25 years old. It is poor, so has lots of scope[8] for catch-up growth: GDP per person (at purchasing-power[9] parity[10]) was $5,500 in 2013, compared with $11,900 in China and $15,000 in Brazil. The economy has been balkanized[11] by local taxes levied[12] at state borders, but
10 cross-party support for a national goods-and-services tax could create a true common market. The potential is there; the question has always been whether it can be unleashed[13]. [...]
The real reason for hope is the prospect of more reforms. Last May Narendra Modi's Bharatiya Janata Party won a huge election victory on a promise of a better-run economy. His government spent its early months putting a rocket up[14] a sluggish[15] civil service and on other useful groundwork. But
15 the true test of its reformist credentials[16] will be Mr Jaitley's budget.
The easy part will be to lock in India's good fortune, with fiscal[17] and monetary discipline. In addition India's public-sector banks need capital and, since the state cannot put up the money, the minister must persuade potential shareholders that they will be run at arm's length[18] from politicians.
If India is to thrive[19], it needs bold reforms and political courage to match. The tried-and-tested
20 development strategy is to move people from penurious[20] farm jobs to more productive work with better pay. China's rise was built on export-led manufacturing. The scope to follow that model is limited. Supply-chain trade growth has slowed, and manufacturing is becoming less labour-intensive as a result of technology. Yet India could manage better than it does now. It has a world-class IT-services industry, which remains too skill-intensive and too small to absorb the 90m–115m often
25 ill-educated youngsters entering the job market in the next decade. The country's best hope is a mixed approach, expanding its participation in global markets in both industry and services. To achieve this Mr Jaitley must focus on three inputs: land, power and labour. [...]
The danger is that, with inflation falling and India enjoying a boost from cheaper energy, the country's leaders duck[21] the tough reforms needed for lasting success. That would be a huge mistake. Mr
30 Modi and Mr Jaitley have a rare chance to turbocharge[22] an Indian take-off. They must not waste it.
(*467 words*)

http://www.economist.com/news/leaders/21644145 – india-has-rare-opportunity-become-worlds-most-dynamic-big-economy-
chance-fly, 21 February 2015 [04.04.2015]

[1] **emerging market** *Schwellenland* – [2] **beacon** ['biːkən] *Leuchtfeuer* – [3] **gloom** unhappiness, hopelessness – [4] **mired** stuck in a difficult situation – [5] **stagflation** a situation, in which economic activity does not increase (= stagnation) even though prices keep rising (= inflation) – [6] **to batter sb./sth.** to repeatedly hit or damage sb./sth. with force – [7] **untold promise** immeasurable potential – [8] **scope** the opportunity or potential for doing sth. – [9] **purchasing power** how much you can buy with a particular currency (*Währung*) –[10] **parity** equality – [11] **to balkanize** to divide sth., esp. a territory, into small, conflicting units – [12] **to levy taxes** *Steuern erheben* – [13] **to unleash** here: to free from restraints or limitations – [14] **to put a rocket up sb.** (*infml.*) to cause sb. to quickly spring into action – [15] **sluggish** slow-moving and lacking energy – [16] **credential** *Berechtigung, Glaubwürdigkeit* – [17] **fiscal** *Steuer-* – [18] **at arm's length** independently, at a distance – [19] **to thrive** to grow, develop and be successful – [20] **penurious** [pəˈnjʊəriəs] (*fml.*) extremely poor – [21] **to duck sth.** here: *sich vor etw. drücken* – [22] **to turbocharge** to start sth. very quickly and with a lot of power

ASSIGNMENTS

1. Present the measures that should be taken in order to unleash India's enormous economic and political potential and allow it to become the world's "most dynamic big economy".
(*Comprehension*)

2. Examine the author's line of argument and explain whether the various suggestions and pieces of advice have a factual and serious background or whether they are merely wishful thinking and rather illusionary.
(*Analysis*)

3. You have a choice here. Choose **one** of the following tasks:

   3.1 "The country's best hope is a mixed approach, expanding its participation in global markets in both industry and services." (ll. 24 ff.)
   Taking into consideration the possible risks and dangers of globalization, discuss whether (or not) the advice given above represents a promising approach for India and is worth trying.
   (*Comment/Evaluation*)

   3.2 Based on the suggestions made in the article, compose a commercial, promoting India's "hidden potentials" and "untold promise".
   Back up your commercial with information and knowledge you have gained in class and write a short shooting script.
   (*(Re-)Creation of text*)

Part B: Mediation

Willi Germund

Spiegelbild* einer kranken Gesellschaft

Indische Regierung verbietet Dokumentarfilm über die Gruppenvergewaltigung einer Studentin

Ein einziger Satz genügt, um das Blut in den Adern gefrieren zu lassen. „Sie brauchen zwei Hände zum Klatschen", sagt der adrette junge Mann in einem frischen, karierten Hemd über eine Vergewaltigung. Mukesh Singh gehörte zu einer fünfköpfigen Bande, die im Dezember des Jahres
5 2012 eine 23-jährige Studentin in einem Bus in der Hauptstadt Delhi entführte und so brutal vergewaltigte, dass sie später an ihren Verletzungen starb. Sie hätte halt nicht „nach neun Uhr abends unterwegs sein sollen", führt Singh lakonisch aus und gibt dem Opfer auch noch die Schuld: „Ein Mädchen trägt viel mehr Verantwortung für eine Vergewaltigung als ein Junge." [...]
Freimütig spricht er vor der Filmkamera der britischen Filmemacherin Leslee Udwin, die Singh
10 für ihren Dokumentarfilm „India's Daughter" mit behördlicher Genehmigung* mehr als 16 Stunden interviewte.
Wie repräsentativ sein steinzeitliches Frauenbild für die knapp 1,3 Milliarden Menschen zählende Nation steht, sei dahingestellt. Einen eigenen Eindruck dürfen sich die Bürger der größten Demokratie der Welt freilich nicht von der abstrusen* Gedankenwelt des Vergewaltigers und Mörders
15 schaffen. Denn die amtierende hindunationalistische Regierung von Premierminister Narendra Modi ließ den Film per Gerichtsbeschluss* am Ganges verbieten. [...]
Im Fall des Dokumentarfilms begründete Innenminister Rajanath Singh sein Vorgehen so: „Das Interview ist hochgradig herabwürdigend und ein Affront gegen die Würde von Frauen." [...]
Die brutale Tat der Bande um Mukesh Singh Ende 2012 hatte im Jahr 2013 eine radikale Reform
20 der Vergewaltigungsgesetze zur Folge.
Indiens Gesellschaft ist heute eher bereit, missbrauchten Frauen Gehör zu schenken als vor zwei Jahren. Aber die unabhängige Parlamentarierin Anu Agha betont in der Hauptstadt Delhi: „Wir müssen zur Kenntnis nehmen, dass Männer in Indien keinen Respekt vor Frauen haben. Bei jeder Vergewaltigung wird der Frau die Schuld zugeschoben." (*290 words*)

Frankfurter Rundschau, 7/8 March 2015, p. 56

Annotations 》》》

Spiegelbild reflection ■ **behördliche Genehmigung** official/governmental approval ■ **abstrus** absurd ■
Gerichtsbeschluss court order

ASSIGNMENT 》》》》》

India has always been a favoured destination for adolescent backpackers and gappers, offering an exciting and diverse culture, as well as interesting insights into one of the world's most important emerging economies.

Against the background of repeated rapes and other violent crimes towards women, an Indian agency that organizes gap years and internships for international students has established an online forum and is now calling for students from all around the world to post comments about how India is perceived in the international media.

Based on the information given in the article, write a text for the online forum in which you outline the journalist's depiction of the current state of Indian society.

| Bewertungsbogen für: _____ | Kurs: _____ |

Part A: Teilaufgabe 1 (Comprehension)

	Anforderungen Der Schüler/die Schülerin ...	maximal erreichbare Punktzahl	erreichte Punkte
1	... skizziert die **Situation von anderen *emerging markets*** und die Gründe für deren Scheitern, z. B. • Chinas eher rückläufigen wirtschaftlichen „Boom", • Brasiliens wirtschaftliche Stagnation bei gleichzeitiger Inflation, • Russlands Rezession, bedingt durch westliche Sanktionen und sinkende Ölpreise, • Südafrikas Probleme mit Korruption und mangelnder Effizienz.	2	
2	... stellt demgegenüber **Indiens wirtschaftliches und politisches Potential** dar und benennt z. B. • den Unternehmergeist der Inder sowie das niedrige Durchschnittsalter der Bevölkerung (ll. 4 f.), • den durch die Armut bedingten Willen zu finanziellem Wachstum (ll. 6 f.), • die politische Unterstützung einer national *goods-and-services tax*, die einen *common market* ermöglichen soll.	2	
3	... zeigt demgegenüber **noch bestehende Probleme** auf und verweist z. B. auf • den eher phlegmatischen und trägen indischen *civil service*, • die Notwendigkeit einer finanziellen Unterstützung von *India's public-sector banks*, • die oft schlecht ausgebildete Jugend Indiens (ll. 23 f.).	3	
4	... arbeitet daraus schlussfolgernd die **notwendigen Maßnahmen** heraus und verweist z. B. auf • die Fortführung der bereits vorgenommene Reformen in Politik und Wirtschaft (ll. 11 ff.), • eine strenge Disziplinierung in Bezug auf Steuer und Finanzen, • eine Ausweitung und globale Anknüpfung des Arbeitsmarktes und des Servicebereiches wie der Industrie (ll. 24 ff.).	3	
5	... erfüllt ein weiteres aufgabenbezogenes Kriterium. (2) •	2	
		10	

Part A: Teilaufgabe 2 (Analysis)

	Anforderungen Der Schüler/die Schülerin ...	maximal erreichbare Punktzahl	erreichte Punkte
1	... verdeutlicht die **Argumentationsstruktur des Textes** und nennt z. B. • die einleitende Darstellung der Negativbeispiele (China, Brasilien, Russland, Südafrika, ll. 2 ff.), • die durch Zahlenmaterial gestützte Hervorhebung von Indiens Potentialen (ll. 5 f.), • die vom Premierminister in der Wahl gegebenen Reformversprechen und die bereits begonnene vielversprechende Arbeit daran (ll. 11 ff.).	4	
2	... analysiert die **sprachlichen Mittel in Zusammenhang mit Indiens möglichem Potenzial** und belegt das z. B. mit • dem kontrastiven Gebrauch von *positive and negative emotional words* (*gloom; battered; mired; stagnation* → *China, Brasil, etc.; scope; unleashed, a rocket up; thrive; turbocharge* → *India*), • dem Gebrauch eines Wortfeldes im Zusammenhang mit Zukunft, Hoffnung etc. (*untold promise; catch-up growth; real reason for hope ...; the prospect of ...; a promise of ...* etc.), • dem abschließenden Hinweis auf mögliche Risiken und Hindernisse (*penurious farm jobs; the scope is limited; growth has slowed; India could manage better ...* etc.).	4	
3	... analysiert vor dem Hintergrund möglicher Risiken **die Lösungsvorschläge** des Autors, z. B. • *the prospect of more reforms* als Signal der Hoffnung, • *fiscal and monetary discipline ... capital ...* als Gegenentwurf zu Korruption und Geldverschwendung, • *bold reforms and political courage* vor dem Hintergrund der Wahlversprechen des Premierministers, • *expanding ... participation in global markets in both service and industry* als Maßnahme der „Risikoverteilung" im globalen Handel.	5	
4	... analysiert unter Berücksichtigung der **sprachlichen Mittel** und der vom Autor **genannten Fakten** die Argumentationsweise und stellt z. B. dar, dass • seine Analyse sich auf diverses Zahlen- und Faktenmaterial stützt, • der Autor Indien eine Art „Vermeidungsstrategie" empfiehlt: die von anderen *emerging markets* gemachten Fehler sollten nicht wiederholt werden, • er wiederholt „*must-do*"-Formulierungen wählt, um seinen Empfehlungen Nachdruck zu verleihen.	5	
5	... erfüllt ein weiteres aufgabenbezogenes Kriterium. (4) •	4	
		18	

Part A: Teilaufgabe 3.1 (Evaluation/Comment)

	Anforderungen Der Schüler/die Schülerin ...	maximal erreichbare Punktzahl	erreichte Punkte
1	... bezieht sich konkret auf die im Text gegebenen **Ratschläge des Autors** und benennt z. B., dass ● Indien nicht dem Beispiel Chinas folgen und sich auf die (einseitige) Massenproduktion von Exportwaren fokussieren sollte (ll. 20 ff.), ● Indien die bereits bestehende *world-class IT-services industry* nutzen und ausbauen sollte (ll. 22 ff.), ● die 90–115 Millionen auf den Arbeitsmarkt drängenden jungen Menschen sowohl in der Industrie als auch in Servicebereich gut ausgebildet und genutzt werden sollten.	3	
2	... greift den im Text betonten **Aspekt der *global markets*** auf und erläutert z. B. – u. a. unter Rückgriff auf unterrichtliche Kenntnisse, dass ● Indien im Servicebereich bereits Erfahrungen mit Globalisierung hat (z. B. durch *Outsourcing, IT-Services* etc.), ● Indien z. B. auf die Erfahrungen im Bereich der Textil – und Gebrauchsgüter zurückgreifen kann, ● Indien bereits global agierende Unternehmen besitzt, die erfolgreich auf internationalen Märkten arbeiten (z. B. Tata).	3	
3	... kommt unter Rückgriff auf unterrichtliche Kenntnisse und Ergebnisse zu einer **Darstellung der Risiken und Chancen der Globalisierung und bezieht sie auf Indien**, z. B. ● die möglichen Risiken im Zusammenhang mit Umweltverschmutzung und -zerstörung sowie einer ausbeuterischen Arbeitspolitik, ● die Chancen, durch ein großes Potential von jungen, wissensbegierigen und risikobereiten Menschen, ● das Risiko einer Ausweitung von sozialen Unterschieden und der Ausgrenzung von sozialen Randgruppen.	4	
4	... kommt in Abwägung der verschiedenen Aspekte zu **einem begründeten Urteil**, z. B., dass ● es in der heutigen Zeit keine Alterative zur Globalisierung gibt – Indien sich aber auch auf nationale Werte und Errungenschaften besinnen sollte, ● Indien vorrangig seine gesellschaftlichen Probleme in den Griff bekommen muss (z. B. Kastensystem, Gewalt gegen Frauen, Korruption etc.), um auch wirtschaftlich stabil und international wettbewerbsfähig zu sein/zu werden.	4	
5	... erfüllt ein weiteres aufgabenbezogenes Kriterium. (4) ●	4	
		14	

Part A: Teilaufgabe 3.2 ((Re-)Creation of text)

	Anforderungen Der Schüler/die Schülerin ...	maximal erreichbare Punktzahl	erreichte Punkte
1	... erstellt ein **Shooting Script,** in dem er/sie die wesentlichen formal-stilistischen Elemente verarbeitet, z. B. ● Regieanweisungen, ● kurze Dialoge, ● einen kurzen Überblick über die Protagonisten des *Commercials*.	3	
2	... entwickelt einen kurzen **Plot** und bezieht sich dabei z. B. auf ● Indiens ungenutzte Potentiale und Möglichkeiten in wirtschaftlicher Hinsicht, ● im Text genannte Zahlen und Beispiele, ● eine abschließende Message/einen Appell an die Inder, sich stark zu machen bzw. an die Welt, in Indien zu investieren.	3	
3	... verarbeitet **charakteristische Elemente der Werbung**, wie z. B. ● einen Slogan und/oder eine griffige und witzige Werbebotschaft, ● Schlüsselbegriffe, Schlagworte, Hochwertworte, ● ein die Story abschließendes Happy End bzw. einen Appell in Indien zu investieren.	4	
4	... übernimmt **weitere „typische" stilistische Elemente der Werbesprache**, z. B. ● Wiederholungen, ● Wortspiele, Puns, ● musikalische Elemente etc.	4	
5	... erfüllt ein weiteres aufgabenbezogenes Kriterium. (4) ●	4	
		14	

Part B: Mediation – Inhalt

	Anforderungen Der Schüler/die Schülerin ...	maximal erreichbare Punktzahl	erreichte Punkte
1	... fasst die Informationen situations- und adressatenbezogen sinngemäß zusammen.	4	
2	... konzentriert sich dabei – bezogen auf den situativen Kontext – auf wesentliche Inhalte.	4	
3	... fügt ggf. für das Verstehen erforderliche detaillierte Erläuterungen hinzu.	5	
4	... bezieht den situativen Kontext jugendlicher Rucksackreisender auf die im Artikel beschriebene Situation. Bezieht auch die deutsche Perspektive mit ein.	5	
5	... erfüllt ein weiteres aufgabenbezogenes Kriterium. (2) •	2	
		18	

Part B: Mediation – Sprache

Sprache (60 %)	Der Schüler/die Schülerin ...	Lösungsqualität	
		maximal erreichbare Punktzahl	erreichte Punkte
Kommunikative Textgestaltung	• richtet seinen/ihren Text konsequent und explizit auf die **Intention** und den **Adressaten** im Sinne der **Aufgabenstellung** aus. • berücksichtigt den **situativen Kontext**. • beachtet die Textsortenmerkmale des geforderten **Zieltextformats**. • erstellt einen sachgerecht **strukturierten** Text. • gestaltet seinen/ihren Text hinreichend ausführlich, aber ohne unnötige Wiederholungen und Umständlichkeiten.	9	
Ausdrucksvermögen/ Verfügbarkeit sprachlicher Mittel	• löst sich vom Wortlaut des Ausgangstextes und formuliert **eigenständig**, ggf. unter Verwendung von Kompensationsstrategien. • verwendet funktional einen sachlich wie stilistisch angemessenen und differenzierten allgemeinen und thematischen **Wortschatz** sowie **Funktionswortschatz**. • verwendet einen variablen und dem jeweiligen Zieltextformat angemessenen **Satzbau**.	9	
Sprachrichtigkeit	• beachtet die Normen der sprachlichen Korrektheit im Sinne einer **gelingenden Kommunikation** in den Bereichen **Wortschatz**, **Grammatik** und **Orthographie**.	9	
	Summe Sprache	27	
	Summe Klausurteil B: Aufgabe 3	45	

Part B: Mediation – Possible Solution

The German journalist paints a rather gloomy and negative picture of Indian society right from the start by calling it "sick".

His assessment is largely based on two aspects.

1. The repeated rapes of Indian women, who are then made responsible for the crime by being accused of having behaved inappropriately, instead of charging and sentencing the brutal rapists.
2. The scandalous censorship of the British documentary "India's Daughter", in which an Indian rapist, Mukesh Singh, was interviewed and did not show any remorse at all.

In contrast to the depiction of this alarming and appalling situation, the journalist informs us that the Indian laws concerning rape were radically reformed in 2013. However, the independent Indian MP Ana Agha states that – despite all the reforms – Indian men do not respect women, and women are still given the blame for being raped.

(141 words)

Topic: Economy, Energy, Efficiency – The World Going Global

Skills: Analysis of a non-fictional text (magazine article); writing a letter to the editor
(*Zieltextformat*); mediation

Texts: **Part A:** The Unbalanced Global Economy – American Shopper (628 words)
Part B: Susanne Amann: Jung und unfair, magazine article (332 words)

Part A: Reading/Writing

The Unbalanced Global Economy – American Shopper

The world is once again relying too much on American consumers to power growth

A global economy running on a single engine is better than one that needs jump leads[1]. The American economy is motoring again, to the relief of exporters from Hamburg to Hangzhou. Firms added more than 1m net new jobs in the past three months, the best showing[2] since 1997. Buoyed up[3]
5 by cheap petrol, Americans are spending; in January consumer sentiment[4] jumped to its highest in more than a decade. The IMF[5] reckons[6] that American growth will hit 3.6 % in 2015, faster than the world economy as a whole. All this is good. But growing dependence on the American economy – and on consumers in particular – has unwelcome echoes.
A decade ago American consumers borrowed heavily and recklessly[7]. They filled their ever-larger
10 houses with goods from China; they fuelled gas-guzzling[8] cars with imported oil. Big exporters recycled their earnings[9] back to America, pushing down interest rates which in turn helped to feed[10] further borrowing. Europe was not that different. There, frugal[11] Germans financed debt binges[12] around the euro area's periphery.
After the financial crisis, the hope was of an end to these imbalances. Debt-addicted Americans and
15 Spaniards would chip away[13] at their obligations[14]; thrifty[15] German and Chinese consumers would start to enjoy life for once. At first, this seemed to be happening. America's trade deficit[16], which was about 6 % of GDP[17] in 2006, had more than halved by 2009.
But now the world is slipping back into some nasty habits[18]. Hair grows faster than the euro zone, and what growth there is depends heavily on exports. The countries of the single currency are run-
20 ning a current-account surplus[19] of about 2.6 % of GDP, thanks largely to exports to America. At 7.4 % of GDP, Germany's trade surplus is as large as it has ever been.
China's growth, meanwhile, is slowing – and once again relying heavily on spending elsewhere. It notched up[20] its own record trade surplus in January. [...]
America's economy is warping[21] as a result. Consumption's contribution to growth in the fourth
25 quarter of 2014 was the largest since 2006. The trade deficit is widening. Strip out[22] oil, and America's trade deficit grew to more than 3 % of GDP in 2014, and is approaching its pre-recession peak[23] of about 4 %.
The world's reliance[24] on America is likely to deepen. Germans are more interested in shipping savings abroad than investing at home. Households and firms in Europe's periphery are overbur-

---

[1] **jump leads** *Starterkabel* – [2] **showing** result – [3] **to buoy sb. up** to make sb. feel more optimistic – [4] **consumer sentiment** measurement of people's confidence in the state of the economy – [5] **IMF** (*abbr.*) International Monetary Fund – [6] **to reckon** *mit etw. rechnen* – [7] **reckless** irresponsible and unconcerned about possible consequences – [8] **gas-guzzling** using a lot of petrol – [9] **to recycle earnings** here: to reinvest profits – [10] **to feed** here: to encourage – [11] **frugal** careful with money – [12] **binge** sth. done to excess – [13] **to chip away at sth.** (*phr. v.*) here: to gradually reduce – [14] **obligation** *Verpflichtung* – [15] **thrifty** careful with money, esp. by avoiding waste – [16] **trade deficit** debt caused by having more imports than exports – [17] **GDP** (*abbr.*) Gross Domestic Product: the total value of goods and services produced by a country in a year – [18] **nasty habit** *schlechte Gewohnheit* – [19] **current account surplus** *Leistungsbilanzüberschuss* – [20] **to notch sth. up** (*phr. v.*) to achieve sth. – [21] **to warp** to alter sth. from what is normal or healthy – [22] **to strip out** (*phr. v.*) here: to exclude from a calculation – [23] **peak** highest point – [24]**reliance on sth.** *Abhängigkeit von etw.*

30 dened[25] with debt, workers' wages squeezed[26] and banks in no mood[27] to lend. Like Germany, Europe as a whole is relying on exports. [...]

Two dangers loom[28]. The short-term worry is that weak exports, a rising dollar and a slowdown in energy investment (because of falling oil prices) will stifle[29] the American expansion. Rather than pull others along, America will be dragged down by their weakness. That is why the Fed[30] should be
35 none too eager to raise interest rates[31]. With inflation below target it has no need to rush to tighten.

The longer-term fear is that growing imbalances will repeat the financial cycle of the 2000s, in which exporters to America once again finance reckless consumer borrowing. The ratio of Americans' debt to income has fallen from a pre-crisis high of more than 120 % to around 100 %, but consumers still have too much incentive[32] to load up on debt. Politicians would do well to get rid of
40 subsidies[33] like tax relief[34] on mortgage interest[35].

But the burden to act[36] does not lie just on America. Leaders from Brussels to Beijing should not allow falling currencies to become a substitute for structural reform, or for efforts to boost spending at home. A strong American economy is a boon[37] to the world. It should not be taken for granted[38].
(*628 words*)

www.economist.com/news/leaders/21643188-world-once-again-relying-too-much-american-consumers-power-growth-american-shopper, 14 February 2015 [04.04.2015]

ASSIGNMENTS

1. Give an outline of the author's analysis of the state of the global economy in general and the U.S. economic recovery in particular.
   (*Comprehension*)

2. Examine the author's stance on the recent economic developments in the USA as well as globally, and explain how the rhetorical devices emphasize the author's intention and the overall message of the article.
   (*Analysis*)

3. You have a choice here. Choose **one** of the following tasks:

   3.1 As the author points out, Americans love to shop and do have the tendency to spend more money than they actually earn. The fear that, due to America's economic recovery, corporations worldwide will increase their exports to the U.S, and that U.S. consumers might recklessly borrow money again is thus not unrealistic.
   However, are Europeans to blame for that behaviour?
   Comment on the author's fears and indirect criticisms of Germany and China because of their strength as export nations.
   (*Comment/Evaluation*)

   3.2 Germany's automotive industry is one of the biggest exporters to the USA. As the CEO of a German car-making company, write a "Letter to the Editor" in response to the article and its implicit reproaches directed at German and other European export businesses and state your company's point of view.
   (*(Re-)Creation of text*)

---

[25] **overburdened** *überbelastet* – [26] **to squeeze wages** *die Löhne drücken* – [27] **to be in no mood to do sth.** *nicht geneigt sein, etw. zu tun* – [28] **to loom** *lauern* – [29] **to stifle** ['staɪf͵l] *im Keim ersticken* – [30] **the Fed** (*abbr.*) Federal Reserve System: the central banking system of the U.S. – [31] **interest rate** *Zinshöhe* – [32] **incentive** *motivation* – [33] **subsidy** Subvention – [34] **tax relief** *Steuerentlastung* – [35] **mortgage interest** ['mɔːɡɪdʒ] *Hypothekenzinsen* – [36] **burden to act** responsibility for dealing with a problem – [37] **boon** *Wohltat* – [38] **to take sth. for granted** *etw. für selbstverständlich halten*

Part B: Mediation

Susanne Amann

Jung und Unfair

Eine neue Studie belegt: Jugendliche wissen viel über die ethischen Probleme bei der Herstellung von Textilien. Ihr Verhalten ändert das aber kaum.

Der Name schreckt ab. „Kleiderkreisel" heißt die Secondhand-Plattform, auf der man gebrauchte Kleider kaufen und verkaufen oder auch einfach leihen kann. Das klingt nach Ökoladen, nach muf-
5 figem* Selbstgestricktem*, nach dem Charme der Achtzigerjahre – trotz einer gelungenen App, modernen Designs und 3,2 Millionen registrierter Mitglieder, die das Angebot nutzen.
2009 wurde die Website gegründet. Die Nutzer sind überwiegend Frauen, die meisten von ihnen zwischen 16 und 29 Jahre alt – und darüber hinaus so etwas wie Trendsetter. [...]
Auch unter Jugendlichen sind sie damit in der Minderheit, wie eine neue Studie der Umweltorga-
10 nisation Greenpeace belegt. Deutsche zwischen 12 und 19 Jahren sind zwar erstaunlich gut über die Probleme bei der Herstellung von Textilien informiert, wie eine repräsentative Umfrage* von Greenpeace unter 500 Jugendlichen zeigt. Ihr Konsumverhalten* ändert das jedoch nicht. Jugendliche kaufen vor allem viel Mode. Mehr noch als die durchschnittlich fünf neuen Kleidungsstücke, die sich der Deutsche Monat für Monat zulegt.
15 Die Umweltorganisation hat Jugendliche nach ihrem Kaufverhalten befragt und dabei festgestellt, dass diese gut über soziale und ökologische Missstände in der Textilindustrie Bescheid wissen. So haben mit 96 Prozent der Befragten nahezu alle davon gehört, dass Arbeiter in der Modeindustrie oft unter unwürdigen* Bedingungen arbeiten. Dass Bekleidung mit Chemikalien behandelt wird, ist 83 Prozent bekannt; immerhin noch 74 Prozent haben von negativen Auswirkungen auf die
20 Umwelt gehört.
Konsequenzen aber ziehen die wenigsten, das eigene Kaufverhalten verändert kaum jemand: nur knapp 13 Prozent der befragten, also knapp jeder Achte, gab an, beim Kauf auf die Herstellungsbedingungen oder die Textilsiegel* zu achten. [...]
Dazu passt, dass die Jugendlichen ihre Mode meist auf klassischem Wege erwerben: Über 80 Pro-
25 zent geben an, ihre Kleidung in den Läden der konventionellen Modeketten zu kaufen, zwischen 50 und 60 Prozent shoppen außerdem bei Onlineanbietern wie Zalando oder Amazon oder den Onlineshops von Marken wir H&M oder Esprit. [...]
„Grün denken, aber konventionell kaufen", fasst Textilexpertin Brodde zusammen.
(*332 words*)

Der Spiegel, 14/2015, 28 March 2015, p. 88

Annotations ⟫

muffig musty, fusty ■ **Selbstgestricktes** hand-knitted clothing ■ **Umfrage** survey ■ **Konsumverhalten** consumer behaviour ■ **Missstand** injustice ■ **unwürdig** degrading, appalling ■ **Textilsiegel** textile label

ASSIGNMENT ⟫⟫

You are spending an exchange year in the USA and your social sciences class is currently discussing the topics of consumption and ecology. You have come across the article given here and want to inform your class about the shopping habits of German teenagers.
Prepare a short presentation in English, in which you include the relevant information provided in the article.

Bewertungsbogen für: _____ Kurs: _____

Part A: Teilaufgabe 1 (Comprehension)

	Anforderungen Der Schüler/die Schülerin ...	maximal erreichbare Punktzahl	erreichte Punkte
1	... umreißt die **wirtschaftliche Situation weltweit** und benennt z. B. • das verlangsamte Wirtschaftswachstum in China (ll. 21 f.), • das größte jemals erreichte Handelsvolumen in Deutschland (l. 20), • die hochverschuldete spanische Wirtschaft (l. 14), • Europas wirtschaftliche Abhängigkeit von Exporten (l. 29).	2	
2	... stellt den **Stand der US economy** dar, z. B. • der Rückgang der Verschuldung (ll. 36 ff.), • die Halbierung des US-Handelsdefizits (ll. 14 f.), • die weiterhin durchgeführte staatliche Subventionierung von Hypotheken (ll. 38 f.).	2	
3	... beschreibt die Darstellung und die **Bedingungen der *economic recovery*** in den USA und erwähnt z. B. • die Schaffung von mehr als 1 Million neuen Arbeitsplätzen im ersten Quartal 2015 (ll. 2 f.), • die wiedererstarkte Konsumlust der Amerikaner insgesamt (ll. 4 ff.), • die Erstarkung des Dollars (l. 31), • die Reduzierung von Importen aus dem Ausland, stattdessen Fokussierung auf heimische Produkte und Märkte (ll. 41 f.).	3	
4	... legt die **durch den neuerlichen Aufschwung entstandenen Risiken** dar sowie Forderungen und Warnungen des Autors, z. B. • die drohende Rückkehr zu ungehemmtem Import und Konsum von Waren aus dem Ausland (ll. 17 f.), • die durch die Erstarkung des Dollars reduzierten US-Exporte und erneute Zunahme des US-Handelsdefizits (ll. 23 ff.), • die Anreize für Amerikaner, auch weiterhin Schulden zu machen, bedingt durch (unnötige) staatliche Subventionen (ll. 35 ff.), • die (indirekte) Warnung an Deutschland und die Welt, Amerika nicht durch eine Schwemme von Exporten erneut zu schwächen (ll. 27 ff.).	3	
5	... erfüllt ein weiteres aufgabenbezogenes Kriterium. (2) •	2	
		10	

Part A: Teilaufgabe 2 (Analysis)

	Anforderungen Der Schüler/die Schülerin ...	maximal erreichbare Punktzahl	erreichte Punkte
1	... untersucht die **Struktur des Textes** und verweist z. B. auf • die geschlossene Form und den Rückbezug in der *Conclusion* auf die *Introduction* (*The world is once again relying too much ...* ➔ *the American economy should not be taken for granted.*), • die inhaltlich klare Strukturierung (Einleitung – Hauptteil – Schluss/*topical order; comparison: before and after the crisis of 2007/2008* ➔ *recovery* ➔ *future economic dangers*), • die thematische Fokussierung in Verbindung mit einem indirekten Appell (*The American economy is motoring again* ➔ *But: ... now the world is slipping back into nasty habits* ➔ *dangers ...*).	4	
2	... analysiert die durchgängig **vergleichende und kontrastierende Darstellung** der Thematik und nennt z. B. • die Gegenüberstellung der Situation vor und nach der Wirtschaftskrise von 2007/2008 (*a decade ago ... now ...; in 2006 ... by 2009 ...*), • die Kontrastierung der wirtschaftlichen Situation und des Handels der USA und Europa bzw. China (*the American economy is motoring ... to the relief of exporters from Hamburg to Hangzhou; American consumer borrowed ... goods from China ... Germans financed debt binges; debt-addicted Americans ... frugal Germans ...*), • die Kontrastierung des Konsumverhaltens der Amerikaner und Deutschen/Europäer bzw. Chinesen (*American consumers borrowed heavily and recklessly; filled their ever-larger houses with goods from China ...; fuelled gas-guzzling cars with imported oil; debt-addicted ↔ frugal Germans; thrifty German and Chinese consumers; Germans are ... shipping savings abroad ...*).	4	

3	... untersucht und erklärt **rhetorische Stilmittel**, z. B. • den durchgängig kontrastiven Gebrauch von *positive and negative emotive words* (*unwelcome echoes; USA: borro-wed recklessly and heavily ... further borrowing; debt binges; slipping back into nasty habits* ↔ *Germany/China: frugal; thrifty; large/record trade surplus; ... start to enjoy life*), • dem durchgängigen Gebrauch von Wortfeldern zu den Themenbereichen *economy* und *consumption* (*GDP, current-account surplus, trade deficit, subsidies, mortgage interest, interest rate, consumer sentiment*), • dem durchgängigen Gebrauch von Zahlenmaterial zur faktischen Untermauerung der Darstellung, • dem Gebrauch von Klimax (z. B. *short-term worry – longer-term fear*).	5	
4	... arbeitet den klar **strukturierten Aufbau des Schlussteils** heraus sowie dessen warnender/appellativer Funktion. Er/sie verweist z. B. auf • den deutlichen Hinweis auf drohende Gefahren und den damit verbundenen (indirekten) Appell zum Handeln (*That is why ...; it has no need to rush to tighten ...; ... the burden to act ... politicians would do well to ... leaders from Brussels to Beijing should ...*), • den Verweis auf die Mechanismen, die zur Krise von 2007/2008 geführt haben (*will repeat the financial cycle of the 2000s*), • die deutliche Warnung und den Appell, nicht nur an die USA, sondern auch an Europa und Asien (*But the burden to act does not lie just on America ... leaders from Brussels to Beijing ... American economy is a boon ... should not be taken for granted*).	5	
5	... erfüllt ein weiteres aufgabenbezogenes Kriterium. (4) •	4	
		18	

Part A: Teilaufgabe 3.1 (Evaluation/Comment)

	Anforderungen	maximal erreichbare Punktzahl	erreichte Punkte
	Der Schüler/die Schülerin ...		
1	... nimmt konkreten Bezug auf die vom Autor angesprochenen **Sorgen, Ängste und Warnungen** und stellt z. B. dar, dass • der amerikanische Konsument sich wieder traut Geld auszugeben (*Americans are spending*), aber immer noch mit den Schulden der Wirtschaftskrise von 2007/2008 zu kämpfen hat (*chip away at their obligations; ratio of Americans' debt income ... about 100%*), • Amerikaner durch niedrige und staatliche subventionierte Hypothekenzinsen dazu verleitet werden, neue Schulden aufzunehmen, • das amerikanische Handelsdefizit wieder zunimmt (*4% in 2014*) und die Exporte nicht stabil sind (*weak exports ...*).	3	
2	... verweist auf die **Sticheleien und (indirekten) Schuldzuweisungen** des Autors und benennt z. B., dass • das neuerliche amerikanische Wirtschaftswachstum weltweite Begehrlichkeiten weckt (*to the relief of exporters from Hamburg to Hangzhou ...*), • die *global economy* nicht realisiert, dass sie den „amerikanischen Motor" braucht (ll. 2 f.), und in *nasty habits* zurückfällt, ohne Rücksicht auf Verluste (*Hair grows faster than the Euro zone ... growth there depends heavily on exports; the countries ... are running a current-account surplus ... thanks largely to exports to America ...*), • Europa und China schon einmal die Überschuldung von Amerika und anderen Ländern unterstützt und verstärkt haben (*Big exports ... helped to feed further borrowing; frugal Germans financed debt binges around the euro area's periphery ...*).	3	
3	... nimmt vor dem Hintergrund unterrichtlicher Ergebnisse und Kenntnisse **kritisch Stellung zu den Einschätzungen** des Autors und verweist z. B. auf • die Tatsache, dass die Finanzkrise 2007/2008 von amerikanischen Banken ausgegangen war und dann die Finanzmärkte weltweit geschädigt hat (und nicht, wie dargestellt, die Welt habe die USA dazu verleitet, irgendetwas zu tun ...), • die offensichtliche Neigung der amerikanischen Konsumenten, über ihre finanziellen Möglichkeiten hinaus zu konsumieren und sich dabei zu überschulden, die nicht anderen (exportierenden) Nationen zum Vorwurf gemacht werden kann, • die Tatsache, dass die als „typisch" amerikanisch geltenden Werte wie *success, wealth, realizing one's goals, unlimited opportunity for prosperity* etc. auch von anderen Nationen übernommen und als Ziele definiert werden.	4	
4	... formuliert vor dem Hintergrund der verschiedenen Überlegungen und Ergebnisse eine **begründete und logische Schlussfolgerung** und führt z. B. an, dass • er/sie sich der Haltung des Autors anschließt, dass *leaders from Beijing to Brussels* nicht nur an bedingungslosen Exporthandel ihrer eigenen Länder denken sollten, sondern den Welthandeln insgesamt im Blick haben sollten, • er/sie die Sichtweise des Autors ablehnt, da gerade die USA selbst z. B. Befürworter des TTIP-Abkommens sind, das weltweiten Handel forcieren will – und dabei nur bedingt Rücksicht auf Interessen z. B. von Schwellenländern nimmt, • er/sie den Aspekt des Autors aufgreift, dass eine *structural reform* (l. 41) notwendig ist – dies dann allerdings für alle Länder weltweit gelten und verbindlich sein muss.	4	
5	... erfüllt ein weiteres aufgabenbezogenes Kriterium. (4) •	4	
		14	

Part A: Teilaufgabe 3.2 ((Re-)Creation of text)

	Anforderungen Der Schüler/die Schülerin ...	maximal erreichbare Punktzahl	erreichte Punkte
1	... nimmt durchgängig die **vorgegebene Perspektive eines *CEO of a German car-making company*** ein, indem er/sie z. B. • die Verantwortung hervorhebt, die eine solch wichtige Industrie für Deutschlands Wirtschaft hat, • auf die lange gemeinsame erfolgreiche Zusammenarbeit beider Handelsnationen hinweist, • die Wertschätzung deutscher Produkte durch den amerikanischen Konsumenten hervorhebt (guter Ruf deutscher Produkte, gute Verkaufszahlen etc.).	3	
2	... greift konkret im Artikel genannte **Kritik und indirekte Vorwürfe** auf und führt z. B. an, dass • es für den Welthandel wichtig ist, dass die USA sich wirtschaftlich stabilisieren und wieder kauf- und handelsfähig sind, • Deutschland (wie auch andere Länder) eine Exportnation ist, allerdings auch im Ausland (z. B. in den USA) produzieren lässt, sowie viele Produkte aus aller Welt importiert, • die Deutschen nicht einseitig „*debt binges*" finanziert, sondern Finanzhilfen zur Unterstützung gegeben haben.	3	
3	... integriert die formal-stilistischen **Elemente eines „Letter to the Editor"**, z. B. • Anrede/Grußformel am Schluss, • klare und strukturierte Bezugnahme auf den Artikel und das Thema, • kurze Selbstvorstellung/Darstellung der eigenen Position und Motivation zum Schreiben/Appell an den Autor etc.	4	
4	... kommt zu einem die Argumente **abwägenden abschließenden Fazit**, indem er/sie z. B. • die Verantwortung der *global corporations* für den Welthandel insgesamt darstellt, • auf die Notwendigkeit der Durchführung von *structural reforms* hinweist (*reduction of debt; support for emerging economies; ecological responsibility*, etc.), • langfristig verantwortungsvolles Handeln fordert (*global corporation in a global village, sustainability*, etc.).	4	
5	... erfüllt ein weiteres aufgabenbezogenes Kriterium. (4) •	4	
		14	

Part B: Mediation – Inhalt

	Anforderungen Der Schüler/die Schülerin ...	maximal erreichbare Punktzahl	erreichte Punkte
1	... fasst die Informationen situations- und adressatenbezogen sinngemäß zusammen, auch unter Berücksichtigung impliziter Aussageabsichten.	4	
2	... konzentriert sich dabei – bezogen auf den situativen Kontext – auf wesentliche Inhalte und wichtige Details.	4	
3	... antizipiert ggf. unter Berücksichtigung des Welt- und Kulturwissens mögliche Missverständnisse und fügt ggf. für das Verstehen erforderliche Erläuterungen hinzu.	5	
4	... greift den in der Aufgabenstellung vorgegebenen situativen und thematischen Kontext auf und stellt einen inhaltlichen Bezug zwischen den soziokulturellen und wirtschaftlichen Gegebenheiten von jungen Leuten in Deutschland und den USA her.	5	
5	... erfüllt ein weiteres aufgabenbezogenes Kriterium. (2) •	2	
		18	

Part B: Mediation – Sprache

Sprache (60 %)	Der Schüler/die Schülerin ...	Lösungsqualität	
		maximal erreichbare Punktzahl	erreichte Punkte
Kommunikative Textgestaltung	• richtet seinen/ihren Text konsequent und explizit auf die **Intention** und den **Adressaten** im Sinne der **Aufgabenstellung** aus. • berücksichtigt den **situativen Kontext**. • beachtet die Textsortenmerkmale des geforderten **Zieltextformats**. • erstellt einen sachgerecht **strukturierten** Text. • gestaltet seinen/ihren Text hinreichend ausführlich, aber ohne unnötige Wiederholungen und Umständlichkeiten.	9	
Ausdrucksvermögen/ Verfügbarkeit sprachlicher Mittel	• löst sich vom Wortlaut des Ausgangstextes und formuliert **eigenständig**, ggf. unter Verwendung von Kompensationsstrategien. • verwendet funktional einen sachlich wie stilistisch angemessenen und differenzierten allgemeinen und thematischen **Wortschatz** sowie **Funktionswortschatz**. • verwendet einen variablen und dem jeweiligen Zieltextformat angemessenen **Satzbau**.	9	
Sprachrichtigkeit	• beachtet die Normen der sprachlichen Korrektheit im Sinne einer **gelingenden Kommunikation** in den Bereichen **Wortschatz**, **Grammatik** und **Orthographie**.	9	
	Summe Sprache	27	
	Summe Klausurteil B: Aufgabe 3	45	

Part B: Mediation – Possible Solution

German teenagers love shopping for new clothes and following the latest fashion trends, just like American teenagers do. And of course, since teenagers usually do not have much money, they also enjoy hunting for bargains and prefer shopping at more affordable stores like H&M or Esprit.

In a recent study, the well-known NGO Greenpeace found out that teenagers, in particular, buy lots of new clothing – typically even more than the five items per month that represents the average for other consumers. Most of the interviewed teenagers also said that they were well informed about the appalling working conditions of textile workers, as well as the huge negative environmental impact caused by the chemical treatment of textiles with toxic substances.

However, despite their general awareness about the negative environmental aspects involved, only 13 % of the teenagers said they would consider paying particular attention to sustainability-criteria or eco-labels when shopping for clothes. Obviously, that's a really frustrating result.

Nevertheless, a very interesting alternative that is presented by the author of the article I read is an Internet platform for second-hand clothes. The online store offers second-hand clothing that can either be bought outright or even just borrowed and currently has about 3.2 million registered members. You can get information or shop on their website and they even offer Apps for download.

I think that that could be an interesting and promising business idea to try here in the U.S. as well. That way, we teenagers could still shop for the latest trends, but be a lot more environmentally-friendly and green at the same time ☺ .

(264 words)

Topic: Economy, Energy, Efficiency – The World Going Global

Skills: Analysis of a non-fictional text (comment, Internet blog); writing a speech script (*Zieltextformat*); mediation

Texts: **Part A:** Mike Kercheval, Why Online Retailers Continue to Open Brick-and-Mortar Stores (471 words)

Part B: Antonia Lange: Aus dem Netz in die Innenstädte, newspaper article (224 words)

Part A: Reading/Writing

Mike Kercheval

Why Online Retailers[1] Continue to Open Brick-and-Mortar Stores[2]

In an age when new technology and the growth of pure online-only retailers have industry analysts questioning the future of brick-and-mortar stores, what are online retailers doing to grow their businesses and gain market share? Why, opening up physical[3] storefronts of course. The benefits that physical spaces provide make up three of the top reasons why online retailers are setting up
5 shop, including: multisensory[4] consumer experiences, better logistics and consumer service offerings and strong, lasting brand relationships[5].

The rise of omni-channel retail strategies[6] in which mobile, online and in-store experiences complement[7], rather than compete with, one another has ushered[8] in a new era for online retailers. Birchbox and Frank & Oak are just a couple of examples of e-tailers[9] that have planted roots to re-
10 main competitive and provide a seamless[10] customer experience across all shopping channels.

And it's no wonder they're buying up real estate[11]; the economics speak for themselves. According to our latest consumer survey, 78 percent of consumers prefer to shop in-store and they spend six times more in-store than online. This is reflected in the fact that the majority of all retail sales still occur in the physical store. In 2013, the U.S. Census Bureau reported that 94 percent of retail sales
15 were conducted[12] in brick-and-mortar stores, while just 6 percent occurred online. Physical stores are simply good business.

Multisensory Consumer Experiences

Nothing beats holding a product in your hand, feeling the fabric[13] and seeing the minute[14] details – something that can't be done online. We found that 73 percent of consumers want to try on or touch
20 merchandise before they make a purchase. Physical shopping centers allow consumers to do just this – interact with a range of products to make informed decisions about what they're buying. Furthermore, physical stores have been busy retrofitting[15] their spaces with technological advancements that make the in-store customer experience more efficient, which effectively eliminates the guessing games encountered online. Is the size or fabric not quite right? Or maybe it fits perfectly,
25 but you want to try on every color option available? These are solvable problems when you are shopping in a physical store. [...]

Just this month, Amazon.com announced it is opening a physical storefront in the middle of New York City, the first of its kind in the company's 20-year history as an online retailing giant. The store will be located in Herald Square, near the famous Macy's department store and the Empire State
30 Building, an area that receives some of the most significant foot traffic[16] in the city. This announcement speaks to[17] the importance of an omni-channel strategy, and certainly could have significant positive effects on the real estate side of the retailing business. [...]

[1] **retailer** a business that sells goods to the public – [2] **brick-and-mortar store** a traditional shop that is located in a real building – [3] **physical** here: real and able to be seen and touched – [4] **multisensory** able to be experienced by more than one of the physical senses of touch, smell, taste, hearing, and sight – [5] **brand relationship** a preference for buying products made by a particular company – [6] **omni-channel retail strategy** system of using many different distribution methods to sell products – [7] **to complement** *ergänzen* – [8] **to usher (in)** to lead the way, introduce – [9] **e-tailer** (*abbr.*) electronic retailer; a business selling products online – [10] **seamless** smooth and without difficulties – [11] **real estate** ['rɪəl ɪˌsteɪt] land and/or buildings – [12] **to conduct an activity** *etw. durchführen* – [13] **fabric** *Faser; Gewebe* – [14] **minute** [maɪˈnjuːt] extremely small – [15] **to retrofit** *nachrüsten* – [16] **foot traffic** *Laufkundschaft* – [17] **to speak to sth.** (*phr. v.*) to signal, show

This is why online retailers are looking to the physical store as an avenue[18] to meaningfully engage[19] customers and build strong, trusted and lasting relationships.

(*471 words*)

http://techcrunch.com/2014/10/31/why-online-retailers-continue-to-open-brick-and-mortar-stores, 31 October 2014 [03.04.2015]

ASSIGNMENTS

1. Describe the recent development of online retailers opening brick-and-mortar stores and offering new multisensory shopping experiences.
   (*Comprehension*)

2. Examine the author's line of argument and use of stylistic devices and explain how these contribute to emphasizing the advantages of the new trend.
   (*Analysis*)

3. You have a choice here. Choose **one** of the following tasks:

   3.1 Comment on the research results from the consumer survey and the Census Bureau's data. Can you believe that, in 2013, only 6 percent of retail sales in the U.S. were online sales? Refer to your personal experiences as a consumer, as well as the ongoing complaints from local retailers who have had to close their businesses because of a lack of customers and not enough sales.
   (*Comment/Evaluation*)

   3.2 You are the spokesman for the association of retailers in your hometown and have been asked to prepare a speech for a meeting of the retail industry in London.
   The local retailers in your area are concerned and upset about the announcement that several online retailers, like Amazon or Zalando, are planning to open physical stores and to buy up real estate in several cities.
   Prepare a speech, in which you refer to the information given in the article and also depict your association's concerns and demands.
   (*((Re-)Creation of text*)

---

[18] **avenue** here: a way of achieving sth. – [19] **to engage** here: to attract, involve

Part B: Mediation

Antonia Lange

Aus dem Netz in die Innenstädte

Internet-Händler zieht es häufiger mit Ladenlokalen in die Fußgängerzonen. Sogar Amazon denkt darüber nach.

Einmal durch Amazon bummeln? Was unvorstellbar klingt, könnte schon bald Realität werden: Klassische Internethändler wagen sich derzeit verstärkt in die nicht-virtuelle Welt – und eröffnen
5 erste stationäre Läden*. Jüngstes Beispiel: Der Internetriese Amazon, der angeblich über einen Laden in New York nachdenkt. Auch in Deutschland lassen sich reine Online-Händler in der Fußgängerzone nieder.

„Es ist tatsächlich so, dass immer mehr Onliner sich in die stationäre Welt begeben", sagt Eva Stüber vom Institut für Handelsforschung* (IFH). „Online kann man datenbasiert etwas über den
10 Kunden lernen, aber das Persönliche geht besser im Geschäft." [...]

„Viele Menschen möchten Produkte, gerade Lebensmittel, ja erstmal anfassen und eventuell probieren vor dem Kauf", sagt Mymuesli-Mitbegründer Max Wittrock. „Das können wir in den Läden bieten und auch beraten." Zugleich rufe das Logo in der Innenstadt die Marke ins Bewusstsein. Wittrock: „Es schadet der Bekanntheit* sicher nicht, wenn viele Menschen jeden Tag an Mymuesli-
15 Läden vorbeilaufen."

Fachleute sehen stationären Läden daher auch als eine Art Ausstellungsfläche* für das Unternehmen. „Ich glaube, dass ein stationäres Handelsgeschäft einen Showroom-Charakter hat und auch eine Markenpräsenz vermittelt", sagt Thomas Harms, Handelsexperte bei Ernst&Young. Vor allem für Modehändler könne sich das lohnen – auch um unnötige Retouren zu vermeiden.
20 Der Online-Händler Zalando ist ebenfalls in der echten Welt angekommen – und betreibt in Berlin und Frankfurt Outlet-Stores.

(*224 words*)

Westdeutsche Zeitung, 26 March 2015, p. 13

Annotations

stationärer Laden brick-and-mortar store; physical store ■ **Handelsforschung** commercial research ■ **Bekanntheit** here: brand awareness ■ **Ausstellungsfläche** display space, showroom

ASSIGNMENTS

You are the German representative for an international association of brick-and-mortar retailers, which is planning a symposium in New York City. In preparation for this conference, the delegates from all participating countries are collecting information that they can exchange about the plans announced by online retailers to open physical stores in many cities worldwide.
Compile a handout in English pointing out relevant developments in Germany, as well as possible conclusions that can be drawn from the situation.

Bewertungsbogen für: _____ Kurs: _____

Part A: Teilaufgabe 1 (Comprehension)

	Anforderungen Der Schüler/die Schülerin ...	maximal erreichbare Punktzahl	erreichte Punkte
1	... umreißt **die neue Verkaufsstrategie des Online-Handels** und stellt z. B. dar, dass • es *omni-channel retail strategies* geben soll, in denen *mobile, online* und *in-store experiences* miteinander verknüpft werden sollen (ll. 7 f.), • die neue Verkaufsstrategie für den Kunden unkomplizierte Kaufhandlungen auf allen Ebenen (online und im Geschäft) ermöglicht, • sich der Online-Handel dadurch eine größere Effizienz, d. h. mehr Absatz erhofft (l. 11 f.).	2	
2	... benennt die genannten **Gründe für die neue Strategie**, z. B. • das Ermöglichen eines „*multisensory*" Einkaufserlebnisses für den Kunden (l. 5), • eine unkompliziertere (und kostengünstigere) Logistik für das Unternehmen, • ein besseres (Waren-)Angebot für den Kunden (l. 5), • dauerhafte Kunden- und Markentreue (ll. 5 f.), • die Reaktion des Online-Handels auf Umfrageergebnisse (l. 11).	2	
3	... beschreibt das **Konzept der neuen *physical stores***, und benennt z. B. • das Ermöglichen eines sinnlichen Kauferlebnisses (ll. 18 ff.), • die Möglichkeit für den Kunden, sich direkt im Geschäft über das Produkt zu informieren (Größe, Farbe, Funktion etc., ll. 24 f.), • das Ermöglichen einer direkten Interaktion mit einer Produktauswahl, auf der die Kaufentscheidung basiert (ll. 23 ff.).	3	
4	... stellt das Beispiel für die **bereits realisierte Umsetzung** dieses neuen Konzepts vor, und stellt dar, dass • Amazon dabei ist, einen Store in New York City zu eröffnen – in einem Bereich, der höchstfrequentierten *foot traffic* aufweist (ll. 29 f.). • dieses neue Geschäftskonzept auch positive Auswirkungen auf die Immobilienpreise haben könnte (ll. 31 f.).	3	
5	... erfüllt ein weiteres aufgabenbezogenes Kriterium. (2) •	2	
		10	

Part A: Teilaufgabe 2 (Analysis)

	Anforderungen Der Schüler/die Schülerin ...	maximal erreichbare Punktzahl	erreichte Punkte
1	... analysiert die **Struktur des Textes** und verdeutlicht z. B., dass • es sich bei dem Text um eine Kombination von *descriptive* und *argumentative text* handelt, der einerseits Informationen und Fakten bietet, andererseits jedoch versucht, den Leser (indirekt) zu beeinflussen, • der Text klar strukturiert ist (Einleitung – Hauptteil/Fakten – *Conclusion*/Schluss), • bereits die Überschrift den Fokus auf den zu erwartenden Inhalt des Textes lenkt.	4	
2	... untersucht die **Argumentationsstruktur (*line of argument*)** des Textes und belegt dies z. B. durch • die bereits in der Einleitung vorgenommene Fokussierung auf die *benefits* der neuen Verkaufsstrategie (*The benefits that physical stores provide ...; experiences ... logistics ... offerings ... brand relationship ...*), • die im Hauptteil dargelegte Begründung der neuen Strategie (*facts, data; advantages compared to online shopping; example: Amazon*), • die abschließende pointierte Zusammenfassung (l. 33 ff.), • die Rahmenstruktur des Textes (einleitende Frage, die pointiert am Ende des Textes beantwortet wird, ll. 1 ff., ll. 33 ff.).	4	
3	... untersucht den Gebrauch von ***stylistic devices* und erklärt deren Funktion**, z. B. • die den Text einleitende Frage, die das Interesse der Leser weckt, indem auf einen (vermeintlichen) Widerspruch verweisen wird (*new technology ... growth of pure online-only retailers ...* vs. *what are online retailers doing to grow their businesses and gain market share* ➔ *opening up physical storefronts; benefits of physical stores*), • den wiederholten Gebrauch von *keywords* und *phrases*, die die Vorteile der neuen Geschäftsstrategie hervorheben (*physical; multisensory; omni-channel retail strategy; a new era* etc.), • den Gebrauch von *positive emotive words* und *comparisons/superlatives* zur Unterstreichung der positiven Qualitäten (*new; growth; benefit; better; good business; more efficient; most significant, effective* etc.).	5	

		maximal	erreichte
4	... konkretisiert die **Botschaft und Intention des Autors** und benennt z. B. • die enge Fokussierung der Darstellung und Reduzierung auf ausschließlich potentiell positive Entwicklungen, • die ausschließliche Betonung der *positive effects* (*more efficient customer experiences; solvable problems; significantly positive effects* etc.), • die aus der Darstellung resultierende Einseitigkeit der Perspektive (z. B. fehlt die Hinterfragung der Folgen für kleinere Geschäfte etc.).	5	
5	... erfüllt ein weiteres aufgabenbezogenes Kriterium. (4) •	4	
		18	

Part A: Teilaufgabe 3.1 (Evaluation/Comment)

	Anforderungen **Der Schüler/die Schülerin ...**	maximal erreichbare Punktzahl	erreichte Punkte
1	... nimmt konkreten **Bezug auf die *consumer survey* von *TechCrunch*** und stellt z. B. dar, dass • gemäß dieser Umfrage 78 % der Konsumenten *in-store shopping* bevorzugen (l. 12), • die Mehrheit der Einzelhandelsumsätze im *physical store* erreicht wird (l. 13), • 73 % der Konsumenten die Ware vor dem Kauf ausprobieren oder anfassen wollen (ll. 19 ff.).	3	
2	... bezieht sich auf **weitere *research results***, z. B. • das U.S. Census Bureau, nach dessen Ergebnissen 94 % aller Einzelhandelskäufe über *physical stores* getätigt werden ➔ nur 6 % wurden online getätigt, • dass Kunden, nach TechCrunch-Recherchen – sechsmal mehr Geld in Geschäften als online ausgeben.	3	
3	... **hinterfragt die dargestellten Daten und Umfrageergebnisse** kritisch und verweist z. B. darauf, dass • sie der Realität in vielen Städten widersprechen (zunehmende Leerstände und Verwahrlosung von Innenstädten und Fußgängerzonen), • die Situation von kleinen Einzelhändlern nun noch kritischer ist, wenn sie nicht nur in Konkurrenz zum Online-Handel stehen, sondern sich auch gegen die Präsenz der *retail giants* behaupten müssen, • die steigenden Immobilienpreise (und Mieten) es für kleinere Unternehmen noch problematischer macht, sich zu behaupten.	4	
4	... kommt zu einem die dargelegten Überlegungen abwägenden und zusammenfassenden **begründeten Resümee**, z. B. • hält er/sie die Daten für nicht der Realität entsprechend und steht einer erneuten Ausweitung der Großkonzerne kritisch gegenüber, • hält er/sie die Daten für aussagekräftig und valide und stimmt den daraus gezogenen Schlussfolgerungen zu.	4	
5	... erfüllt ein weiteres aufgabenbezogenes Kriterium. (4) •	4	
		18	

Part A: Teilaufgabe 3.2 ((Re-)Creation of text)

	Anforderungen **Der Schüler/die Schülerin ...**	maximal erreichbare Punktzahl	erreichte Punkte
1	... versetzt sich durchgängig in **die Rolle des *local retailer*** und benennt z. B. • die (wirtschaftlichen) Probleme der kleinen Geschäfte, mit den Einzelhandelsgiganten zu konkurrieren, • die vielen Leerstände in Städten und den dann entstehenden Teufelskreis von Verwahrlosung – weiteren Geschäftsaufgaben – der Zunahme von Kriminalität etc., • die Unmöglichkeit, sowohl mit dem Internethandel als auch mit Handelsketten zu konkurrieren.	3	
2	... bezieht sich konkret auf die im Text genannten **„Vorteile" für den Kunden** und führt z. B. demgegenüber an, dass • er/sie Zweifel an der Validität des Zahlenmaterials hat, weil es nicht der beobachteten Realität entspricht, • die Kombination von Online-Handel und Ladenlokalen in den Innenstädten strategisch auf Synergie-Effekte abzielt und die Online-Daten der Kunden ausnutzt, • die ohnehin für den Einzelhandel bereits problematischen „Riesen" Amazon und Zalando nun auch in den Innenstädten den Verdrängungskampf forcieren.	3	
3	... formuliert **mögliche Forderungen**, die sich aus den dargestellten Fakten ergeben und benennt z. B., dass • die Vielfalt des Angebots in den (Innen-)Städten gewahrt und wiederbelebt werden und kleinere und mittlere Läden unterstützt werden müssen (z. B. durch Steuererleichterungen), • die Städte darauf verzichten sollten, neben den bereits bestehenden Handelsketten noch weitere *retail giants* in die Innenstädte zu holen, weil sie rücksichtslos andere verdrängen, • es in den Innenstädten für Kunden mehr Anreize zum Einkaufsbummel und verweilen geben muss, • es evt. eine Quotierung für *retail giants* im innerstädtischen Bereich geben sollte.	4	

4	... verfasst einen **dem Zieltextformat entsprechendes** *speech script*, das z. B. die folgenden formal-stilistischen Elemente beinhaltet <ul><li>klare Strukturierung (*introduction – main part – conclusion*),</li><li>Argumente, Beispiele, Fakten zur Untermauerung der eigenen Position,</li><li>ein gewisses Maß an Rhetorisierung und rhetorischen Stilmitteln,</li><li>ein pointierter Abschluss (Appell, Vorblick etc.).</li></ul>	4	
5	... erfüllt ein weiteres aufgabenbezogenes Kriterium. (4) <ul><li></li></ul>	4	
		14	

Part B: Mediation – Inhalt

	Anforderungen	maximal erreichbare Punktzahl	erreichte Punkte
	Der Schüler/die Schülerin ...		
1	... fasst die Informationen situations- und adressatenbezogen sinngemäß zusammen.	4	
2	... konzentriert sich dabei – bezogen auf den situativen Kontext – auf wesentliche Inhalte.	4	
3	... fügt ggf. für das Verstehen erforderliche detaillierte Erläuterungen hinzu.	5	
4	... bezieht den situativen Kontext internationaler Onlinehandelshäuser sowie Einzelhandelsrepräsentanten auf die im Artikel beschriebene Situation. Bezieht auch die deutsche Perspektive mit ein.	5	
5	... erfüllt ein weiteres aufgabenbezogenes Kriterium. (2) <ul><li></li></ul>	2	
		18	

Part B: Mediation – Sprache

		Lösungsqualität	
Sprache (60 %)	**Der Schüler/die Schülerin ...**	maximal erreichbare Punktzahl	erreichte Punkte
Kommunikative Textgestaltung	<ul><li>richtet seinen/ihren Text konsequent und explizit auf die **Intention** und den **Adressaten** im Sinne der **Aufgabenstellung** aus.</li><li>berücksichtigt den **situativen Kontext**.</li><li>beachtet die Textsortenmerkmale des geforderten **Zieltextformats**.</li><li>erstellt einen sachgerecht **strukturierten** Text.</li><li>gestaltet seinen/ihren Text hinreichend ausführlich, aber ohne unnötige Wiederholungen und Umständlichkeiten.</li></ul>	9	
Ausdrucksvermögen/ Verfügbarkeit sprachlicher Mittel	<ul><li>löst sich vom Wortlaut des Ausgangstextes und formuliert **eigenständig**, ggf. unter Verwendung von Kompensationsstrategien.</li><li>verwendet funktional einen sachlich wie stilistisch angemessenen und differenzierten allgemeinen und thematischen **Wortschatz** sowie **Funktionswortschatz**.</li><li>verwendet einen variablen und dem jeweiligen Zieltextformat angemessenen **Satzbau**.</li></ul>	9	
Sprachrichtigkeit	<ul><li>beachtet die Normen der sprachlichen Korrektheit im Sinne einer **gelingenden Kommunikation** in den Bereichen **Wortschatz**, **Grammatik** und **Orthographie**.</li></ul>	9	
	Summe Sprache	27	
	Summe Klausurteil B: Aufgabe 3	45	

Part B: Mediation – Possible Solution

Association of German Retailers
Representative: XXX

… May 2015

Online Retailers Opening Physical Stores in German Cities

General background
- a growing number of traditional online-retailers are planning to open physical stores as well
- Amazon is planning to open a store in New York City

Developments in Germany
- the German Institute for Trade Research/Commercial Research has confirmed this trend for Germany as well
- major online retailers are hoping for synergetic effects, for example, by collecting data about customers online and using this information to better serve their customers personally in physical stores
- Max Wittrock, the co-founder of the German online retailer Mymuesli believes that
  a) stores with company logos in pedestrian shopping areas raise customer awareness of the brand,
  b) physical stores give customers the chance to have a sensory product experience while also getting advice from a shop assistant.
- experts plan to use their stores as "showrooms" in order to increase and reinforce a strong brand presence
- online fashion retailers are particularly pleased with this new development as they hope to avoid unnecessary and costly returns by allowing customers to easily try on different colours, sizes and designs so they can make an informed choice from the start
- the online retail giant Zalando has already opened "outlet stores" in Berlin and Frankfurt

Conclusion
- traditional local retailers will have to cope with even more competition in the future
- the online retail giants are synergizing customer data collected online with complementary emotional and multisensory shopping experiences for their customers in their physical stores
- in combination with predatory pricing, this development will most likely lead to and ever fiercer, cut-throat competition
- we need to find a way to stop this development
- this is a do-or-die moment for smaller German brick-and-mortar retailers

(301 words)

Topic:	Science (Fiction) and Technology – Towards a Better World?!
Skills:	Analysis of a non-fictional text (magazine article); writing an interview (*Zieltextformat*); mediation
Texts:	**Part A:** Reproductive Medicine: A Dad and Two Mums (610 words)
	Part B: Laura Höflinger: Babys für alle, magazine article (287 words)

Part A: Reading/Writing

Reproductive Medicine: A Dad and Two Mums

MPs[1] vote in favour of children with three genetic parents

Every year around a hundred children are born in Britain with seriously damaged mitochondria[2], those parts of a living cell that synthesise[3] the chemical fuel that powers the rest of it. It is often a death sentence. Those who survive live a debilitating[4] existence in which the tissues[5] of their bod-
5   ies – brains, muscles, nerves and the rest – are chronically short of the energy they need to function. There is no cure. But there might be a way to help the roughly 2,500 women whose future children would be at risk. On February 3rd the House of Commons voted, by 382 to 182, to make Britain the first country in the world to permit "mitochondrial donation[6]", a form of in-vitro fertilisation (IVF) designed to ensure that those children can be born free of the condition.
10 It was a free, unwhipped[7] vote because, despite the potential benefits, the issue is contentious[8]. The procedure involves transplanting the nucleus[9] from an egg cell with damaged mitochondria into another egg with healthy ones. That second egg is provided by a donor.
Mitochondria are different from other cellular components. They are the distant descendants of free-living bacteria that, in the deep evolutionary past, became symbiotic[10] with the cells they now
15 inhabit. As such, they contain their own tiny genomes, separate from the main human genome that resides in the nucleus. A baby created via mitochondrial donation will thus have genes from three people – its mother, its father, and the woman who donated the egg.
The amounts in question[11] are small. Humans have about 22,000 genes. Mitochondria have 37, all of which are concerned with the nuts and bolts[12] of low-level biochemistry. So the small slice of
20 mitochondrial DNA from the donor should not affect things like eye colour, height or personality, which will be influenced by the child's parents in the usual way. But since all the mitochondria in a person's body are descended from the original few in the egg, women born via the procedure will pass the modifications to their children in turn[13].
The noisiest opposition came from traditionalists and the religious – a weakening lobby in a coun-
25 try that is becoming ever more secular[14], and one that in this case was divided. The Church of England supports the idea in theory, although it wants more research, and some priests have spoken out against it. The Roman Catholic church is opposed, as it is to all forms of IVF; Britain's Muslims are split. Polls[15] suggest that a majority of the public, once informed about the procedure, are in favour.
30 IVF clinics will not rush to offer it. Assuming the bill clears[16] the House of Lords, mitochondrial donation will remain illegal until October. Clinics will need a licence from the Human Fertilisation and Embryology Authority, which regulates fertility medicine, as well as specific permission to treat each couple. Any children born as a result will be followed up, to check for unforeseen complications.

---

[1] **MP** (*abbr.*) Member of Parliament – [2] **mitochondria** [ˌmaɪtəʊˈkɒndrɪə] the powerhouse of the cell – [3] **to synthesise** [ˈsɪnθəsaɪz] to form a more complex (chemical) substance by combining individual parts – [4] **to debilitate** to weaken – [5] **tissue** [ˈtɪʃuː] a large collection of similar cells that work together to perform a specific function in an organism, *Gewebe* – [6] **donation** *Spende* – [7] **unwhipped vote** a vote (*Abstimmung*), in which the government has not taken any formal position on the question being voted on – [8] **contentious** [kənˈtenʃəs] causing or likely to cause disagreement – [9] **nucleus** [ˈnjuːklɪəs] the central part of an atom or cell – [10] **symbiotic** [ˌsɪmbaɪˈɒtɪk] dependent on each other, often to the benefit of both – [11] **in question** (*fml.*) under discussion – [12] **the nuts and bolts** the basic working components or practical aspects – [13] **in turn** *wiederum* – [14] **secular** not concerned with or devoted to religion – [15] **poll** *Meinungsumfrage* – [16] **to clear** here: to be officially approved and accepted

35 Doug Turnbull, a scientist at the University of Newcastle who has led much of the research into mitochondrial donation, reckons[17] that about 150 families a year could benefit. But he thinks that, while the technique is new and relatively untried, only a minority will go for[18] it. Much will depend on whether the NHS[19] agrees to pay, as it does for some but not all IVF patients. Yet the ranks of British early adopters[20] could be swelled[21] by couples from overseas. By the end of this year, Britain
40 is likely to be the only place in the world where they will be able to have children who can hope to lead ordinary, healthy lives.

(*610 words*)

www.economist.com/news/britain/21642156-mps-vote-favour-children-three-genetic-parents-dad-and-two-mums, 7 February 2015 [04.04.2015]

ASSIGNMENTS

1. Present the reasons for the controversial discussion about "mitochondrial donation" as depicted in the text.
What finally led to the House of Commons' vote in favour of this form of IVF?
(*Comprehension*)

2. Analyse the stylistic devices employed in the article and explain their function and effect. Pay particular attention to the type of text and the choice of words.
(*Analysis*)

3. You have a choice here. Choose **one** of the following tasks:

3.1 Evaluate the British House of Commons' decision to permit "mitochondrial donation".
State whether (or not) you agree with the legal approval of this genetic technology.
(*Comment/Evaluation*)

3.2 Against the background of the controversial discussion on "mitochondrial donation" in the U.K., compile an interview, in which the various opposing views are discussed, e. g. in a video conference.
Possible participants could be a member of the House of Commons, affected parents, a representative of the Church of England and of the Roman Catholic Church, a scientist, etc.
((*Re-*) *Creation of text*)

---

[17] **to reckon** *schätzen* – [18] **to go for sth.** (*phr. v.*) here: to accept or be interested in sth. – [19] **NHS** (*abbr.*) National Health Service; the public healthcare system in Britain – [20] **early adopter** sb. who starts using a new technology or product as soon as it becomes available – [21] **to swell** to increase in size or number

Part B: Mediation

Laura Höflinger

Babys für alle

Tausende von Euros kostet eine künstliche Befruchtung – jetzt will ein belgischer Arzt den Preis so weit senken, dass sich auch arme Afrikanerinnen ihren Kinderwunsch erfüllen können.

Bis 2050 soll die Bevölkerung Afrikas um 1,3 Milliarden Menschen wachsen, und Willem Ombelet arbeitet daran, dass es auch ganz sicher so kommt. [...]

5 Mehr als 3000 Euro kostet eine künstliche Befruchtung in Deutschland. In Großbritannien sind es sogar umgerechnet 7000 Euro. Ombelet will den Preis für ein Baby auf 200 Euro drücken.

„In manchen Ländern Afrikas sind 300 Euro inklusive Personalkosten* realistisch", sagt er. „In Deutschland natürlich nicht. Aber weniger als 1000 Euro – das ist sicherlich machbar." [...]

Doch wenn er auf Kongressen seine Idee vortrug, kamen kaum mehr als 20 Zuhörer. Es waren
10 Tagungen über Gesundheit in Afrika, also saßen die restlichen 700 Besucher in Vorträgen über HIV, Tuberkulose, Malaria. Es ging schließlich um Länder, in denen eine Frau durchschnittlich fünf Kinder bekommt – wer will da eine IVF-Klinik für Arme eröffnen?

Die Frage ist doch: Haben Entwicklungsländer nicht eher ein Problem mit Empfängnisverhütung* als mit Empfängnis?

15 Diesen Gedanken findet Ombelet ignorant. Einem weißen Pärchen würde man dies wohl nie an den Kopf werfen: Tut mir leid, es gibt schon zu viele von euch. [...]

In vielen ländlichen Gebieten werden kinderlose Frauen verstoßen*, die Ehen annulliert, die Schuld sowieso immer der Frau zugeschoben. In manchen Gegenden verliert sie sogar ihren Namen*.

20 Der Wert einer Frau wird in diesen Gesellschaften an ihrer Gebärfähigkeit* gemessen. Entsprechend sind Kinderlose in Entwicklungsländern eher depressiv, suizidgefährdet, ärmer, häufiger mit HIV infiziert. Im Alter fehlt ihnen die Absicherung. [...]

Es gehe ihm, sagt Ombelet, auch nicht darum, einer Familie die Zeugung* von möglichst vielen Babys zu ermöglichen. Eher gehe es um ein Kind, vielleicht zwei.

(*287 words*)

Der Spiegel, 13/2015, 21 March 2015, p. 122

Annotations »»

Personalkosten personnel costs ■ **Empfängnisverhütung** contraception ■ **verstoßen werden** to be cast out ■ **den Namen verlieren** to lose one's reputation ■ **Gebärfähigkeit** child-bearing ability ■ **Zeugung** conception

ASSIGNMENT

You are working as an intern for the United Nations Youth Development Programme and are helping to organize an international conference on the situation of young women in Africa. At the end of the conference, the different delegates are expected to decide on the distribution of funds to certain projects and initiatives.

Write a synopsis in English of the article at hand, in which you present the pros and cons of IVF for African women with regard to:

- economic aspects
- social aspects
- the demographic development of Africa
- the (lacking) emancipation of African women
- HIV/Aids

Bewertungsbogen für: _____	Kurs: _____

Part A: Teilaufgabe 1 (Comprehension)

	Anforderungen Der Schüler/die Schülerin ...	maximal erreichbare Punktzahl	erreichte Punkte
1	... umreißt die **wesentlichen Aspekte**, die der Artikel thematisiert und benennt z. B. • die schweren gesundheitlichen Folgen von *damaged mitochondria*, • die wissenschaftlichen und medizinischen Hintergründe von *mitochondrial donation*, • die gesellschaftliche, politische und ethische Diskussion in Großbritannien im zukünftigen Umgang mit dem Thema.	2	
2	... stellt die genannten **Gründe für die aktuelle Diskussion** in Großbritannien dar und verweist z. B. darauf, dass • ca. 2 500 britische Frauen von dem Risiko, evt. Kinder mit *damaged mitochondria* zu gebären, betroffen sind, • die Mitochondrienschädigung für die betroffenen Kinder oft den Tod oder eine chronische Schwächung des Gehirns, der Muskeln und Nerven zur Folge hat, • die komplexe und kostenintensive Behandlung nur für ca. 150 Familien pro Jahr in Frage käme.	2	
3	... beschreibt das im Artikel dargestellte **Verfahren der *mitochondrial donation***, z. B., dass • eine gesunde Spender-Eizelle in eine geschädigte Eizelle implantiert wird (ll. 10 f.), • eine Mitochondrienzelle eine Genome enthält – sodass das Kind die Gene von drei Menschen erhält: seinen Eltern und der Frau, die die Eizelle gespendet hat (ll. 16 f.), • die wenigen in den Spender-Mitochondrien enthaltenen Gene nicht die Physis eines Menschen bestimmen – wohl aber weitervererbt werden können.	3	
4	... arbeitet die **kontroverse politische und gesellschaftliche Debatte in Großbritannien** heraus und stellt z. B. dar, dass • das *House of Commons* in deutlicher Mehrheit (382 zu 182 Stimmen) seine Zustimmung gegeben hat, • nach Umfrageergebnissen die Mehrheit der Bevölkerung sowie die Church of England der Therapie zustimmt, • die katholische Kirche sich generell gegen IVF ausspricht, • die britischen Muslime geteilter Meinung sind.	3	
5	... erfüllt ein weiteres aufgabenbezogenes Kriterium. (2) •	2	
		10	

Part A: Teilaufgabe 2 (Analysis)

	Anforderungen Der Schüler/die Schülerin ...	maximal erreichbare Punktzahl	erreichte Punkte
1	... **kategorisiert den vorliegenden Artikel als *expository text***, der z. T. auch argumentative Elemente aufweist, und belegt dies z. B. durch • das komplexe und komplizierte medizinische Thema, das vermittelt wird, • die *topical order* der dargelegten Aspekte, • den emotionalen und daher indirekt appellativen Charakter der Überschrift (*A Dad and Two Mums*) sowie des den Artikel abschließenden Satzes (*Britain is likely to be the only country ...*).	4	
2	... analysiert die **Darstellung der medizinischen Fachinformationen** und verweist z. B. auf • die einleitende Fokussierung auf die schweren Folgeschäden (*seriously damaged ... There is no cure ...*), • die *step-by-step* Beschreibung der Behandlung sowie der genetischen Konsequenzen (*transplanting the nucleus ... that second egg is provided by a donor ... a baby will thus have genes from three people ...; ll. 10 – 17*), • die Experteneinschätzung, dass (nur) ca. 150 Familien in den Genuss der Behandlung kommen werden bzw. dafür in Frage kommen (ll. 35 ff.).	4	
3	... analysiert die *choice of words* und verweist z. B. auf • die bis auf wenige Ausnahmen durchgängig gebrauchte *formal language*, die den expositorischen Charakter des Textes unterstreicht (*a debilitating existence; contentious, cellular compnents*, etc.), • das durchgängig eingeflochtene medizinische Fachvokabular (*mitochondria, nucleus, synthesise*, etc.), das den Autor als Experten ausweist, • die Verweise auf medizinische Autoritäten bzw. offizielle staatliche Institutionen, die dem Thema einen seriösen und offiziellen Hintergrund geben.	5	

	Anforderungen	maximal erreichbare Punktzahl	erreichte Punkte
4	... untersucht **weitere Stilmittel**, die die Wirkung des Textes verstärken und bezieht sich z. B. auf • metaphorische Formulierungen (*a death sentence; the nuts and bolts of ...; the noisiest opposition*), • *positive and negative emotive words/phrases* (*seriously damaged; death sentence; no cure ↔ ordinary healthy lives*), • den Gebrauch von einschränkenden und relativierenden *conditionals* und Adverbien (*around a hundred; there might be ...; should not affect ...;* etc.).	5	
5	... erfüllt ein weiteres aufgabenbezogenes Kriterium. (4) •	4	
		18	

Part A: Teilaufgabe 3.1 (Evaluation/Comment)

	Anforderungen Der Schüler/die Schülerin ...	maximal erreichbare Punktzahl	erreichte Punkte
1	... greift die im Artikel genannte **Entscheidung des *House of Commons*** auf und benennt z. B. • die deutliche Mehrheit der Stimmen (382 zu 182) im House of Commons und die erwartete Zustimmung im House of Lords (ll. 30 f.), • dass Großbritannien das einzige Land in der Welt ist, das zur Zeit dieser Behandlung zugestimmt hat (ll. 39 f.) • die dargestellte mehrheitliche Zustimmung in der Bevölkerung, der Church of England und einem Teil der muslimischen Bevölkerung (ll. 25 f.).	3	
2	... formuliert seine **Zustimmung zur Entscheidung des *House of Commons*** und führt z. B. an, dass • die schweren gesundheitlichen Folgen für die Betroffenen die Behandlung rechtfertigen (ll. 3 ff.), • die geringe Zahl der in Frage kommenden Familien keine dramatische Explosion der Kosten (NHS) zur Folge hätte und daher vertretbar ist, • die zu erwartenden Risiken oder *side-effects* offenbar sehr minimal sind (ll. 20 f.).	3	
3	... **hinterfragt die Entscheidung** des britischen Unterhauses und benennt z. B. • die grundsätzlich zu berücksichtigen Bedenken in Teilen der Bevölkerung, • die Unausgereiftheit der Methode (*new and relatively untried*), • den medizinisch enorm hohen Aufwand sowie das Risiko von *unforeseen complications*.	4	
4	... kommt in Abwägung der beschriebenen Aspekte zu einer **Schlussfolgerung**, die sich plausibel aus den entwickelten Gedanken ergibt, z. B. • lehnt er/sie die Behandlung wegen mangelnder Erprobung ab, • stimmt er/sie der Behandlung mit Blick auf die möglichen schweren Gesundheitsschäden von Betroffenen zu, • fordert er/sie mehr Forschung, um etwaige Risiken oder Komplikationen auszuschließen.	4	
5	... erfüllt ein weiteres aufgabenbezogenes Kriterium. (4) •	4	
		14	

Part A: Teilaufgabe 3.2 ((Re-)Creation of text)

	Anforderungen Der Schüler/die Schülerin ...	maximal erreichbare Punktzahl	erreichte Punkte
1	... versetzt sich durchgängig in die **Situation des Interviewers** und gibt einen Überblick über den Stand der Diskussion/der Problematik und benennt z. B. • das klare Votum des *House of Commons*, • das Krankheitsbild sowie die schweren gesundheitlichen Folgen, • die Strittigkeit des Themas sowie die Kritik und Ablehnung der Behandlung durch Teile der Bevölkerung sowie offizielle Stellen.	3	
2	... lässt **Betroffene zu Wort kommen, die gegen die Durchführung** der *mitochondrial donation* sind, z. B. • Vertreter der katholischen Kirche, Muslime, die religiöse und/oder ethische Bedenken haben, • Politiker oder Vertreter des NHS, die Bedenken wegen der zu erwartenden hohen Kosten haben, • Wissenschaftler, die noch weitere/intensivere Forschung fordern, bevor die Behandlung „praxistauglich" ist.	3	
3	... lässt demgegenüber **Vertreter aus Politik, Gesellschaft, der Kirche etc.** zu Wort kommen, die die **Durchführung der Behandlung befürworten**, z. B. • einen Arzt/Wissenschaftler, der das Procedere darstellt, • einen Politiker, der auf die hohen Kosten der Behandlung von Menschen mit *damaged mitochondria* hinweist, • Familien/Eltern von Kindern, die unter den Folgen einer *damaged mitochondria* leiden, die durch eine solche Behandlung hätten verhindert werden können.	4	

4	... integriert die **formal-stilistischen Elemente des Zieltextformats Interview**, z. B. • eine neutrale, wertungsfreie und unemotionale Haltung gegenüber den Interviewpartnern bzw. der Thematik, • eine klare Strukturierung des Interviews (Einleitung (Thema, Gesprächspartner) – strukturierte Fragesequenz – Abschluss), • eine strategisch geschickte Fragestellung sowie Antworten und (Re-)Agieren auf die Interviewpartner.	4	
5	... erfüllt ein weiteres aufgabenbezogenes Kriterium. (4) •	4	
		14	

Part B: Mediation – Inhalt

	Anforderungen Der Schüler/die Schülerin ...	maximal erreichbare Punktzahl	erreichte Punkte
1	... fasst die Informationen situations- und adressatenbezogen sinngemäß zusammen, auch unter Berücksichtigung impliziter Aussageabsichten.	4	
2	... Konzentriert sich dabei – bezogen auf den situativen Kontext – auf wesentliche Inhalte und wichtige Details.	4	
3	... antizipiert ggf. unter Berücksichtigung des Welt- und Kulturwissens mögliche Missverständnisse und fügt ggf. für das Verstehen erforderliche Erläuterungen hinzu.	5	
4	... greift den in der Aufgabenstellung vorgegebenen situativen und thematischen Kontext auf und stellt einen inhaltlichen Bezug zwischen den soziokulturellen Gegebenheiten in Deutschland und Afrika bzw. den teilnehmenden Delegierten in den USA her.	5	
5	... erfüllt ein weiteres aufgabenbezogenes Kriterium. (4) •	2	
		18	

Part B: Mediation – Sprache

Sprache (60 %)	Der Schüler/die Schülerin ...	Lösungsqualität	
		maximal erreichbare Punktzahl	erreichte Punkte
Kommunikative Textgestaltung	• richtet seinen/ihren Text konsequent und explizit auf die **Intention** und den **Adressaten** im Sinne der **Aufgabenstellung** aus. • berücksichtigt den **situativen Kontext**. • beachtet die Textsortenmerkmale des geforderten **Zieltextformats**. • erstellt einen sachgerecht **strukturierten** Text. • gestaltet seinen/ihren Text hinreichend ausführlich, aber ohne unnötige Wiederholungen und Umständlichkeiten.	9	
Ausdrucksvermögen/ Verfügbarkeit sprachlicher Mittel	• löst sich vom Wortlaut des Ausgangstextes und formuliert **eigenständig**, ggf. unter Verwendung von Kompensationsstrategien. • verwendet funktional einen sachlich wie stilistisch angemessenen und differenzierten allgemeinen und thematischen **Wortschatz** sowie **Funktionswortschatz**. • verwendet einen variablen und dem jeweiligen Zieltextformat angemessenen **Satzbau**.	9	
Sprachrichtigkeit	• beachtet die Normen der sprachlichen Korrektheit im Sinne einer **gelingenden Kommunikation** in den Bereichen **Wortschatz**, **Grammatik** und **Orthographie**.	9	
	Summe Sprache	27	
	Summe Klausurteil B: Aufgabe 3	45	

Part B: Mediation – Possible Solution

Belgian gynaecologist and IVF expert Willem Ombelet wants to drive down the price for artificial insemination or in vitro fertilization for African women to 200 – 300 euros, which would include the costs for the medical treatment, as well as for personnel. In comparison, an IVF treatment in Germany costs around 3,000 euros, and in the UK, it even costs the equivalent of 7,000 euros.

Critics of the idea refer to the prognosis that, by 2050, the African population will have grown by 1.3 million people and argue that fighting diseases such as HIV, tuberculosis and malaria seems to be much more important than helping to conceive more children.

However, Ombelet states that it is not his aim to foster over-population. He also points out that IVF could ultimately help women to avoid becoming infected with HIV. In addition, Ombelet explains that this treatment would enable women who are unable to bear children to secure their social status and not end up being shunned or cast out from their villages and communities. Africa is still very traditional and many communities define a woman's social status and "value" by her capacity to bear children.

Accordingly, in many rural areas, women who are presumed to be infertile are shunned or cast out, and their marriages annulled. As a result, such women often become depressive and suicidal, descend into poverty and later lack any form of old age security.

In conclusion, Ombelet's idea of making IVF more easily available for infertile African women could help to;
- secure their social status,
- improve their health – and the health of their children,
- fight the spread of HIV/Aids,
- allow them to be more independent,
- minimize the risk of them falling prey to prejudiced and unjust social repression.

(287 words)

Topic: Modern Media – Social, Smart and Spying?!/The World of Work

Skills: Analysis of a non-fictional text (newspaper); writing a formal letter (*Zieltextformat*); mediation

Texts: **Part A:** Rosemary Bennett: Longer Hours, More Stress? Welcome to the Digital World (476 words)
Part B: Guido Kleinhubbert: Das Volkslaster, magazine article (277 words)

Part A: Reading/Writing

Rosemary Bennett

Longer Hours, More Stress? Welcome to the Digital World

Smartphones, tablets, and other digital devices have resulted in longer working hours, higher stress levels and blurred[1] boundaries between personal and working life, according to a large-scale study. It found that the digital revolution has been almost entirely negative for the health and happiness of employees. The only clear advantage identified was a greater ability to attend moveable[2]
5 family events such as a school sports day.

These one-off events[3] were more than out-weighed by reduced time spent with the family. Researchers to the University of Surrey examined 65 big studies on the subject, covering the experiences of about 50,000 employees. They found that handing out work phones and other gadgets[4] to staff generally came with an expectation that employees were available for work at all times.
10 Few companies have clear policies about the limits of contacting staff in their free time, making it a virtual free-for-all[5].

Svenja Schlachter, a researcher at the University of Surrey, said that many more companies needed to address the issue – or face the consequences of having a burnt-out workforce.

"In the absence of a policy written down in black and white, employees tended to take guidance[6]
15 from their manager or their colleagues. If mangers sent emails late at night, staff felt they were required to answer them," she said.

"Employees generally showed great enthusiasm at first when they received phones from work but very quickly they felt an expectation was established that meant they had to be always available. They lost a sense of control and in the long-run it became a burden." [...]
20 Overall smartphone technology is thought to have led to white-collar employees[7] working an average of a full working day extra each week, and managers up to two days a week more.

Family life emerged as the greatest casualty[8] of digital technology, with parents being often distracted or breaking off during the evening, at weekends and on holiday to deal with work emails and calls.
25 A handful of German companies have led the way in putting restrictions in place[9] to protect the personal life of staff. Volkswagen, BMW and Puma stop their company servers from forwarding emails to staff half an hour after the end of the working day, making it clear that employees are not meant to check them at night or during weekends.

Ms Schlachter said that the research suggested that individuals dealt with interruptions to their
30 personal life in different ways, some ruminating[10] for hours over a single work email, while others simply put it to the back of their mind until the morning. However, the general trend appeared to be negative, with long-term problems for health and happiness.

---

[1] **blurred** vague, unclear – [2] **moveable** able to be moved, e. g. delayed – [3] **one-off event** *einmaliges Ereignis* –
[4] **gadget** here: a small electronic device, *Gerät* – [5] **free-for-all** a disorderly situation without clear limits or rules –
[6] **guidance** ['gaɪdəns] help or advice about how to act – [7] **white-collar employee** sb. who works in an office –
[8] **casualty** ['kæʒjuəlti] here: sth. that is affected or harmed by a certain situation – [9] **to put sth. in place** *etw. einrichten* – [10] **to ruminate** to think carefully and for a long period about sth.

She said: "Staying 'switched on' might increase flexibility and efficiency at first glance, but in the long run it can result in longer work hours and be detrimental[11] to wellbeing due to stress and
35 work-life balance issues."

(*476 words*)

The Times, 8 January 2015

ASSIGNMENTS

1. Give an outline of the advantages and negative impacts of digital technology on employees.
   (*Comprehension*)

2. Examine the author's stance on "the digital world" by analysing the structure of the text, the use of particular devices, as well as examples given and referred to in the text.
   (*Analysis*)

3. You have a choice here. Choose **one** of the following tasks:

   3.1 "Staying 'switched on' might increase flexibility and efficiency at first glance, but in the long run it can result in longer work hours and be detrimental to wellbeing due to stress and work-life balance issues."
   Comment on Ms Schachter's concluding assumption, taking into consideration your own experiences of being "switched on", as well as relevant aspects mentioned in the text.
   (*Comment/Evaluation*)

   3.2 Although the company you work for allows its staff to have flexible office and work hours and to choose between working at home or in the office, since the company handed out smartphones and tablets to all its workers, the pressure on employees to work extra hours in their free time has continually risen over time.
   Now, the works council (*Betriebsrat*) has decided to take a stand by writing a formal letter to the CEO of the company, in which they present the problematic situation and call for change and improvement.
   (*(Re-) Creation of text*)

[11] **detrimental** [ˌdetrɪˈmentəl] (*fml.*) causing harm and damage

Part B: Mediation

Guido Kleinhubbert

Das Volkslaster*

Millionen Menschen nutzen jede Gelegenheit, zum Smartphone zu greifen. Forscher vergleichen das Verhalten mit dem von Nikotinabhängigen und warnen vor Schäden.

Das Verhalten von Millionen Nutzern hat längst suchtartige Züge angenommen – und zwar nicht nur das von Teenagern, sondern auch das von Menschen jenseits der 40. Sie schauen morgens mit
5 schläfrigen Augen zunächst aufs Handydisplay – und abends als Allerletztes. Sie greifen Hunderte Male am Tag zu ihren Mobilgeräten und schaffen es nicht einmal, sie bei Treffen mit Freunden in der Tasche zu lassen. Oft scheint eine ähnliche Gier* im Spiel zu sein wie bei Kettenrauchern*, und manchmal gefährdet diese Gier nicht nur die eigene Gesundheit, sondern wie beim Qualmen auch die der Mitmenschen. [...]
10 „So wie es das Rauchen tut, hilft der Griff zum Smartphone natürlich, Zeit totzuschlagen, zum Beispiel an Bus- und U-Bahnhaltestellen", sagt Montag. Außerdem werde die Beschäftigung mit dem kleinen Taschencomputer oft als eine Art Belohnung empfunden: Statt des Nikotinkicks warte dann eben eine nette Nachricht oder eine Runde „Quizduell". [...]
Psychologe Montag glaubt, dass iPhones und andere Geräte zunehmend zu einer „Produktivitäts-
15 bremse" werden. Nicht nur, weil sie körperliche Schäden verursachen können. Sondern auch, weil starke Smartphone-Nutzung den Schulunterricht stört und jeden Tag Millionen Stunden Arbeitszeit mit den Geräten verplempert werden. Laut einer US-Studie beschäftigt sich jeder vierte amerikanische Arbeitnehmer während eines durchschnittlichen Arbeitstags etwa eine Stunde lang mit seinem privaten Smartphone. [...]
20 Während die Smartphone-Nutzung am Arbeitsplatz lediglich eine Art Betrug* ist, kann sie im Straßenverkehr potentiell tödlich sein. Immer wieder passieren schwere Unfalle, weil Männer und Frauen am Autosteuer nicht auf ihr Smartphone verzichten wollen. Abgelenkt* von SMS oder Telefonaten, überfahren sie Radler, krachen gegen Bäume oder driften in den Gegenverkehr* ab.
(*277 words*)

Der Spiegel, 13/2015, 21 March 2015, pp. 62 f.

Annotations ⟫⟫

Laster vice ∎ **Gier** craving for sth. ∎ **Kettenraucher** chain smoker ∎ **Betrug** fraud, deception ∎ **abgelenkt von etw. sein** to be distracted by sth. ∎ **Gegenverkehr** oncoming traffic

ASSIGNMENT

Your American pen pal Sam has sent you some funny YouTube videos about "distracted walking". This phenomenon has become a serious issue in the U.S. in recent times because of the ever-increasing number of accidents caused by the excessive use of smartphones. Not long after you came across the given article that was published in *Der Spiegel*.
Write an e-mail in English to your friend, in which you outline what German scientists and psychologists have observed and think about the permanent use of smartphones and the impact of this behaviour.

© Schöningh Verlag, Best.-Nr. 040158

Bewertungsbogen für: _____ Kurs: _____

Part A: Teilaufgabe 1 (Comprehension)

	Anforderungen Der Schüler/die Schülerin ...	maximal erreichbare Punktzahl	erreichte Punkte
1	... gibt einen **Überblick über die dargestellte Situation** und benennt z. B., dass • viele Firmen ihren Angestellten *digital devices* wie Smartphones oder Tablets zur Verfügung stellen (ll. 7 ff.), • eine Studie der University of Surrey herausgefunden hat, dass diese Geräte einen starken negativen Einfluss auf das Privatleben der Angestellten haben (ll. 6 ff.), • es einige deutsche Firmen gibt, die versuchen, diesem Negativtrend entgegenzuwirken (ll. 25 ff.).	2	
2	... arbeitet die **tatsächlichen oder erhofften Vorteile** dieser Firmenpolitik heraus, z. B., dass • Arbeitnehmer ihre Arbeitszeit flexibler und räumlich unabhängig gestalten können (ll. 33 f.), • Arbeitnehmer selbstständiger und effizienter arbeiten können (ll. 9 f.), • Arbeitnehmer ihr Familienleben und ihre Arbeit besser in Einklang bringen können (l. 5 f.).	2	
3	... stellt demgegenüber die **in der Studie herausgefundenen Nachteile** heraus, z. B., dass • sich Privat- und Berufsleben vermengen, sodass schließlich keine Trennung mehr möglich ist (Folge: *burn-out*, l. 13), • Arbeitnehmer ständig verfügbar und erreichbar sind (Folge: Anstieg der Überstunden, ll. 20 f.), • sich Arbeitnehmer ständig verpflichtet fühlen, bereit stehen zu müssen und damit das Privatleben vollkommen von der Arbeit dominiert wird (ll. 18 ff.).	3	
4	... benennt die **dargestellten Folgen**, z. B. • das verstärkte Empfinden von Stress und *burn-out* (ll. 19 f.), • längerfristige negative Folgen für Gesundheit und *happiness* (ll. 31 f.), • den Verlust von Familien- und Privatleben (ll. 22 f.).	3	
5	... erfüllt ein weiteres aufgabenbezogenes Kriterium. (2) •	2	
		10	

Part A: Teilaufgabe 2 (Analysis)

	Anforderungen Der Schüler/die Schülerin ...	maximal erreichbare Punktzahl	erreichte Punkte
1	... arbeitet die **Struktur des Textes** heraus und benennt z. B. • den überwiegend informativ-deskriptiven Charakter des Artikels (*informative, matter-of-fact style, relatively unemotional*), • die ironisch-humorvolle Überschrift, die sich auf die unmittelbare Situation vieler Menschen bezieht und so Aufmerksamkeit und Interesse weckt, • den klaren Aufbau (Einleitung – Hauptteil (*results of the study; examples*) – Schluss (*conclusion; reference to the introduction*)) sowie *cause-effect*-Darstellung (*longer working hours, stress → negative impact on health and happiness*, etc).	4	
2	... verdeutlicht die **Funktion der dargestellten Beispiele** und stellt z. B. dar, dass • Forscher 65 Studien zum Thema ausgewertet haben (→ *reliability; validity of results; credibility of author*), • einige (allgemein bekannte) deutsche Firmen das Problem erkannt haben und an ihre Angestellten nach dem offiziellen Feierabend keine E-Mails versenden, um keinen Druck aufzubauen.	4	
3	... untersucht die verwendeten **Stilmittel und verdeutlicht ihre Funktion**, z. B. • das wiederholte Zitieren einer Forscherin, Svenja Schlachter, der University of Surrey (→ *credibility, seriousness*), • der Hinweis auf den Umfang der Studien (*65 big studies; 50,000 employees → validity, credibility of data*), • die Kontrastierung von wenigen *advantages* mit vielen *disadvantages* (*only one clear advantage identified ... ↔ almost entirely negative; more than out-weighed by ...*).	5	
4	... untersucht **weitere Stilmittel** und bezieht sie auf die **Sichtweise des Autors**, z. B. • die eindeutig negative Einleitung in die Thematik, die in einem zusammenfassenden Schluss rückbezogen wird (ll. 1 ff., ll. 29 ff.), • die eindringliche und akkumulative Darstellung der vielen negativen Folgen und der daraus resultierende Handlungsbedarf (*longer working hours; higher stress levels ... blurred boundaries → negative for ... health ... happiness; always available → loss of control → burden*), • den Einsatz von überwiegend *negative emotive words* in der Darstellung der Folgen dieser Firmenpolitik (*stress; blurred; negative; burnt-out ...; lost ... control; burden; greatest casualty, detrimental*, etc.).	5	
5	... erfüllt ein weiteres aufgabenbezogenes Kriterium. (4) •	4	
		18	

Part A: Teilaufgabe 3.1 (Evaluation/Comment)

	Anforderungen Der Schüler/die Schülerin ...	maximal erreichbare Punktzahl	erreichte Punkte
1	... greift die **Ambivalenz der dargestellten Situation** auf und stellt z. B. dar, dass ● die moderne digitale Technologie zunächst einen Zuwachs an Flexibilität und Effizienz vermuten ließ, ● bei genauerem Hinsehen das Gegenteil der Fall ist, nämlich ein deutliches Mehr an Arbeitszeit und Stress, was sich negative auf die Gesundheit und das Wohlbefinden auswirkt.	3	
2	... nimmt Bezug auf **im Text genannte Beispiele** und benennt z. B. ● die ursprüngliche Begeisterung der Mitarbeiter über die technischen Geräte (ll. 17 f.), die jedoch schnell einem Gefühl der Belastung gewichen ist (ll. 18 f.), ● die nicht mehr mögliche Trennung zwischen Beruflichem und Privatem (ll. 22 f.), die zu Stress und Burn-out führt (ll. 31 f.), ● die Gefahr der Ausbeutung und Ausnutzung der Mitarbeiter durch den Arbeitgeber.	3	
3	... nimmt Bezug auf **eigene Erfahrungen im Umgang mit digitaler Technik** und benennt z. B., dass ● das permanent „staying switched-on" einem zunächst das Gefühl vermittelt, „mitten im Geschehen zu stehen", gebraucht zu werden, „wichtig zu sein" (➔ Vermittlung von positiven Gefühlen), ● man sehr viel Zeit aufwendet/verschwendet, ohne es jedoch konkret zu merken, ● das dauerhafte „online" sein einen schließlich überlastet und erschöpft.	4	
4	... kommt zu einer **kritischen Abwägung und Einschätzung** der genannten Aspekte und benennt z. B., dass ● er/sie die Firmenpolitik von VW/BMW/Puma für sinnvoll und praktikabel hält, ● es wichtig ist, in einer Firma klare Vereinbarungen zu treffen, die für alle verbindlich sind, ● es auch in den Familien klare Absprachen und Vereinbarungen bzgl. der „work-life balance" der Familienmitglieder geben sollte, um ein zufriedenstellendes Privat- und Familienleben zu ermöglichen.	4	
5	... erfüllt ein weiteres aufgabenbezogenes Kriterium. (4) ●	4	
		14	

Part A: Teilaufgabe 3.2 ((Re-)Creation of text)

	Anforderungen Der Schüler/die Schülerin ...	maximal erreichbare Punktzahl	erreichte Punkte
1	... bezieht sich konkret auf die **genannten Probleme** und stellt z. B. dar, dass ● die Angestellten einen hohen Erwartungsdruck empfinden, permanent verfügbar zu sein und Überstunden zu machen, ● die flexiblen Arbeitszeiten einem „Dauereinsatz" gewichen sind, ● es bei den Angestellten bereits Burn-out-Symptome und Krankheitsfälle gibt.	3	
2	... benennt demgegenüber **die ursprünglich hohe Erwartungshaltung auf beiden Seiten**, z. B. ● das Gefühl auf Seiten der Angestellten „wichtig zu sein" und das Gefühl zu haben, flexibel, „modern" und effizient zu arbeiten, ● das Empfinden der Angestellten, sich die Arbeitszeit noch selbstverantwortlicher einteilen zu können, ● die Hoffnung/Erwartung der Firma, dass die Angestellten noch engagierter und verantwortungsvoller arbeiten.	3	
3	... stellt gegenüber dem Unternehmen **schlussfolgernd bestimmte Forderungen und Verbesserungswünsche** auf, z. B., dass ● klare und verbindliche Vereinbarungen verschriftlicht werden, ● an das Herausgeben von technischen Geräten keine selbstverständliche oder automatische (häusliche) Mehrarbeit geknüpft wird, ● das Unternehmen dem Beispiel von VW/BMW/Puma folgt und nach Ende der offiziellen Arbeitszeit keine E-Mails etc. weitergeleitet werden.	5	
4	... formuliert einen **sach- und adressatengerecht gestalteten „formal letter"**, indem er/sie z. B. ● durch eine knappe Selbstvorstellung einleitet, ● die Motivation zum Schreiben/den Anlass verdeutlicht, ● die formal-stilistischen Aspekte berücksichtigt (Anrede, Gliederung in thematische Abschnitte, Abschluss/Grußformel, Standard English).	4	
5	... erfüllt ein weiteres aufgabenbezogenes Kriterium. (4) ●	4	
		14	

Part B: Mediation – Inhalt

	Anforderungen Der Schüler/die Schülerin ...	maximal erreichbare Punktzahl	erreichte Punkte
1	... fasst die Informationen situations- und adressatenbezogen sinngemäß zusammen.	4	
2	... konzentriert sich dabei – bezogen auf den situativen Kontext – auf wesentliche Inhalte.	4	
3	... fügt ggf. für das Verstehen erforderliche detaillierte Erläuterungen hinzu.	5	
4	... bezieht den situativen Kontext jugendlicher/erwachsener Smartphonenutzer (die Perspektive seines Freundes Sam) auf die im Artikel beschriebene Situation. Bezieht auch die deutsche Perspektive mit ein.	5	
5	... erfüllt ein weiteres aufgabenbezogenes Kriterium. (2) •	2	
		18	

Part B: Mediation – Sprache

Sprache (60 %)	Der Schüler/die Schülerin ...	Lösungsqualität	
		maximal erreichbare Punktzahl	erreichte Punkte
Kommunikative Textgestaltung	• richtet seinen/ihren Text konsequent und explizit auf die **Intention** und den **Adressaten** im Sinne der **Aufgabenstellung** aus. • berücksichtigt den **situativen Kontext**. • beachtet die Textsortenmerkmale des geforderten **Zieltextformats**. • erstellt einen sachgerecht **strukturierten** Text. • gestaltet seinen/ihren Text hinreichend ausführlich, aber ohne unnötige Wiederholungen und Umständlichkeiten.	9	
Ausdrucksvermögen/ Verfügbarkeit sprachlicher Mittel	• löst sich vom Wortlaut des Ausgangstextes und formuliert **eigenständig**, ggf. unter Verwendung von Kompensationsstrategien. • verwendet funktional einen sachlich wie stilistisch angemessenen und differenzierten allgemeinen und thematischen **Wortschatz** sowie **Funktionswortschatz**. • verwendet einen variablen und dem jeweiligen Zieltextformat angemessenen **Satzbau**.	9	
Sprachrichtigkeit	• beachtet die Normen der sprachlichen Korrektheit im Sinne einer **gelingenden Kommunikation** in den Bereichen **Wortschatz**, **Grammatik** und **Orthographie**.	9	
	Summe Sprache	27	
	Summe Klausurteil B: Aufgabe 3	45	

Part B: Mediation – Possible Solution

Hi Sam,

Thanks a lot for the funny videos you sent about people bumping into others or running into cyclists because of "distracted walking". ☺

I couldn't help laughing in some cases, but actually, such accidents are not really funny, because some of the people got seriously hurt and ended up in hospital, and that's really sad.

Coincidentally, I happened to come across a magazine article on more or less the same topic soon after – and guess what? – it's not just teenagers who are forever using their smartphones … even people, who are older than 40 are turning into smartphone addicts … who'd have thought!

A scientist quoted in the article compared the smartphone addiction to chain smoking: Just as people smoke a cigarette when they're bored or waiting for a train or bus, the same goes for using their smartphones to kill time. And for some people, using their smartphone and checking messages is the very first thing they do in the morning and the last thing they do before going to bed. What a waste of time! I mean, I really like sending and receiving messages or talking to friends, but I think that's a bit over the top.

According to a U.S. study, 25 % of American employees even spend a whole hour during their working day dealing with their private smartphones instead of working. I guess, they'd better hope they don't get caught, since they might then end up in serious trouble.

Towards the end of the article, the author also pointed out that there has been a rise in the number of fatal car accidents, with drivers crashing into trees or oncoming traffic while they were phoning or texting. Some even ran over cyclists or pedestrians, because they were so distracted by their smartphone and weren't paying proper attention to the traffic.

So if America is anything like Germany, it seems we both need to watch out and keep clear, not just of "distracted walkers", but also of "distracted drivers" if we want to stay in one piece ! ;-)

Bye for now,

XXX

(346 words)

Topic: Starting off and Starting out – Learning, Studying and Working

Skills: Analysis of a non-fictional text (magazine article); writing a letter to the editor (*Zieltextformat*); mediation

Texts: **Part A:** The World Is Going to University (489 words)
Part B: Aleksandra Bakmaz: Mut zur Lücke zwischen den Examina, newspaper article (334 words)

Part A: Reading/Writing

The World Is Going to University

More and more money is being spent on higher education. Too little is known about whether it is worth it

The modern research university, a marriage[1] of the Oxbridge college[2] and the German research institute, was invented in America, and has become the gold standard[3] for the world. Mass higher
5 education started in America in the 19th century, spread to Europe and East Asia in the 20th and is now happening pretty much everywhere except sub-Saharan Africa. The global tertiary enrolment[4] ratio[5] – the share of the student-age population at university – went up from 14% to 32% in the two decades to 2012; in that time, the number of countries with a ratio of more than half rose from five to 54. University enrolment is growing faster even than demand[6] for that ultimate consumer good,
10 the car. The hunger for degrees is understandable: these days they are a requirement[7] for a decent job and an entry ticket to the middle class.

There are, broadly, two ways of satisfying this huge demand. One is the continental European approach of state funding and provision[8], in which most institutions have equal resources and status. The second is the more market-based American model, of mixed private-public funding and provi-
15 sion, with brilliant, well-funded institutions at the top and poorer ones at the bottom.

The world is moving in the American direction. More universities in more countries are charging[9] students tuition fees. And as politicians realise that the "knowledge economy"[10] requires top-flight[11] research, public resources are being focused on a few privileged institutions and the competition to create world-class universities is intensifying.
20 In some ways, that is excellent. The best universities are responsible for many of the discoveries that have made the world a safer, richer and more interesting place. But costs are rising. OECD[12] countries spend 1.6% of GDP[13] on higher education, compared with 1.3% in 2000. If the American model continues to spread, that share will rise further. America spends 2.7% of its GDP on higher education. [...]
25 Some governments and institutions are trying to shed light on[14] educational outcomes. A few American state-university systems already administer a common test to graduates. Testing is spreading in Latin America. Most important, the OECD, whose PISA[15] assessments of secondary education gave governments a jolt[16], is also having a go[17]. It wants to test subject-knowledge and reasoning ability, starting with economics and engineering, and marking[18] institutions as well as

[1] **marriage** here: joining together – [2] **Oxbridge college** morphological blend from Oxford and Cambridge; used to refer to two traditional British universities renowned for their superior social and intellectual status – [3] **gold standard** here: model of excellence, *Maßstab* – [4] **tertiary enrolment** *Immatrikulation in eine Universität* – [5] **ratio** the relationship between two different things, e. g. here: the number of students who could study at a university and those who are actually enrolled – [6] **demand** *Nachfrage* – [7] **requirement** *Voraussetzung* – [8] **funding and provision** *Finanzierung und Bereitstellung* – [9] **to charge students tuition fees** to make students pay money for the teaching they receive at a university, college, etc. – [10] **knowledge economy** economy based on creating, using and trading information to produce growth – [11] **top-flight** highest in standard or quality – [12] **OECD** (*abbr.*) Organisation for Economic Co-operation and Development – made up of 34 countries, the OECD is committed to promoting democracy and the market economy to stimulate global economic progress and world trade – [13] **GDP** (*abbr.*) Gross Domestic Product: the total value of goods and services produced by a country in a year – [14] **to shed light on sth.** *Aufschluss geben über etw.* – [15] **PISA** (*abbr.*) Programme for International Student Assessment: a worldwide study organized by the OECD to test the scholastic performance of 15-year-old students in mathematics, science and reading – [16] **to give sb. a jolt** *jdm. einen Ruck geben* – [17] **to have a go** (*infml.*) to try sth.

30 countries. Asian governments are keen[19], partly because they believe that a measure of the quality of their universities will help them in the market for international students; rich countries, which have more to lose and less to gain, are not. Without funding and participation from them, the effort will remain grounded[20].

Governments need to get behind[21] these efforts. America's market-based system of well-funded,
35 highly differentiated universities can be of huge benefit to society if students learn the right stuff. If not, a great deal of money will be wasted.

(*489 words*)

www.economist.com/news/leaders/21647285-more-and-more-money-being-spent-higher-education-too-little-known-about-whether-it, 28 March 2015 [04.04.2015]

ASSIGNMENT 1

1. Present the different models of "tertiary education" along with the resulting benefits and problems of each one as depicted by the author.
(*Comprehension*)

2. Examine and analyse the stylistic devices employed in the article and explain how they underline the author's intention and the overall message of the text.
(*Analysis*)

3. You have a choice here. Choose **one** of the following tasks:

3.1 Against the background of your personal situation as a student about to start tertiary education, give an assessment of the two main models presented.
Which model – the European or the American one – do you consider to be more efficient and successful? Which kind of university would you prefer to enroll in?
(*Comment/Evaluation*)

3.2 Article 26 of the *Universal Declaration of Human Rights* states:
"Everyone has the right to education. Education shall be free, at least in the elementary and fundamental stages. [...] Technical and professional education shall be made generally available and higher education shall be equally accessible to all on the basis of merit*".

Against the background of this universal right, write a "Letter to the Editor" in which you state your opinion about "Going to University" in response to the article.
((*Re-*)*Creation of text*)

[18] **to mark** *benoten, Zensuren geben* – [19] **keen** wanting to do sth. very much – [20] **grounded** unable to take off or start – [21] **to get behind sth.** to support a project or plan

*on the basis of merit (*fml.*) as the result of demonstrated ability, effort, performance or achievement rather than wealth or connections

Part B: Mediation

Aleksandra Bakmaz

Mut zur Lücke zwischen den Examina

Keine Lust mehr auf die Hochschule? Das geht vielen so, die gerade die Bachelorarbeit abgegeben haben. Direkt in den Job einsteigen und ganz auf den Master verzichten wollen viele aber auch nicht. Warum nicht zwischen dem ersten und dem zweiten Abschluss eine Pause einlegen? Ein Gap Year – also Lücken-Jahr – ist dann eine Option. [...]

5 **Praktikum** Wer noch nicht genau weiß, wohin er beruflich will, sollte das Gap Year nutzen, um sich auf dem Arbeitsmarkt umzusehen. Praktika bieten die Möglichkeit, mehrere Firmen kennenzulernen. Studenten sammeln so Praxiserfahrung. Gleichzeitig haben sie eine berufliche Orientierungshilfe, erklärt Peter Piolot von der zentralen Studienberatung* der Universität zu Köln. Viele wissen nicht, wohin es nach dem Master gehen soll. „Eine Auszeit nach dem Bachelor ist die ideale
10 Möglichkeit, um in unterschiedliche Bereiche zu schnuppern* und eigene Vorlieben besser kennenzulernen."

Wer sein Ziel schon fest vor Augen hat, sollte dagegen keine Zeit mit Praktika vergeuden. Meistens sind ohnehin während des Studiums Hospitanzen* Pflicht*. „Es gibt auch andere Möglichkeiten, um Berufserfahrung zu sammeln", erklärt Jutta Boenig. Sie ist Vorstandsvorsitzende der
15 deutschen Gesellschaft für Karriereberatung in Überlingen am Bodensee. Dazu gehören etwa freie Mitarbeiten* und Auftragsarbeiten*.

Auslandsaufenthalt In Frankreich die Esskultur genießen und unbeschwert durch das Land reisen? So sollte der Auslandsaufenthalt während eines Gap Year nicht aussehen. „Besser ist es, ein freiwilliges soziales Jahr zu absolvieren", sagt Joachim Sauer. Er ist Präsident des Bundesverbands
20 der Personalmanager in Berlin. Faulenzen am Strand von Malibu oder in einer südamerikanischen Großstadt – wer nicht erklären kann, was er Sinnvolles im Auslandsaufenthalt gemacht hat, sammelt damit auch keine Pluspunkte.

Die Beschäftigung mit anderen Kulturen – etwa durch soziales Engagement* – kommt dagegen gut an. Auch Nebenjobs wie Erntehelfer oder Kellner können für Personaler* interessant sein. „Al-
25 les, was die Persönlichkeit schärft, ist von Vorteil", erklärt Joachim Sauer. Wer die finanziellen Mittel für einen längeren Auslandsaufenthalt hat, plant am besten mindestens drei Monate ein. Ein paar Wochen zu reisen, das wirkt häufig lediglich wie ein verlängerter Urlaub. Schwieriger sei es dagegen, über längere Zeitspannen hinweg zurechtzukommen. [...]

(*334 words*)

www.rp-online.de/panorama/wissen/bildung/mut-zur-luecke-zwischen-den-examina-aid-1.4946459, 18 March 2015 [04.04.2015]

Annotations »»»

Studienberatung student counselling ■ **schnuppern** here: to try out/to test (different professions) ■ **Hospitanz** to sit in on a course ■ **Pflicht/verpflichtend** compulsory ■ **freie Mitarbeit** freelance work ■ **Auftragsarbeit** commissioned work, contract work ■ **soziales Engagement** volunteer engagement ■ **Personaler** personnel manager, human resources manager

ASSIGNMENT »»»

What is the best strategy for spending the time after graduating from school and before enrolling at a university in a useful and efficient way? Students from all over the world are exchanging their ideas and experiences on an Internet forum called "Mind the Gap".

Using the information and advice given in the article, explain some of the "do's and don'ts" and possible pitfalls of Gap years to your fellow international students and write a post for the forum's website.

| Bewertungsbogen für: _____ | Kurs: _____ |

Part A: Teilaufgabe 1 (Comprehension)

	Anforderungen	maximal erreichbare Punktzahl	erreichte Punkte
	Der Schüler/die Schülerin ...		
1	... gibt einen kurzen **Überblick über die Ursprünge und die Ausbreitung** moderner *research universities*, z. B. benennt er/sie • die Anfänge im Amerika des 19. Jahrhunderts als eine Mischung aus britischem College und deutschem Forschungsinstitut (ll. 3 ff.), • den enormen Zuwachs an Studenten weltweit (1992 – 2012: 14 % ➜ 32 %), • die globale Ausbreitung des „Bildungsmodells Universität" von den USA nach Europa und Ostasien (Ausnahme: *sub-Saharan Africa*, ll. 3 ff.).	2	
2	... stellt die **verschiedenen Modelle universitärer Ausbildung** heraus, z. B. • das kontinental-europäische Modell, in dem staatlich finanzierte Universitäten mit möglichst gleichen/vergleichbaren Angeboten einen ähnlichen Status haben (ll. 10 ff.), • das amerikanische, eher marktorientierte Modell, einer Mischung aus privaten und öffentlich finanzierten Universitäten, das ein großes Gefälle bzgl. der finanziellen Möglichkeiten der Universitäten zur Folge hat (ll. 12 ff.).	2	
3	... skizziert die **aus den unterschiedlichen Systemen resultierenden *benefits* and *problems***, und benennt z. B., dass • öffentliche Mittel auf wenige privilegierte Universitäten fokussiert werden, von denen man sich Spitzenforschung und erstklassige Forschungsergebnisse erhofft (ll. 18 ff.), • dem amerikanischen Modell folgend, die OECD-Länder zunehmend mehr für *higher education* ausgeben (*1.6 % of GDP; USA: 2.7 %*), • durch dieses System ein Konkurrenzkampf unter den Universitäten entsteht, der zunimmt (ll. 17 ff.).	3	
4	... benennt weitere **Folgen dieses Trends auf dem „internationalen Bildungsmarkt"**, z. B. • eine Zunahme an Testverfahren für Studenten, um die Besten herauszufiltern (ll. 23 f.), • dass die Universitäten weltweit um eine Verbesserung ihrer Leistungen im Wettbewerb stehen (ll. 16 f.), • das zunehmende „Buhlen" um leistungsstarke Studenten, wobei reiche Länder weltweit im Vorteil sind (ll. 29 ff.).	3	
5	... erfüllt ein weiteres aufgabenbezogenes Kriterium. (2) •	2	
		10	

Part A: Teilaufgabe 2 (Analysis)

	Anforderungen	maximal erreichbare Punktzahl	erreichte Punkte
	Der Schüler/die Schülerin ...		
1	... verdeutlicht die **Strukturierung des Artikels** und belegt dies z. B. durch • die klare thematische Untergliederung des Textes (kritische Einleitung – Hauptteil (Zahlen, Beispiele) – Schlussfolgerung), • die zeitlich-strukturelle Unterteilung des Artikels in: Vergangenheit (*19th century*) – Situation in der Gegenwart (*USA, Europe, OECD countries, Asia*) – Zukunft (Bedingungen, Forderungen).	4	
2	... analysiert die **rhetorischen Stilmittel** und verdeutlicht deren Funktion, z. B. • den Gebrauch von *contrast* und *comparison* (*more and more money vs. little is known ...; university enrolment ... faster than ... the car; more to lose and less to gain*, etc.). • die Darstellung von Fakten und Zahlenmaterial zur Untermauerung der Seriosität des Autors (14 %; 32 % ... etc.), • der Gebrauch von *accumulation* und *climax* (*America ... 19th century ➜ Europe and East Asia ... 20th century ... now ... pretty much everywhere; safer, richer and more interesting; the best universities*).	4	
3	... untersucht **weitere Stilmittel** und verweist z. B. auf • den durchgängigen Gebrauch von Fachbegriffen (*tertiary enrolment ratio; OECD; PISA*, etc. ➜ *expert knowledge, credibility*), • den Einsatz von kontrastiv eingesetzten *word fields* zu *economy* und *education*, • den Gebrauch von *irony* als Mittel der kritisch-distanzierten Darstellung (*modern research ... a marriage of ...; pretty much everywhere except sub-Saharan Africa; faster than ... ultimate consumer good, the car*; etc.).	5	

4	... arbeitet die **Aussage (*message*) und Autorintention** heraus und nennt z. B., dass • der Autor einen kritisch-ironischen Blick auf den wachsenden „Bildungsmarkt" wirft, bei dem es um beträchtliche finanzielle Summen geht (*knowledge economy, GDP*, etc.), • der Autor dafür plädiert, ein Markt-orientiertes Bildungssystem zu entwickeln, das hochwertig und effizient arbeitet, • der Autor an die Verantwortung der ausbildenden Institute appelliert, durch eine hochqualitative Ausbildung die Welt zu einem *„safer, richer and more interesting place"* zu machen.	5	
5	... erfüllt ein weiteres aufgabenbezogenes Kriterium. (4) •	4	
		18	

Part A: Teilaufgabe 3.1 (Evaluation/Comment)

	Anforderungen Der Schüler/die Schülerin ...	maximal erreichbare Punktzahl	erreichte Punkte
1	... nimmt **konkreten Bezug auf zentrale inhaltliche Aspekte** des Artikels und verweist z. B. darauf, dass • es die in Europa üblichen staatlich subventionierten Universitäten gibt, die sich dem Gleichheitsprinzip verpflichtet fühlen (ll. 10 f.), • demgegenüber das amerikanische System auf zusätzliche private Zuwendungen setzt, die ein *top-bottom*-Spektrum zur Folge haben (ll. 12 f.), • das amerikanische System auf Wettbewerb setzt, der Spitzenleistungen und *world-class universities* hervorbringen soll.	3	
2	... kommentiert die **Vorteile der beiden Systeme**, z. B. • die stärkere Leistungs- und Qualitätsorientierung (ll. 16 f.), • die durch den Wettbewerb erreichte *world-class quality* (ll. 17 f.), • die Fokussierung auf das *educational outcome*, • die Berücksichtigung auch von ärmeren/armen Studenten im europäischen Modell.	3	
3	... benennt und hinterfragt die **möglichen Nachteile der beiden Systeme**, z. B. • das Entstehen einer *„survival of the fittest"*-Mentalität, die finanziell schwächere Länder oder Studenten nicht berücksichtigt, • die Abhängigkeit der Universitäten von privaten Finanzhilfen oder Sponsoren (die dann evt. auch Einfluss auf die Studieninhalte nehmen können), • das möglicherweise nicht-Erreichen von Spitzenforschung im europäischen System, weil die entsprechenden finanziellen Mittel fehlen.	4	
4	... kommt in Abwägung der verschiedenen Aspekte zu einer **Schlussfolgerung**, z. B., dass • auch höhere Schulbildung (bei entsprechender Begabung) für jedermann zugänglich sein sollte, • zunächst der Staat für die Finanzierung von Ausbildung zuständig ist, sich aber Unternehmen durch Spenden beteiligen können/sollten, • man eine Mischung aus beiden Systemen andenken sollte.	4	
5	... erfüllt ein weiteres aufgabenbezogenes Kriterium. (4) •	4	
		14	

Part A: Teilaufgabe 3.2 ((Re-)Creation of text)

	Anforderungen Der Schüler/die Schülerin ...	maximal erreichbare Punktzahl	erreichte Punkte
1	... nimmt **konkreten Bezug auf Artikel 26** und benennt z. B. • das allen Menschen zustehende Grundrecht auf Erziehung und Bildung, die frei zugänglich ist, • dass auch *higher education* frei zugänglich sein sollte, allerdings basierend auf den entsprechenden Fähigkeiten, • dass der Begriff *„equally accessible"* auch für Menschen aus armen Regionen der Welt gilt, sowohl in Industrieländern, als auch in *„sub-Saharan Africa"* (ll. 4 f.).	3	
2	... bezieht die in **Artikel 26 genannten Grundrechte auf Aspektes des Textes** und stellt z. B. dar, dass • es sich eine *„knowledge economy"* nicht leisten kann, unter Umständen ganze Kontinente und Regionen der Welt nicht mit adäquater Bildung zu versorgen, • im Zeitalter der Globalisierung *technical and professional education* von existenzieller Bedeutung sind, • nur im gegenseitigen Austausch von *„knowledge"* ein Rückschritt zu einer imperialistischen Grundhaltung überwunden werden kann.	3	

3	... kommt zu einer **kritischen Hinterfragung** der im Text dargestellten Fokussierung, z. B. indem er/sie • darstellt, dass ein ausschließlich amerikanisch orientiertes System z. B. den Forderungen der *Declaration of Human Rights* widerspricht, • betont, dass ein überwiegend staatlich finanziertes System mangels fehlender finanzieller Mittel zum Scheitern verurteilt ist, • formuliert, dass ein Testen von „*subject-knowledge and reasoning ability*" (ll. 26 f.) in Kombination mit privater und staatlicher Unterstützung von ärmeren Studenten ein vielversprechendes Modell sein könnte.	4	
4	... formuliert einen **sach- und adressatengerecht gestalteten Brief**, indem er/sie z. B. • durch eine knappe Selbstvorstellung einleitet, • seine/ihre Motivation zum Schreiben verdeutlicht, • die formalstilistischen Aspekte eines „*Letter to the Editor*" berücksichtigt (Anrede, Gliederung in thematische Abschnitte, Abschluss/Grußformel).	4	
5	... erfüllt ein weiteres aufgabenbezogenes Kriterium. (4) •	4	
		14	

Part B: Mediation – Inhalt

	Anforderungen Der Schüler/die Schülerin ...	maximal erreichbare Punktzahl	erreichte Punkte
1	... fasst die Informationen situations- und adressatenbezogen sinngemäß zusammen.	4	
2	... konzentriert sich dabei – bezogen auf den situativen Kontext – auf wesentliche Inhalte.	4	
3	... fügt ggf. für das Verstehen erforderliche detaillierte Erläuterungen hinzu.	5	
4	... bezieht den situativen Kontext von Abiturienten/Gap Years auf die im Artikel beschriebene Situation. Bezieht auch die deutsche Perspektive mit ein.	5	
5	... erfüllt ein weiteres aufgabenbezogenes Kriterium. (2) •	2	
		18	

Part B: Mediation – Sprache

Sprache (60 %)	Der Schüler/die Schülerin ...	Lösungsqualität	
		maximal erreichbare Punktzahl	erreichte Punkte
Kommunikative Textgestaltung	• richtet seinen/ihren Text konsequent und explizit auf die **Intention** und den **Adressaten** im Sinne der **Aufgabenstellung** aus. • berücksichtigt den **situativen Kontext**. • beachtet die Textsortenmerkmale des geforderten **Zieltextformats**. • erstellt einen sachgerecht **strukturierten** Text. • gestaltet seinen/ihren Text hinreichend ausführlich, aber ohne unnötige Wiederholungen und Umständlichkeiten.	9	
Ausdrucksvermögen/ Verfügbarkeit sprachlicher Mittel	• löst sich vom Wortlaut des Ausgangstextes und formuliert **eigenständig**, ggf. unter Verwendung von Kompensationsstrategien. • verwendet funktional einen sachlich wie stilistisch angemessenen und differenzierten allgemeinen und thematischen **Wortschatz** sowie **Funktionswortschatz**. • verwendet einen variablen und dem jeweiligen Zieltextformat angemessenen **Satzbau**.	9	
Sprachrichtigkeit	• beachtet die Normen der sprachlichen Korrektheit im Sinne einer **gelingenden Kommunikation** in den Bereichen **Wortschatz**, **Grammatik** und **Orthographie**.	9	
	Summe Sprache	27	
	Summe Klausurteil B: Aufgabe 3	45	

Part B: Mediation – Possible Solution

Taking time out for a *Gap year* offers great opportunities for discovering the world and finding out more about yourself, in particular, your professional and personal strengths and weaknesses.

However, career advisers and personnel managers warn that young people should be careful not to just waste their time "hanging out" and doing nothing or simply taking an extended holiday to relax abroad. If you want to add bonus points to your CV, you should be able to present your time out as something meaningful.

An internship, for example, can be a really good opportunity not only to gain practical work experience, but also to get further orientation about your potential professional skills. Further alternatives include working as a freelancer or doing commissioned work for a certain time.

Of course, many young people want to spend time abroad in order to improve their foreign language skills and to learn about other countries and cultures. Nevertheless, they should be careful not to evoke the impression of having spent the time there just holidaying and "enjoying life". Therefore, for a trip abroad, you plan to stay for at least three months, and you should be able to provide references or certification for any jobs or work that you do while there.

The president of the German Association of Personnel Managers, Joachim Sauer, recommends young people demonstrating social commitment or working as fruit pickers or waiting staff because these kinds of jobs help to sharpen and focus a person's personality, as well as providing insights into different areas of life – to put it in a nutshell: such activities serve to broaden a young person's horizons.

(271 words)

> **Topic:** Science (Fiction) and Technology – Towards a Better World?!
>
> **Skills:** Analysis of a fictional text (novel); continuation of a fictional text (*Zieltextformat*); mediation
>
> **Texts:** **Part A:** Matt Haig: Echo Boy (444 words)
> **Part B:** Alexander Jung, Thomas Schulz: Der Maschinen-Schwarm, magazine article
> (353 words)

Part A: Reading/Writing

Matt Haig

Echo Boy

I heard my parents arguing. Not arguing. Niggling[1]. But I couldn't hear what it was about. Maybe it was about Alissa. Our Echo.

She had only lived with us for a little over a month. My mother thought we should have got her sooner – straight after the accident, in fact – but Dad had been determined[2] to struggle on with
5 nothing more than Travis, our old house robot. Dad had been pretty clear that he didn't like having Alissa around very much. To be fair, I didn't either.

She was too human. Too real-looking. It creeped[3] me out.

She came into my room. She looked at me sternly[4], even though I knew an Echo couldn't really feel stern. She had been designed to look like a thirty-year-old human woman with blonde hair and fea-
10 tures that were pretty, but not threateningly[5] so. She had a perfectly wholesome face, with a smooth shining Echo skin. Echo skin is not quite like human skin, just as Echo blood is not quite human blood, but the freaky thing for me was how similar she looked to an actual human. She was flesh and blood. I was used to Travis, of course, but robots were different. Alissa was as flesh and blood as I was, except for the small centimetre cube of hardware and circuitry[6] inside her brain.
15 "You have the first lesson of the day – Mandarin – in thirty-five minutes. You need to start getting ready."

She stayed standing there a little too long.

"OK. I'll ... be ready."

I was a slow waker, so I commanded the curtains to open and just stared at the grey, rain-streaked
20 world. There were other houses, but we didn't really know our neighbours.

This was even before I put on my info-lenses. Sometimes I didn't want enhancements[7], or informa-tion. The news had been depressing lately.

The re-emergence of cholera across Europe.

The energy crisis.
25 The deaths of terraformers[8] on Mars.

Hurricanes. Tsunamis.

Echo Stuff.

The government was wiping out[9] homes in the deserts of Andalusia[10].

Sometimes – like that morning – I just wanted to see the world as it actually was, in all its rain-rav-
30 aged[11] glory. So – no mind-wires, no info-lenses.

I was never really a full-on body-tech person. Well, that's kind of a lie. It was hard for me to be a body-tech person, as my dad was very suspicious about most types of technological advancement. For instance, he basically thought that Echos would one day take over, and we'd be wiped out. Ac-cording to him, none of the big tech companies cared for human life, no matter what they said, and
35 he got quite cross[12] if I ever showed too much interest. *(444 words)*

Matt Haig: Echo Boy. The Bodley Head, London, 2014, pp. 7 ff.

[1] **to niggle** to criticize sb. about small details – [2] **determined** [dɪˈtɜːmɪnd] *fest entschlossen* – [3] **to creep sb. out** (*infml.*) to make sb. feel uncomfortable or afraid – [4] **stern** very serious, *streng* – [5] **threatening** [ˈθretənɪŋ] *bedroh-lich* – [6] **circuitry** system of electric wiring, *Schaltkreise* – [7] **enhancement** sth. that makes sth. better or more effi-cient – [8] **terraformer** sb. who works to engineer a different planet so that it will be able to support human life – [9] **to wipe out sth.** to destroy sth. completely – [10] **Andalusia** an autonomous region in the south-west of Spain – [11] **ravaged** spoiled, destroyed – [12] **cross** angry

Note: One of the protagonists and narrators of the science fiction novel *Echo Boy* is 15-year-old Audrey, whose family – like most American families – has a so-called Echo (<u>E</u>nhanced <u>C</u>omputerised <u>H</u>umanoid <u>O</u>rganism) called Alissa.

ASSIGNMENTS

1. Point out Audrey's observations of and reflections on Echos, technical enhancements and the state of world she lives in.
   (*Comprehension*)

2. Examine the use of narrative and stylistic devices and explain how they convey and underline Audrey's perceptions of herself and her surroundings.
   (*Analysis*)

3. You have a choice here. Choose **one** of the following tasks:

   3.1 Assess whether the novel the excerpt is taken from describes more a utopia or a dystopia. Justify your assessment by referring to the knowledge about utopias and dystopias that you gained in class, as well as hints and clues given in the text itself.
   (*Comment/Evaluation*)

   3.2 Audrey mentions her parents arguing and suspects that it may be about Alissa – the family's Echo.
   Both of them have a very different opinion about house robots and particularly about Echos. Based on the clues given in the excerpt, imagine what they might have been saying to each other and write a dialogue that reflects their opposing views.
   (*(Re-)Creation of text*)

Part B: Mediation

Alexander Jung, Thomas Schulz

Der Maschinen-Schwarm

In den vergangenen Monaten haben sowohl Stephen Hawking* als auch Bill Gates* vor einer neuen Maschinenintelligenz gewarnt, die zur Gefahr für die Menschheit* werden könne. Schon in den nächsten Jahren würden Roboter zu vielen mechanischen Arbeiten in der Lage sein, sei es, Früchte zu pflücken oder Krankenhauspatienten umzubetten, so Gates. „Sobald Computer und Roboter
5 ein Niveau erreichen, auf dem Sehen und Bewegen einfach funktionieren, wird das extrem genutzt werden." Auf lange Sicht, sagt der Microsoft-Gründer, bestehe die Gefahr, dass Maschinen die Menschheit generell überflügelten*.

Solch apokalyptische Visionen scheinen heute noch weit entfernt. Allerdings zeichnet sich in der Robotik tatsächlich „ein neues Paradigma*" ab, sagt Ken Goldberg. „Es gibt nicht einfach mehr
10 brutale Rechenkraft*, sondern ganz neue, große Ideen." Goldberg ist Professor für Robotik an der University of California in Berkeley, er leitet eine neue Roboter-Forschungsallianz von kalifornischen Universitäten. Das Silicon Valley ist nur wenige Kilometer entfernt.

Lange hätten Industrie und Wissenschaft Roboter nur als autonome Maschinen betrachtet, die separat programmiert und gesteuert werden, sagt Goldberg. Doch durch das Internet und allge-
15 genwärtige Netzwerke sowie Datenverbindungen könnten Roboter nun extern mit Informationen aus der Datenwolke versorgt werden und voneinander lernen. Die neue Forschungsrichtung heißt deswegen Cloud-Robotik. „Über die Cloud können Maschinen auf riesige Mengen von Rechenkraft zugreifen, Daten teilen und ganz neue mathematische Berechnungen anstellen", sagt Goldberg.

Roboter sind damit in der Lage, erheblich schneller zu lernen. „Ganz vereinfacht lässt sich sagen:
20 Ein Roboter kann 10 000 Stunden etwas lernen, oder 10 000 Roboter können das Gleiche in einer Stunde lernen", so Goldberg. Es sei inzwischen bewiesen, dass eine Gruppe lernender Maschinen bessere Entscheidungen trifft als eine einzelne. Daraus ließen sich mathematische Modelle entwickeln, die Roboter zu weit komplexeren Aufgaben befähigten. [...]

Google hat inzwischen acht Robotik-Firmen übernommen; darunter auch Boston Dynamics, ein
25 Unternehmen, das unter anderem für das Pentagon an Robotik-Projekten arbeitete. Es hat neben vierbeinigen Robotern, die bis zu 46 Kilometer pro Stunde schnell rennen können, auch humanoide, zweibeinig laufende Maschinen entwickelt. [...]

Aber wo geht die Entwicklung hin, wenn sich der technologische Fortschritt weiter beschleunigt? Werden Maschinen den Menschen dann tatsächlich schon in wenigen Jahrzehnten weitgehend
30 überflüssig machen, wie manche Experten warnen?

(353 words)

www.spiegel.de/spiegel/print/d-131928425.html, 21 March 2015 [04.04.2015]

Annotations »»

Stephen Hawking (*1942) British theoretical physicist and cosmologist ■ **Bill Gates** (*1955) American business magnate; founder of Microsoft ■ **Menschheit** humanity ■ **überflügeln** to outdo, to surpass ■ **Paradigma** paradigm; a model of sth. ■ **Rechenkraft** computing power

ASSIGNMENT

Your school is participating in an e-Twinning project about "the field of robotics and its impact on society" with an American high school in California. Together with your Californian e-pal, Steven, you have chosen to focus on the topic of "humanoids/androids", i.e. robots that are designed to look like a real person.

After reading this online article, you decide to write an e-mail to Steven, in which you outline and juxtapose the expected benefits and risks of the new types of humanoid robots.

Bewertungsbogen für: _____ Kurs: _____

Part A: Teilaufgabe 1 (Comprehension)

	Anforderungen Der Schüler/die Schülerin ...	maximal erreichbare Punktzahl	erreichte Punkte
1	... skizziert die in dem Textauszug dargestellten **Rahmenbedingungen**, z. B., dass • die beschrieben Situation morgens, unmittelbar nach dem Aufwachen, stattfindet, • die 15-jährige Ich-Erzählerin ihre Abneigung gegenüber Alissa, dem neuen Echo der Familie, beschreibt, • Audrey offensichtlich in einer Technologie-dominierten, jedoch sehr krisengeschüttelten Welt lebt, • Audreys Vater Echos ablehnt und ihnen misstraut.	2	
2	... umreißt **Audreys Darstellung von Alissa, dem Echo ihrer Familie**, und erwähnt z. B., dass • Alissa in erschreckender Weise einem Menschen ähnelt; in diesem Fall einer 30-jährigen, gut aussehenden Frau „nachgebaut" wurde, • Alissa die Funktion einer Hausangestellten hat, die z. B. Audrey morgens weckt und sie auf den anstehenden Unterricht (Mandarin) hinweist, • Audrey Alissa u. a. deswegen nicht mag, weil sie einen strengen und missbilligenden Gesichtsausdruck hat und sich ihrer Meinung nach zu lange in ihrem Zimmer aufhält.	2	
3	... stellt die **modernen Technologien** heraus, die Audrey nutzt, z. B. • das Öffnen der Vorhänge in ihrem Zimmer durch ein akkustisches Signal, • sogenannte *info-lenses* und *mind-wires*, die neueste Nachrichten und Informationen vermitteln.	3	
4	... arbeitet heraus, wie Audrey die **Situation in der Welt/die neuesten Nachrichten** wiedergibt, z. B., dass • es eine Energiekrise gibt, • sich Cholera wieder in Europa verbreitet hat, • es gefährliche Unwetter (*hurricanes, tsunamis*) sowie Dürren (*deserts in Andalusia*) gibt, • es Tote bei Arbeiten auf dem Mars gegeben hat.	3	
5	... erfüllt ein weiteres aufgabenbezogenes Kriterium. (2) •	2	
		10	

Part A: Teilaufgabe 2 (Analysis)

	Anforderungen Der Schüler/die Schülerin ...	maximal erreichbare Punktzahl	erreichte Punkte
1	... arbeitet die **erzählerischen Stilmittel** heraus und erklärt deren Funktion, z. B. • die Erzählperspektive (*first-person narrator: I heard my parents ...; I couldn't know ...; It creeped me out ...* etc.); *limited point of view*: nur ihre Gedanken/Perspektive werden dargestellt, • die Darstellungsart: *scenic mode of presentation*, • den Tagebuch- und Alltagscharakter der Darstellung: fast völliger Verzicht auf Dialog; oft kurze, elliptische Satzkonstruktionen; *insertions* und *comments* (*... to be fair, I didn't either; well. That's kind of a lie ...*).	4	
2	... arbeitet **weitere Stilmittel** heraus, die **Audreys persönliche Wahrnehmung** unterstreichen und benennt z. B. • den Einsatz von Humor und Ironie (*Dad had been determined to struggle on ...; She was too human: Too real-looking. It creeped me out ...; I just wanted to see the world ... in all its rain-ravaged glory ...*), • die z. T. umgangssprachlichen Kommentierungen (*To be fair ...; It creeped me out ..., the freaky thing...* etc.), • den fast durchgängigen Gebrauch von *simple past* als typischer *narrative tense*.	4	
3	... untersucht **weitere Stilmittel** in Zusammenhang mit Audreys Darstellung der **Umgebung**, z. B. • den Gebrauch von fast ausschließlich *negative emotive words* zur Darstellung des *state of the planet* und der *surroundings* (*grey, rain-streaked world, depressing; cholera; energy crisis; deaths* etc.), • die Darstellung der offenbar bedrohlichen Situation insgesamt (*Echos would one day take over; we'd be wiped out; none of the tech companies cared for human life*), • die kontrastive Beschreibung von Echos (*blonde hair; pretty; perfectly wholesome face; smooth, shining Echo skin*, etc.) und der Umwelt insgesamt (*depressing, grey; rain-streaked; hurricanes, tsunamis, cholera* etc.).	5	
4	... analysiert **Audreys Beschreibung von Alissa** und der (indirekten) Darstellung der Bedrohung, die von ihr ausgeht, z. B. • ihr zu perfektes (und damit inhumanes) Äußeres (*pretty; perfectly wholesome face; smooth shining Echo skin ... she was flesh and blood ...*), • ihr ernsthafter, fast eindringlicher Blick (*she looked at me sternly ...*), • ihre fast statische Art zu sprechen und ihr (zu langes) Verweilen im Zimmer (*You have ... You need to ...; she stayed standing there a little too long ...*).	5	

5	... erfüllt ein weiteres aufgabenbezogenes Kriterium. (4) ●	4	
		20	

Part A: Teilaufgabe 3.1 (Evaluation/Comment)

	Anforderungen Der Schüler/die Schülerin ...	maximal erreichbare Punktzahl	erreichte Punkte
1	... nimmt Bezug auf **charakteristische Merkmale einer Utopie** und führt dabei z. B. an, dass ● Utopien oft Paradies-ähnliche, perfekte Umgebungen oder Gesellschaften sind, in denen Menschen in Harmonie und materiellem Überfluss leben, ● moderne, z. T. futuristische Technologie das Leben der Menschen unterstützt, vereinfacht etc., ● utopische Gesellschaften oft insulär oder von der Welt abgeschieden leben.	3	
2	... nimmt Bezug auf **charakteristische Merkmale einer Dystopie** und benennt z. B. ● die oft zerstörerische oder gefährliche Umgebung (z. B. Krieg, Umweltkatastrophen, Seuchen etc.), ● eine von einem diktatorischen Regime und/der Technologie unterdrückte, oft überwachte und kontrollierte Gesellschaft, ● die Existenz eines kritischen, das System in Frage stellenden Protagonisten, der i. d. R. ein Außenseiter ist.	3	
3	... bezieht die charakteristischen Merkmale einer **Dystopie/Utopie auf den Romanausschnitt** und verdeutlicht z. B., dass ● die überwiegenden Merkmale den Text als Dystopie ausweisen (*disasters, diseases, potentially dangerous technology* etc.), ● die Technik eine dominante und potentiell kontrollierende Funktion hat (*too human ... creeped me out; looked at me sternly* etc.), ● die (potenzielle) Außenseiterstellung des Protagonisten oder zentraler Figuren (*Dad ... didn't like having Alissa around ... I didn't either ... I just wanted to see the world as it was ...*).	4	
4	... kommt zu einer **begründeten Einschätzung**, die sich schlüssig aus den Ausführungen ergibt, z. B. ● benennt er/sie den dystopischen Charakter des Romanauszugs, der (indirekt) auf weitere Katastrophen hinweist, ● weist er/sie auf die Elemente von Science Fiction hin, die sowohl utopischen als auch dystopischen Charakter haben können, ● benennt er/sie die angedeuteten Katastrophen und Gefahren als spannungserzeugendes Element.	4	
5	... erfüllt ein weiteres aufgabenbezogenes Kriterium. (4) ●	4	
		14	

Part A: Teilaufgabe 3.2 ((Re-)Creation of text)

	Anforderungen Der Schüler/die Schülerin ...	maximal erreichbare Punktzahl	erreichte Punkte
1	... versetzt sich in **die Lage von Audreys Eltern** und berücksichtigt dabei z. B. ● ihre kontroverse Sichtweise und Meinung von *robots* und *Echos*, ● die generell skeptische Haltung von Audreys Vater (ll. 5 f.), ● die Gewöhnung des Vaters an Travis, den alten *house robot* (ll. 4 f.).	3	
2	... greift die **Perspektive des Vaters** auf und stellt z. B. dar, dass ● er jeder Art von technologischer Entwicklung/Veränderung mit Argwohn gegenübersteht (ll. xxx), ● er der Meinung ist, dass Echos gefährlich und bedrohlich für die Menschen sind, ● er glaubt, dass die Technologiekonzerne sich nicht um menschliches Leben kümmern, sondern ausschließlich an Echos interessiert sind.	3	
3	... greift die **Perspektive von Audreys Mutter** auf und berücksichtigt dabei z. B., dass ● sie daran interessiert ist, Hilfe und Erleichterung durch Roboter zu haben, ● sie sich auf einen Unfall bezieht, der möglicherweise körperliche Beeinträchtigungen nach sich zieht, sodass ein Roboter/Echo für die alltägliche Hausarbeit hilfreich ist.	4	
4	... verfasst einen **Dialog** und berücksichtigt dabei z. B., dass ● beide Charaktere im Gespräch interagieren, ● *spoken English* verwendet wird (z. B. *short forms, colloquialisms, exclamations* etc.), ● beide Charaktere z. B. emotional aufgebracht sind (*use of irony, reproaches* etc.).	4	
5	... erfüllt ein weiteres aufgabenbezogenes Kriterium. (4) ●	4	
		18	

Part B: Mediation – Inhalt

	Anforderungen **Der Schüler/die Schülerin ...**	maximal erreichbare Punktzahl	erreichte Punkte
1	... fasst die Informationen situations- und adressatenbezogen sinngemäß zusammen.	4	
2	... konzentriert sich dabei – bezogen auf den situativen Kontext – auf wesentliche Inhalte.	4	
3	... fügt ggf. für das Verstehen erforderliche detaillierte Erläuterungen hinzu.	5	
4	... bezieht den situativen Kontext bzgl. des Einflusses und der Entwicklung von Humanoiden und Androiden auf die im Artikel beschriebene Situation. Bezieht auch die deutsche Perspektive mit ein.	5	
5	... erfüllt ein weiteres aufgabenbezogenes Kriterium. (2) •	2	
		18	

Part B: Mediation – Sprache

Sprache (60 %)	Der Schüler/die Schülerin ...	Lösungsqualität	
		maximal erreichbare Punktzahl	erreichte Punkte
Kommunikative Textgestaltung	• richtet seinen/ihren Text konsequent und explizit auf die **Intention** und den **Adressaten** im Sinne der **Aufgabenstellung** aus. • berücksichtigt den **situativen Kontext**. • beachtet die Textsortenmerkmale des geforderten **Zieltextformats**. • erstellt einen sachgerecht **strukturierten** Text. • gestaltet seinen/ihren Text hinreichend ausführlich, aber ohne unnötige Wiederholungen und Umständlichkeiten.	9	
Ausdrucksvermögen/ Verfügbarkeit sprachlicher Mittel	• löst sich vom Wortlaut des Ausgangstextes und formuliert **eigenständig**, ggf. unter Verwendung von Kompensationsstrategien. • verwendet funktional einen sachlich wie stilistisch angemessenen und differenzierten allgemeinen und thematischen **Wortschatz** sowie **Funktionswortschatz**. • verwendet einen variablen und dem jeweiligen Zieltextformat angemessenen **Satzbau**.	9	
Sprachrichtigkeit	• beachtet die Normen der sprachlichen Korrektheit im Sinne einer **gelingenden Kommunikation** in den Bereichen **Wortschatz**, **Grammatik** und **Orthographie**.	9	
	Summe Sprache	27	
	Summe Klausurteil B: Aufgabe 3	45	

Part B: Mediation – Possible Solution

Hi Steven,

Thanks again for recommending the novel *Echo Boy* to me – it was really fun reading it, although at times, a little scary as well! ☺

And guess what? By chance, I also just came across a really interesting article about androids and artificial intelligence, and it quotes several experts who have warned that humanoids may end up taking over the world and making human beings redundant. That also sounds really creepy!

Bill Gates and Stephen Hawking, for example, predict that robots will eventually outsmart humans, and could become a great threat to humanity. Ken Goldberg, a Professor of Robotics at Berkeley, on the other hand, expects to see many great new ideas and advances in Cloud robotics. He says that a huge swarm of robots which is synchronized with the Cloud is capable of learning and executing VERY complex tasks in a VERY short period of time. WOW!

Another interesting fact from the article is that Google has already taken over eight robotics companies. One of them – Boston Dynamics – is a company that, in addition to developing four-legged robots capable of running 46kms per hour, has now even managed to build robots that are able to walk on two legs just like us.

Although Hawking and Gates are worried that, in just a few decades, human work and intelligence might not be needed any longer, Gates did also point out that robots will soon be able to take on a lot of useful, but unpleasant or difficult manual work, such as fruit-picking or moving hospital patients from one bed to another.

Of course, even the experts can't really be sure about what's actually going to happen, but I certainly hope that robots or androids don't end up becoming as independent as described in *Echo Boy* because that would be really freaky … ☺

Bye for now,

XXX

(307 words)

Appendix >>>>

Bewertungsraster

1. Lesen/Schreiben (integriert)

2. Lesen/Schreiben (integriert) + Hör-/Hörsehverstehen (isoliert)

3. Lesen/Schreiben (integriert) + Mediation (isoliert)

Kriterielle Bewertung des Bereichs „Sprachliche Leistung/Darstellungsleistung"
Bewertungsraster Englisch Einführungsphase und Q 1/2
Lesen + Schreiben

Kommunikative Textgestaltung – Kriterien	Lösungsqualität	
Der Schüler/die Schülerin ...	maximal erreichbare Punkte	erreichte Punkte
1 Aufgabenbezug ... richtet seinen Text konsequent und explizit auf die Aufgabenstellung aus. • eindeutiger Aufgabenbezug in allen drei Teilaufgaben • Beachtung der Anforderungsbereiche (siehe Operatoren)	6	
2 Textformate ... beachtet die Konventionen der jeweils geforderten Zieltextformate. • **Aufgabe 1:** Quellenangaben zum Ausgangstext: Autor, Titel, Textsorte, Thema, Publikation, Ort und Jahr, ggf. Ausgabe/Auszug, Intention/Zielgruppe; keine Zitate und i. d. R. keine Textverweise • **Aufgaben 1 und 2:** sachlich-neutraler Stil/Register; verdichtendes Wiedergeben, Darstellen und Erläutern (expositorisch-darstellendes Schreiben) • **Aufgabe 3.1:** subjektiv-wertender Stil/Register; Erörtern, Begründen, Schlussfolgern und argumentativ sinnvolle Textstruktur mit einem gewissen Maß an Rhetorisierung (argumentierendes Schreiben) • **Aufgaben 1–3.1:** *present tense* als Tempus der Textbesprechung; keine *short forms* • **Aufgabe 3.2:** Bezug auf klar definierte Normen der Textsorte (anwendungs-/produktionsorientiertes kreatives Schreiben), z. B. bei Rede/Debattenbeitrag: Adressatenbezug durch Bezugnahme auf das Vorwissen und den Erfahrungshorizont des Adressaten	6	
3 Textaufbau ... erstellt einen sachgerecht strukturierten Text. • Geschlossenheit des Gesamttextes (Aufgaben 1, 2 und 3.1, bzw. Aufgaben 1 und 2 in Vorbereitung von 3.2) • sach- und intentionsgerechte Untergliederung in grafisch erkennbare Sinnabschnitte • inhaltlich-thematische Geschlossenheit der Sinnabschnitte und Herstellung eindeutiger Bezüge • leserfreundliche Verknüpfung der Sinnabschnitte und Gedanken (z. B. durch gliedernde Hinweise, Aufzählung, Vor- und Rückverweise, zusammenfassende Wiederaufnahme zentraler Punkte, Konnektoren)	8	
4 Ökonomie ... gestaltet seinen Text hinreichend ausführlich, aber ohne unnötige Wiederholungen und Umständlichkeiten. • Beschränkung auf relevante bzw. exemplarische Punkte/Details/Zitate • Vermeidung von Redundanz, z. B. durch Rückverweise auf bereits Dargelegtes (statt Wiederholung) • abstrahierende Zusammenfassung mit konkreten, exemplarischen Belegen (statt langwieriger, textchronologischer Bearbeitung) • Bereitstellung und ggf. Erläuterung verständnisrelevanter Informationen	6	
5 Belegtechnik ... belegt seine Aussagen durch eine funktionale Verwendung von Verweisen und Zitaten. • Gebrauch von Textverweisen (Zeilenangabe, Hinweise auf Absatz) zur Orientierung des Lesers • der Darstellungsabsicht angemessener Gebrauch wörtlicher Zitate aus dem Ausgangstext (Aufgaben 2 und 3) • Konventionen des Zitierens: z. B. durch Zeilenangabe, Absatzangabe, wörtliches Zitieren, sinngemäßes Zitieren (Paraphrase), ggf. unter Kennzeichnung von Auslassungen oder Ergänzungen, Wechsel zwischen in den Satz eingebauten Zitaten, eingeleiteten Zitaten und Zitaten in Klammern	4	

Ausdrucksvermögen/Verfügbarkeit sprachlicher Mittel – Kriterien	Lösungsqualität	
Der Schüler/die Schülerin ...	maximal erreichbare Punkte	erreichte Punkte
6 Eigenständigkeit ... löst sich vom Wortlaut des Ausgangstextes und formuliert eigenständig. • Wiedergaben von Inhalten/Sachverhalten in „eigenen Worten" • keine wörtliche Wiedergabe auswendig gelernter Textpassagen (z. B. aus der Sekundärliteratur) • Hinweis: Ein punktuell das Sprachmaterial des Ausgangstextes kreativ verarbeitendes Vorgehen ist durchaus erwünscht.	6	
7 Allgemeiner und thematischer Wortschatz ... bedient sich eines sachlich wie stilistisch angemessenen und differenzierten allgemeinen und thematischen Wortschatzes. Inhalts- und Strukturwörter: • treffende und präzise Bezeichnung von Personen, Dingen und Sachverhalten, Berücksichtigung von Bedeutungsnuancen (auch Modalitäten) • stilistisch angemessene Wortwahl (*register: formal, neutral, informal*) • Variation der Wortwahl, Vermeidung von „Allerweltswörtern" (z. B. *think, want, good, thing*)	8	

	Ausdrucksvermögen/Verfügbarkeit sprachlicher Mittel – Kriterien	Lösungsqualität	
	Der Schüler/die Schülerin ...	maximal erreichbare Punkte	erreichte Punkte
8	**Funktions- und Textinterpretationswortschatz** ... bedient sich eines sachlich wie stilistisch angemessenen und differenzierten Textbesprechungs- und Textproduktionswortschatzes. ● **Aufgabe 1:** Vokabular zur Wiedergabe und Zusammenfassung von Inhalten ● **Aufgabe 2:** Vokabular der Textanalyse (auch Filmanalyse, Analyse von Karikaturen, Grafiken etc.) ● **Aufgabe 3.1:** Vokabular der Meinungsäußerung/Bewertung ● **Aufgabe 3.2:** Anpassung des Wortschatzes an das geforderte Textformat	6	
9	**Satzbau** ... bedient sich eines variablen und dem jeweiligen Zieltextformat angemessenen Satzbaus. ● durchgängig klare Syntax, Verständlichkeit beim ersten Lesen (Überschaubarkeit, Eindeutigkeit der Bezüge, Satzlogik) ● dem jeweiligen Zieltextformat angemessene Satzmuster: z. B. Hypotaxe (Konjunktional-, Relativ-, indirekte Fragesätze), Parataxe, Aktiv- und Passivkonstruktionen, Gerundial-, Partizipial- und Infinitivkonstruktionen, Adverbiale	10	

	Sprachrichtigkeit – Kriterien	Lösungsqualität	
	Der Schüler/die Schülerin ...	maximal erreichbare Punkte	erreichte Punkte
	... beachtet die Normen der sprachlichen Korrektheit (siehe Orientierung).		
10	Wortschatz	12	
11	Grammatik	12	
12	Orthographie	6	
		30	
	Summe sprachliche Leistung/Darstellungsleistung	**90**	

	Gesamtpunkte	Lösungsqualität	
		maximal erreichbare Punkte	erreichte Punkte
	Summe Darstellungsleistung/sprachliche Leistung	**90**	
	Summe inhaltliche Leistung	**60**	
	Summe insgesamt (Inhalt und Darstellung/Sprache)	**150**	
	aus der Punktsumme resultierende Note		

	Bewertungsschlüssel																
Punkte = %	29 – 0	39 – 30	48 – 40	57 – 49	67 – 58	74 – 68	82 – 75	89 – 83	97 – 90	104 – 98	112 – 105	119 – 113	127 – 120	134 – 128	142 – 135	150 – 143	**Ziffernote**
Note	6	5-	5	5+	4-	4	4+	3-	3	3+	2-	2	2+	1-	1	1+	

Eine Klausurleistung, die in einem der beiden Anforderungsbereiche, *Inhalt* und *Sprache* eine ungenügende Leistung darstellt, kann insgesamt nicht mit mehr als drei Notenpunkten bewertet werden.
Eine ungenügende Leistung im *inhaltlichen Bereich* liegt vor, wenn in diesem **weniger als 8 Punkte** erreicht werden.
Eine ungenügende Leistung im *sprachlichen Bereich* liegt vor, wenn in ihm **weniger als 12 Punkte** erreicht werden.

Die Klausur wird mit der Note _____ (_____ Punkte) bewertet.

Orientierungsangaben für die Sprachrichtigkeit
Bewertungsraster Englisch Einführungsphase und Q 1/2
Lesen + Schreiben

Sprachrichtigkeit

Der Schüler/die Schülerin ...	maximal erreichbare Punktzahl
... beachtet die Normen der sprachlichen Korrektheit.	**30**

10. Wortschatz

0 Punkte	2–5 Punkte	6–9 Punkte	10–12 Punkte
In nahezu jedem Satz sind Schwächen im korrekten Gebrauch der Wörter feststellbar. Die Mängel im Wortgebrauch erschweren das Lesen und Textverständnis erheblich und verursachen Missverständnisse.	Einzelne Sätze sind frei von lexikalischen Verstößen. Fehler beim Wortgebrauch beeinträchtigen z. T. das Lesen und Verstehen.	Vereinzelt ist eine falsche Wortwahl feststellbar. Abschnitte bzw. Textpassagen sind weitgehend frei von lexikalischen Verstößen.	Der Wortgebrauch (Struktur- und Inhaltswörter) ist über den gesamten Text hinweg korrekt.

Maximal erreichbare Punktzahl: 12

11. Grammatik

0 Punkte	2–5 Punkte	6–9 Punkte	10–12 Punkte
In nahezu jedem Satz ist wenigstens ein Verstoß gegen die grundlegenden Regeln der Grammatik feststellbar. Diese erschweren das Lesen erheblich und verursachen Missverständnisse.	Einzelne Sätze sind frei von Verstößen gegen grundlegende Regeln der Grammatik. Grammatikfehler beeinträchtigen z. T. das Lesen und Verstehen.	Es sind vereinzelt Verstöße gegen die Regeln der Grammatik feststellbar. Jedoch sind Abschnitte bzw. Textpassagen weitgehend frei von Grammatikfehlern. Das Lesen des Textes wird durch die auftretenden Grammatikfehler nicht erschwert.	Der Text ist weitgehend frei von Verstößen gegen die Regeln der Grammatik. Wenn Grammatikfehler auftreten, betreffen sie den komplexen Satz und sind ein Zeichen dafür, dass die Schülerin/der Schüler Risiken beim Verfassen des Textes eingeht, um sich dem Leser differenziert mitzuteilen.

Maximal erreichbare Punktzahl: 12

12. Orthographie (Rechtschreibung und Zeichensetzung)

0 Punkte	1–2 Punkte	3–4 Punkte	5–6 Punkte
In nahezu jedem Satz ist wenigstens ein Verstoß gegen die Regeln der Orthographie feststellbar. Die Orthographiefehler erschweren das Lesen erheblich und verursachen Missverständnisse.	Einzelne Sätze sind frei von Verstößen gegen orthographische Normen. Orthographiefehler beeinträchtigen z. T. das Lesen und Verstehen.	Es sind durchaus Orthographiefehler feststellbar. Jedoch sind Abschnitte bzw. Textpassagen weitgehend ohne Verstoß gegen orthographische Normen. Das Lesen des Textes wird durch die auftretenden Orthographiefehler nicht wesentlich beeinträchtigt.	Der gesamte Text ist weitgehend frei von Verstößen gegen orthographische Normen. Wenn vereinzelt Orthographiefehler auftreten, haben sie den Charakter von Flüchtigkeitsfehlern, d. h., sie deuten nicht auf Unkenntnis von Regeln hin.

Maximal erreichbare Punktzahl: 6

Bewertungsraster Englisch Einführungsphase und Q 1/2
Lesen + Schreiben

Bewertungsbogen für: _____ Kurs: _____

Die Fachkonferenz trifft Vereinbarungen zum Bewertungsschlüssel; der Fachlehrer/die Fachlehrerin konkretisiert und ergänzt klausurspezifisch im Teilleistungsbereich Inhalt die Lösungen und Kriterien (vgl. Klausurformate gemäß Lehrplan Englisch SII 1999).

Inhalt (40 %)	Der Schüler/die Schülerin ...	mögliche Punkte	erreichte Punkte
Aufgabe 1: *(Comprehension)*	Kriterium 1: ...		
	Kriterium 2: ...	16	
	Kriterium 3: ...		
Aufgabe 2: *(Analysis)*	Kriterium 1: ...		
	Kriterium 2: ...	24	
	Kriterium 3: ...		
Aufgabe 3: *(Comment/Evaluation/ (Re-)Creation of text)*	Kriterium 1: ...		
	Kriterium 2: ...	20	
	Kriterium 3: ...		
	Summe Inhalt:	**60**	

Sprache (60 %)	Der Schüler/die Schülerin ...	mögliche Punkte	erreichte Punkte
Kommunikative Textgestaltung [30 P.]	**Aufgabenbezug:** ... richtet seinen Text konsequent und explizit im Sinne der Aufgabenstellung auf die Intention und den Adressaten aus.	6	
	Textformate: ... richtet seinen Text auf die Aufgabenstellungen aus und beachtet die Konventionen der jeweils geforderten Zieltextformate: • Aufgabe 1: u. a.: Quellenangabe zum Ausgangstext, keine Zitate/Textverweise, *present tense* • Aufgabe 2: u. a. sachlich-neutraler Stil, Textverweise u. Zitate, *present tense* • Aufgabe 3: u. a. subjektiv-wertender Stil (3.1), bzw. Berücksichtigung der Normen der Textsorte (3.2)	6	
	Textaufbau: ... erstellt einen sachgerecht strukturierten leserfreundlichen Text, u. a. durch sprachliche Verknüpfungen, Absätze als erkennbare Sinnabschnitte etc.	8	
	Ökonomie: ... formuliert hinreichend ausführlich, aber ohne unnötige Wiederholungen und Umständlichkeiten (auch unter funktionaler Verwendung von Verweisen/Zitaten).	6	
	Belegtechnik: funktionale Verwendung von Textverweisen und Zitaten	4	
Ausdrucksvermögen/ Verfügbarkeit sprachlicher Mittel [30 P.]	**Eigenständigkeit:** ... löst sich vom Ausgangstext und formuliert eigenständig.	6	
	Themenwortschatz: ... bedient sich eines sachlich wie stilistisch angemessenen wie differenzierten (allgemeinen, thematischen, analytischen) Wortschatzes.	8	
	Funktions- und Interpretationswortschatz: ... bedient sich eines sachlich wie stilistisch angemessenen und differenzierten Wortschatzes.	6	
	Satzbau: ... bedient sich eines variablen und dem jeweiligen Zieltextformat angemessenen Satzbaus.	10	
Sprachrichtigkeit [30 P.]	**Wortschatz**	12	
	Grammatik	12	
	Orthografie	6	
	Summe Sprache:	**90**	
	Insgesamt:	**150**	

Bewertungsschlüssel																	
Punkte = %	29 – 0	39 – 30	48 – 40	57 – 49	67 – 58	74 – 68	82 – 75	89 – 83	97 – 90	104 – 98	112 – 105	119 – 113	127 – 120	134 – 128	142 – 135	150 – 143	**Ziffernote**
Note	6	5-	5	5+	4-	4	4+	3-	3	3+	2-	2	2+	1-	1	1+	

Eine Klausurleistung, die in einem der beiden Anforderungsbereiche, *Inhalt* und *Sprache* eine ungenügende Leistung darstellt, kann insgesamt nicht mit mehr als drei Notenpunkten bewertet werden.

Eine ungenügende Leistung im *inhaltlichen Bereich* liegt vor, wenn in diesem **weniger als 8 Punkte** erreicht werden.

Eine ungenügende Leistung im *sprachlichen Bereich* liegt vor, wenn in ihm **weniger als 12 Punkte** erreicht werden.

Die Klausur wird mit der Note _____ (_____ Punkte) bewertet.

Kriterielle Bewertung des Bereichs „Sprachliche Leistung/Darstellungsleistung"
Bewertungsraster Englisch Einführungsphase und Q 1/2
Part B: Hör-/Hörsehverstehen (20 %)

	Kommunikative Textgestaltung – Kriterien	Lösungsqualität	
	Der Schüler/die Schülerin ...	maximal erreichbare Punkte	erreichte Punkte
1	**Aufgabenbezug** ... richtet seinen Text konsequent und explizit auf die Aufgabenstellung aus. • eindeutiger Aufgabenbezug in allen drei Teilaufgaben • Beachtung der Anforderungsbereiche (siehe Operatoren)	6	
2	**Textformate** ... beachtet die Konventionen der jeweils geforderten Zieltextformate. • **Aufgabe 1:** Quellenangaben zum Ausgangstext: Autor, Titel, Textsorte, Thema, Publikation, Ort und Jahr, ggf. Ausgabe/Auszug, Intention/Zielgruppe; keine Zitate und i. d. R. keine Textverweise • **Aufgaben 1 und 2:** sachlich-neutraler Stil/Register; verdichtendes Wiedergeben, Darstellen und Erläutern (expositorisch-darstellendes Schreiben) • **Aufgabe 3.1:** subjektiv-wertender Stil/Register; Erörtern, Begründen, Schlussfolgern und argumentativ sinnvolle Textstruktur mit einem gewissen Maß an Rhetorisierung (argumentierendes Schreiben) • **Aufgaben 1–3.1:** *present tense* als Tempus der Textbesprechung; keine *short forms* • **Aufgabe 3.2:** Bezug auf klar definierte Normen der Textsorte (anwendungs-/produktionsorientiertes kreatives Schreiben), z. B. bei Rede/Debattenbeitrag: Adressatenbezug durch Bezugnahme auf das Vorwissen und den Erfahrungshorizont des Adressaten	5	
3	**Textaufbau** ... erstellt einen sachgerecht strukturierten Text. • Geschlossenheit des Gesamttextes (Aufgaben 1, 2 und 3.1, bzw. Aufgaben 1 und 2 in Vorbereitung von 3.2) • sach- und intentionsgerechte Untergliederung in grafisch erkennbare Sinnabschnitte • inhaltlich-thematische Geschlossenheit der Sinnabschnitte und Herstellung eindeutiger Bezüge • leserfreundliche Verknüpfung der Sinnabschnitte und Gedanken (z. B. durch gliedernde Hinweise, Aufzählung, Vor- und Rückverweise, zusammenfassende Wiederaufnahme zentraler Punkte, Konnektoren)	5	
4	**Ökonomie** ... gestaltet seinen Text hinreichend ausführlich, aber ohne unnötige Wiederholungen und Umständlichkeiten. • Beschränkung auf relevante bzw. exemplarische Punkte/Details/Zitate • Vermeidung von Redundanz, z. B. durch Rückverweise auf bereits Dargelegtes (statt Wiederholung) • abstrahierende Zusammenfassung mit konkreten, exemplarischen Belegen (statt langwieriger, textchronologischer Bearbeitung) • Bereitstellung und ggf. Erläuterung verständnisrelevanter Informationen	5	
5	**Belegtechnik** ... belegt seine Aussagen durch eine funktionale Verwendung von Verweisen und Zitaten. • Gebrauch von Textverweisen (Zeilenangabe, Hinweise auf Absatz) zur Orientierung des Lesers • der Darstellungsabsicht angemessener Gebrauch wörtlicher Zitate aus dem Ausgangstext (Aufgaben 2 und 3) • Konventionen des Zitierens: z. B. durch Zeilenangabe, Absatzangabe, wörtliches Zitieren, sinngemäßes Zitieren (Paraphrase), ggf. unter Kennzeichnung von Auslassungen oder Ergänzungen, Wechsel zwischen in den Satz eingebauten Zitaten, eingeleiteten Zitaten und Zitaten in Klammern	3	

	Ausdrucksvermögen/Verfügbarkeit sprachlicher Mittel – Kriterien	Lösungsqualität	
	Der Schüler/die Schülerin ...	maximal erreichbare Punkte	erreichte Punkte
6	**Eigenständigkeit** ... löst sich vom Wortlaut des Ausgangstextes und formuliert eigenständig. • Wiedergaben von Inhalten/Sachverhalten in „eigenen Worten" • keine wörtliche Wiedergabe auswendig gelernter Textpassagen (z. B. aus der Sekundärliteratur) • Hinweis: Ein punktuell das Sprachmaterial des Ausgangstextes kreativ verarbeitendes Vorgehen ist durchaus erwünscht.	5	

	Ausdrucksvermögen/Verfügbarkeit sprachlicher Mittel – Kriterien	Lösungsqualität	
	Der Schüler/die Schülerin ...	maximal erreichbare Punkte	erreichte Punkte
7	**Allgemeiner und thematischer Wortschatz** ... bedient sich eines sachlich wie stilistisch angemessenen und differenzierten allgemeinen und thematischen Wortschatzes. Inhalts- und Strukturwörter: • treffende und präzise Bezeichnung von Personen, Dingen und Sachverhalten, Berücksichtigung von Bedeutungsnuancen (auch Modalitäten) • stilistisch angemessene Wortwahl (*register: formal, neutral, informal*) • Variation der Wortwahl, Vermeidung von „Allerweltswörtern" (z. B. *think, want, good, thing*)	6	
8	**Funktions- und Textinterpretationswortschatz** ... bedient sich eines sachlich wie stilistisch angemessenen und differenzierten Textbesprechungs- und Textproduktionswortschatzes. • **Aufgabe 1:** Vokabular zur Wiedergabe und Zusammenfassung von Inhalten • **Aufgabe 2:** Vokabular der Textanalyse (auch Filmanalyse, Analyse von Karikaturen, Grafiken etc.) • **Aufgabe 3.1:** Vokabular der Meinungsäußerung/Bewertung • **Aufgabe 3.2:** Anpassung des Wortschatzes an das geforderte Textformat	5	
9	**Satzbau** ... bedient sich eines variablen und dem jeweiligen Zieltextformat angemessenen Satzbaus. • durchgängig klare Syntax, Verständlichkeit beim ersten Lesen (Überschaubarkeit, Eindeutigkeit der Bezüge, Satzlogik) • dem jeweiligen Zieltextformat angemessene Satzmuster: z. B. Hypotaxe (Konjunktional-, Relativ-, indirekte Fragesätze), Parataxe, Aktiv- und Passivkonstruktionen, Gerundial-, Partizipial- und Infinitivkonstruktionen, Adverbiale	8	

	Sprachrichtigkeit – Kriterien	Lösungsqualität	
	Der Schüler/die Schülerin ...	maximal erreichbare Punkte	erreichte Punkte
	... beachtet die Normen der sprachlichen Korrektheit (siehe Orientierung).		
10	Wortschatz	10	
11	Grammatik	10	
12	Orthographie	4	
		24	
	Summe sprachliche Leistung/Darstellungsleistung	**72**	

	Gesamtpunkte	Lösungsqualität	
		maximal erreichbare Punkte	erreichte Punkte
	Summe Darstellungsleistung/sprachliche Leistung	72	
	Summe inhaltliche Leistung	48	
	Summe Teilaufgabe Hör-/Hörsehverstehen	30	
	Summe insgesamt (Inhalt und Sprache/Darstellung)	150	
	aus der Punktsumme resultierende Note		

	Bewertungsschlüssel																Ziffernote
Punkte = %	29 – 0	39 – 30	48 – 40	57 – 49	67 – 58	74 – 68	82 – 75	89 – 83	97 – 90	104 – 98	112 – 105	119 – 113	127 – 120	134 – 128	142 – 135	150 – 143	
Note	6	5-	5	5+	4-	4	4+	3-	3	3+	2-	2	2+	1-	1	1+	

Eine Klausurleistung, die in einem der beiden Anforderungsbereiche, *Inhalt* und *Sprache* eine ungenügende Leistung darstellt, kann insgesamt nicht mit mehr als drei Notenpunkten bewertet werden.
Eine ungenügende Leistung im *inhaltlichen Bereich* liegt vor, wenn in diesem **weniger als 8 Punkte** erreicht werden.
Eine ungenügende Leistung im *sprachlichen Bereich* liegt vor, wenn in ihm **weniger als 12 Punkte** erreicht werden.

Die Klausur wird mit der Note _____ (_____ Punkte) bewertet.

Orientierungsangaben für die Sprachrichtigkeit
Bewertungsraster Englisch Einführungsphase und Q 1/2
Part B: Hör-/Hörsehverstehen (20 %)

Sprachrichtigkeit

Der Schüler/die Schülerin ...	maximal erreichbare Punktzahl
... beachtet die Normen der sprachlichen Korrektheit.	**24**

10. Wortschatz

0 Punkte	2–4 Punkte	5–7 Punkte	8–10 Punkte
In nahezu jedem Satz sind Schwächen im korrekten Gebrauch der Wörter feststellbar. Die Mängel im Wortgebrauch erschweren das Lesen und Textverständnis erheblich und verursachen Missverständnisse.	Einzelne Sätze sind frei von lexikalischen Verstößen. Fehler beim Wortgebrauch beeinträchtigen z. T. das Lesen und Verstehen.	Vereinzelt ist eine falsche Wortwahl feststellbar. Abschnitte bzw. Textpassagen sind weitgehend frei von lexikalischen Verstößen.	Der Wortgebrauch (Struktur- und Inhaltswörter) ist über den gesamten Text hinweg korrekt.

Maximal erreichbare Punktzahl: 10

11. Grammatik

0 Punkte	2–4 Punkte	5–7 Punkte	8–10 Punkte
In nahezu jedem Satz ist wenigstens ein Verstoß gegen die grundlegenden Regeln der Grammatik feststellbar. Diese erschweren das Lesen erheblich und verursachen Missverständnisse.	Einzelne Sätze sind frei von Verstößen gegen grundlegende Regeln der Grammatik. Grammatikfehler beeinträchtigen z. T. das Lesen und Verstehen.	Es sind vereinzelt Verstöße gegen die Regeln der Grammatik feststellbar. Jedoch sind Abschnitte bzw. Textpassagen weitgehend frei von Grammatikfehlern. Das Lesen des Textes wird durch die auftretenden Grammatikfehler nicht erschwert.	Der Text ist weitgehend frei von Verstößen gegen die Regeln der Grammatik. Wenn Grammatikfehler auftreten, betreffen sie den komplexen Satz und sind ein Zeichen dafür, dass die Schülerin/der Schüler Risiken beim Verfassen des Textes eingeht, um sich dem Leser differenziert mitzuteilen.

Maximal erreichbare Punktzahl: 10

12. Orthographie (Rechtschreibung und Zeichensetzung)

0 Punkte	1 Punkt	2–3 Punkte	4 Punkte
In nahezu jedem Satz ist wenigstens ein Verstoß gegen die Regeln der Orthographie feststellbar. Die Orthographiefehler erschweren das Lesen erheblich und verursachen Missverständnisse.	Einzelne Sätze sind frei von Verstößen gegen orthographische Normen. Orthographiefehler beeinträchtigen z. T. das Lesen und Verstehen.	Es sind durchaus Orthographiefehler feststellbar. Jedoch sind Abschnitte bzw. Textpassagen weitgehend ohne Verstoß gegen orthographische Normen. Das Lesen des Textes wird durch die auftretenden Orthographiefehler nicht wesentlich beeinträchtigt.	Der gesamte Text ist weitgehend frei von Verstößen gegen orthographische Normen. Wenn vereinzelt Orthographiefehler auftreten, haben sie den Charakter von Flüchtigkeitsfehlern, d. h., sie deuten nicht auf Unkenntnis von Regeln hin.

Maximal erreichbare Punktzahl: 4

Bewertungsraster Englisch Einführungsphase und Q 1/2
Part B: Hör-/Hörsehverstehen (20 %)

Bewertungsbogen für: _____ Kurs: _____

Die Fachkonferenz trifft Vereinbarungen zum Bewertungsschlüssel; der Fachlehrer/die Fachlehrerin konkretisiert und ergänzt klausurspezifisch im Teilleistungsbereich Inhalt die Lösungen und Kriterien (vgl. Klausurformate gemäß Lehrplan Englisch SII 1999).			
Inhalt (40 %)	**Der Schüler/die Schülerin ...**	mögliche Punkte	erreichte Punkte
Aufgabe 1: *(Comprehension)*	Kriterium 1: ...		
	Kriterium 2: ...	12	
	Kriterium 3: ...		
Aufgabe 2: *(Analysis)*	Kriterium 1: ...		
	Kriterium 2: ...	20	
	Kriterium 3: ...		
Aufgabe 3: *(Comment/Evaluation/ (Re-)Creation of text)*	Kriterium 1: ...		
	Kriterium 2: ...	16	
	Kriterium 3: ...		
	Summe Inhalt:	48	

Sprache (60 %)	**Der Schüler/die Schülerin ...**	mögliche Punkte	erreichte Punkte
Kommunikative Textgestaltung [24 P.]	**Aufgabenbezug:** ... richtet seinen Text konsequent und explizit im Sinne der Aufgabenstellung auf die Intention und den Adressaten aus.	6	
	Textformate: ... richtet seinen Text auf die Aufgabenstellungen aus und beachtet die Konventionen der jeweils geforderten Zieltextformate: ● Aufgabe 1: u. a.: Quellenangabe zum Ausgangstext, keine Zitate/Textverweise, *present tense* ● Aufgabe 2: u. a. sachlich-neutraler Stil, Textverweise u. Zitate, *present tense* ● Aufgabe 3: u. a. subjektiv-wertender Stil (3.1), bzw. Berücksichtigung der Normen der Textsorte (3.2)	5	
	Textaufbau: ... erstellt einen sachgerecht strukturierten leserfreundlichen Text, u. a. durch sprachliche Verknüpfungen, Absätze als erkennbare Sinnabschnitte etc.	5	
	Ökonomie: ... formuliert hinreichend ausführlich, aber ohne unnötige Wiederholungen und Umständlichkeiten (auch unter funktionaler Verwendung von Verweisen/Zitaten).	5	
	Textbelege: funktionale Verwendung von Textverweisen und Zitaten	3	
Ausdrucksvermögen/ Verfügbarkeit sprachlicher Mittel [24 P.]	**Eigenständigkeit:** ... löst sich vom Ausgangstext und formuliert eigenständig.	5	
	Themenwortschatz: ... bedient sich eines sachlich wie stilistisch angemessenen wie differenzierten (allgemeinen, thematischen, analytischen) Wortschatzes.	6	
	Funktions- und Interpretationswortschatz: ... bedient sich eines sachlich wie stilistisch angemessenen und differenzierten Wortschatzes.	5	
	Satzbau: ... bedient sich eines variablen und dem jeweiligen Zieltextformat angemessenen Satzbaus.	8	
Sprachrichtigkeit [24 P.]	Wortschatz	10	
	Grammatik	10	
	Orthografie	4	
	Summe Sprache:	72	
	Summe Teilaufgabe Hör-/Hörsehverstehen:	30	
	Insgesamt:	**150**	

Bewertungsschlüssel																
Punkte = %	29 – 0	39 – 30	48 – 40	57 – 49	67 – 58	74 – 68	82 – 75	89 – 83	97 – 90	104 – 98	112 – 105	119 – 113	127 – 120	134 – 128	142 – 135	150 – 143	**Ziffernote**
Note	6	5-	5	5+	4-	4	4+	3-	3	3+	2-	2	2+	1-	1	1+	

Eine Klausurleistung, die in einem der beiden Anforderungsbereiche, *Inhalt* und *Sprache* eine ungenügende Leistung darstellt, kann insgesamt nicht mit mehr als drei Notenpunkten bewertet werden.

Eine ungenügende Leistung im *inhaltlichen Bereich* liegt vor, wenn in diesem **weniger als 8 Punkte** erreicht werden.

Eine ungenügende Leistung im *sprachlichen Bereich* liegt vor, wenn in ihm **weniger als 12 Punkte** erreicht werden.

Die Klausur wird mit der Note _____ (_____ Punkte) bewertet.

Kriterielle Bewertung des Bereichs „Sprachliche Leistung/Darstellungsleistung"
Bewertungsraster Englisch Einführungsphase und Q 1/2
Part B: Mediation (30 %)

Kommunikative Textgestaltung – Kriterien	Lösungsqualität	
Der Schüler/die Schülerin ...	maximal erreichbare Punkte	erreichte Punkte
1 Aufgabenbezug ... richtet seinen Text konsequent und explizit auf die Aufgabenstellung aus. • eindeutiger Aufgabenbezug in allen drei Teilaufgaben • Beachtung der Anforderungsbereiche (siehe Operatoren)	6	
2 Textformate ... beachtet die Konventionen der jeweils geforderten Zieltextformate. • **Aufgabe 1:** Quellenangaben zum Ausgangstext: Autor, Titel, Textsorte, Thema, Publikation, Ort und Jahr, ggf. Ausgabe/Auszug, Intention/Zielgruppe; keine Zitate und i. d. R. keine Textverweise • **Aufgaben 1 und 2:** sachlich-neutraler Stil/Register; verdichtendes Wiedergeben, Darstellen und Erläutern (expositorisch-darstellendes Schreiben) • **Aufgabe 3.1:** subjektiv-wertender Stil/Register; Erörtern, Begründen, Schlussfolgern und argumentativ sinnvolle Textstruktur mit einem gewissen Maß an Rhetorisierung (argumentierendes Schreiben) • **Aufgaben 1–3.1:** *present tense* als Tempus der Textbesprechung; keine *short forms* • **Aufgabe 3.2:** Bezug auf klar definierte Normen der Textsorte (anwendungs-/produktionsorientiertes kreatives Schreiben), z. B. bei Rede/Debattenbeitrag: Adressatenbezug durch Bezugnahme auf das Vorwissen und den Erfahrungshorizont des Adressaten	4	
3 Textaufbau ... erstellt einen sachgerecht strukturierten Text. • Geschlossenheit des Gesamttextes (Aufgaben 1, 2 und 3.1, bzw. Aufgaben 1 und 2 in Vorbereitung von 3.2) • sach- und intentionsgerechte Untergliederung in grafisch erkennbare Sinnabschnitte • inhaltlich-thematische Geschlossenheit der Sinnabschnitte und Herstellung eindeutiger Bezüge • leserfreundliche Verknüpfung der Sinnabschnitte und Gedanken (z. B. durch gliedernde Hinweise, Aufzählung, Vor- und Rückverweise, zusammenfassende Wiederaufnahme zentraler Punkte, Konnektoren)	4	
4 Ökonomie ... gestaltet seinen Text hinreichend ausführlich, aber ohne unnötige Wiederholungen und Umständlichkeiten. • Beschränkung auf relevante bzw. exemplarische Punkte/Details/Zitate • Vermeidung von Redundanz, z. B. durch Rückverweise auf bereits Dargelegtes (statt Wiederholung) • abstrahierende Zusammenfassung mit konkreten, exemplarischen Belegen (statt langwieriger, textchronologischer Bearbeitung) • Bereitstellung und ggf. Erläuterung verständnisrelevanter Informationen	4	
5 Belegtechnik ... belegt seine Aussagen durch eine funktionale Verwendung von Verweisen und Zitaten. • Gebrauch von Textverweisen (Zeilenangabe, Hinweise auf Absatz) zur Orientierung des Lesers • der Darstellungsabsicht angemessener Gebrauch wörtlicher Zitate aus dem Ausgangstext (Aufgaben 2 und 3) • Konventionen des Zitierens: z. B. durch Zeilenangabe, Absatzangabe, wörtliches Zitieren, sinngemäßes Zitieren (Paraphrase), ggf. unter Kennzeichnung von Auslassungen oder Ergänzungen, Wechsel zwischen in den Satz eingebauten Zitaten, eingeleiteten Zitaten und Zitaten in Klammern	3	

Ausdrucksvermögen/Verfügbarkeit sprachlicher Mittel – Kriterien	Lösungsqualität	
Der Schüler/die Schülerin ...	maximal erreichbare Punkte	erreichte Punkte
6 Eigenständigkeit ... löst sich vom Wortlaut des Ausgangstextes und formuliert eigenständig. • Wiedergaben von Inhalten/Sachverhalten in „eigenen Worten" • keine wörtliche Wiedergabe auswendig gelernter Textpassagen (z. B. aus der Sekundärliteratur) • Hinweis: Ein punktuell das Sprachmaterial des Ausgangstextes kreativ verarbeitendes Vorgehen ist durchaus erwünscht.	4	
7 Allgemeiner und thematischer Wortschatz ... bedient sich eines sachlich wie stilistisch angemessenen und differenzierten allgemeinen und thematischen Wortschatzes. Inhalts- und Strukturwörter: • treffende und präzise Bezeichnung von Personen, Dingen und Sachverhalten, Berücksichtigung von Bedeutungsnuancen (auch Modalitäten) • stilistisch angemessene Wortwahl (*register: formal, neutral, informal*) • Variation der Wortwahl, Vermeidung von „Allerweltswörtern" (z. B. *think, want, good, thing*)	6	

181

	Ausdrucksvermögen/Verfügbarkeit sprachlicher Mittel – Kriterien	Lösungsqualität	
	Der Schüler/die Schülerin ...	maximal erreichbare Punkte	erreichte Punkte
8	**Funktions- und Textinterpretationswortschatz** ... bedient sich eines sachlich wie stilistisch angemessenen und differenzierten Textbesprechungs- und Textproduktionswortschatzes. • **Aufgabe 1:** Vokabular zur Wiedergabe und Zusammenfassung von Inhalten • **Aufgabe 2:** Vokabular der Textanalyse (auch Filmanalyse, Analyse von Karikaturen, Grafiken etc.) • **Aufgabe 3.1:** Vokabular der Meinungsäußerung/Bewertung • **Aufgabe 3.2:** Anpassung des Wortschatzes an das geforderte Textformat	4	
9	**Satzbau** ... bedient sich eines variablen und dem jeweiligen Zieltextformat angemessenen Satzbaus. • durchgängig klare Syntax, Verständlichkeit beim ersten Lesen (Überschaubarkeit, Eindeutigkeit der Bezüge, Satzlogik) • dem jeweiligen Zieltextformat angemessene Satzmuster: z. B. Hypotaxe (Konjunktional-, Relativ-, indirekte Fragesätze), Parataxe, Aktiv- und Passivkonstruktionen, Gerundial-, Partizipial- und Infinitivkonstruktionen, Adverbiale	7	

	Sprachrichtigkeit – Kriterien	Lösungsqualität	
	Der Schüler/die Schülerin ...	maximal erreichbare Punkte	erreichte Punkte
	... beachtet die Normen der sprachlichen Korrektheit (siehe Orientierung).		
10	Wortschatz	9	
11	Grammatik	8	
12	Orthographie	4	
		21	
	Summe sprachliche Leistung/Darstellungsleistung	63	

	Gesamtpunkte	Lösungsqualität	
		maximal erreichbare Punkte	erreichte Punkte
	Summe Darstellungsleistung/sprachliche Leistung	63	
	Summe inhaltliche Leistung	42	
	Teilaufgabe Mediation: Inhalt	18	
	Teilaufgabe Mediation: sprachliche Leistung/Darstellung	27	
	Summe Teilaufgabe Mediation	45	
	Summe insgesamt (Inhalt und Sprache/Darstellung)	150	
	aus der Punktsumme resultierende Note		

Bewertungsschlüssel																	
Punkte = %	29 – 0	39 – 30	48 – 40	57 – 49	67 – 58	74 – 68	82 – 75	89 – 83	97 – 90	104 – 98	112 – 105	119 – 113	127 – 120	134 – 128	142 – 135	150 – 143	Ziffernote
Note	6	5-	5	5+	4-	4	4+	3-	3	3+	2-	2	2+	1-	1	1+	

Eine Klausurleistung, die in einem der beiden Anforderungsbereiche, *Inhalt* und *Sprache* eine ungenügende Leistung darstellt, kann insgesamt nicht mit mehr als drei Notenpunkten bewertet werden.
Eine ungenügende Leistung im *inhaltlichen Bereich* liegt vor, wenn in diesem **weniger als 8 Punkte** erreicht werden.
Eine ungenügende Leistung im *sprachlichen Bereich* liegt vor, wenn in ihm **weniger als 12 Punkte** erreicht werden.

Die Klausur wird mit der Note _____ (_____ Punkte) bewertet.

Orientierungsangaben für die Sprachrichtigkeit
Bewertungsraster Englisch Einführungsphase und Q 1/2
Part B: Mediation (30 %)

Sprachrichtigkeit

Der Schüler/die Schülerin ...	maximal erreichbare Punktzahl
... beachtet die Normen der sprachlichen Korrektheit.	21

10. Wortschatz

0 Punkte	2–3 Punkte	4–6 Punkte	7–9 Punkte
In nahezu jedem Satz sind Schwächen im korrekten Gebrauch der Wörter feststellbar. Die Mängel im Wortgebrauch erschweren das Lesen und Textverständnis erheblich und verursachen Missverständnisse.	Einzelne Sätze sind frei von lexikalischen Verstößen. Fehler beim Wortgebrauch beeinträchtigen z. T. das Lesen und Verstehen.	Vereinzelt ist eine falsche Wortwahl feststellbar. Abschnitte bzw. Textpassagen sind weitgehend frei von lexikalischen Verstößen.	Der Wortgebrauch (Struktur- und Inhaltswörter) ist über den gesamten Text hinweg korrekt.

Maximal erreichbare Punktzahl: 9

11. Grammatik

0 Punkte	2–3 Punkte	4–6 Punkte	7–8 Punkte
In nahezu jedem Satz ist wenigstens ein Verstoß gegen die grundlegenden Regeln der Grammatik feststellbar. Diese erschweren das Lesen erheblich und verursachen Missverständnisse.	Einzelne Sätze sind frei von Verstößen gegen grundlegende Regeln der Grammatik. Grammatikfehler beeinträchtigen z. T. das Lesen und Verstehen.	Es sind vereinzelt Verstöße gegen die Regeln der Grammatik feststellbar. Jedoch sind Abschnitte bzw. Textpassagen weitgehend frei von Grammatikfehlern. Das Lesen des Textes wird durch die auftretenden Grammatikfehler nicht erschwert.	Der Text ist weitgehend frei von Verstößen gegen die Regeln der Grammatik. Wenn Grammatikfehler auftreten, betreffen sie den komplexen Satz und sind ein Zeichen dafür, dass die Schülerin/der Schüler Risiken beim Verfassen des Textes eingeht, um sich dem Leser differenziert mitzuteilen.

Maximal erreichbare Punktzahl: 8

12. Orthographie (Rechtschreibung und Zeichensetzung)

0 Punkte	1 Punkt	2–3 Punkte	4 Punkte
In nahezu jedem Satz ist wenigstens ein Verstoß gegen die Regeln der Orthographie feststellbar. Die Orthographiefehler erschweren das Lesen erheblich und verursachen Missverständnisse.	Einzelne Sätze sind frei von Verstößen gegen orthographische Normen. Orthographiefehler beeinträchtigen z. T. das Lesen und Verstehen.	Es sind durchaus Orthographiefehler feststellbar. Jedoch sind Abschnitte bzw. Textpassagen weitgehend ohne Verstoß gegen orthographische Normen. Das Lesen des Textes wird durch die auftretenden Orthographiefehler nicht wesentlich beeinträchtigt.	Der gesamte Text ist weitgehend frei von Verstößen gegen orthographische Normen. Wenn vereinzelt Orthographiefehler auftreten, haben sie den Charakter von Flüchtigkeitsfehlern, d. h., sie deuten nicht auf Unkenntnis von Regeln hin.

Maximal erreichbare Punktzahl: 4

Bewertungsraster Englisch Einführungsphase und Q 1/2
Part B: Mediation (30 %)

Bewertungsbogen für: _____ Kurs: _____

Die Fachkonferenz trifft Vereinbarungen zum Bewertungsschlüssel; der Fachlehrer/die Fachlehrerin konkretisiert und ergänzt klausurspezifisch im Teilleistungsbereich Inhalt die Lösungen und Kriterien (vgl. Klausurformate gemäß Lehrplan Englisch SII 1999).

Inhalt (40 %)	Der Schüler/die Schülerin …	mögliche Punkte	erreichte Punkte
Aufgabe 1: *(Comprehension)*	Kriterium 1: …		
	Kriterium 2: …	10	
	Kriterium 3: …		
Aufgabe 2: *(Analysis)*	Kriterium 1: …		
	Kriterium 2: …	18	
	Kriterium 3: …		
Aufgabe 3: *(Comment/Evaluation/ (Re-)Creation of text)*	Kriterium 1: …		
	Kriterium 2: …	14	
	Kriterium 3: …		
	Summe Inhalt:	42	

Sprache (60 %)	Der Schüler/die Schülerin …	mögliche Punkte	erreichte Punkte
Kommunikative Textgestaltung [21 P.]	**Aufgabenbezug:** … richtet seinen Text konsequent und explizit im Sinne der Aufgabenstellung auf die Intention und den Adressaten aus.	6	
	Textformate: … richtet seinen Text auf die Aufgabenstellungen aus und beachtet die Konventionen der jeweils geforderten Zieltextformate: ● Aufgabe 1: u. a.: Quellenangabe zum Ausgangstext, keine Zitate/Textverweise, *present tense* ● Aufgabe 2: u. a. sachlich-neutraler Stil, Textverweise u. Zitate, *present tense* ● Aufgabe 3: u. a. subjektiv-wertender Stil (3.1), bzw. Berücksichtigung der Normen der Textsorte (3.2)	4	
	Textaufbau: … erstellt einen sachgerecht strukturierten leserfreundlichen Text, u. a. durch sprachliche Verknüpfungen, Absätze als erkennbare Sinnabschnitte etc.	4	
	Ökonomie: … formuliert hinreichend ausführlich, aber ohne unnötige Wiederholungen und Umständlichkeiten (auch unter funktionaler Verwendung von Verweisen/Zitaten).	4	
	Belegtechnik: funktionale Verwendung von Textverweisen und Zitaten	3	
Ausdrucksvermögen/ Verfügbarkeit sprachlicher Mittel [21 P.]	**Eigenständigkeit:** … löst sich vom Ausgangstext und formuliert eigenständig.	4	
	Themenwortschatz: … bedient sich eines sachlich wie stilistisch angemessenen wie differenzierten (allgemeinen, thematischen, analytischen) Wortschatzes.	6	
	Funktions- und Interpretationswortschatz: … bedient sich eines sachlich wie stilistisch angemessenen und differenzierten Wortschatzes.	4	
	Satzbau: … bedient sich eines variablen und dem jeweiligen Zieltextformat angemessenen Satzbaus.	7	
Sprachrichtigkeit [21 P.]	**Wortschatz**	9	
	Grammatik	8	
	Orthografie	4	
	Summe Sprache:	63	
	Teilaufgabe Mediation/Inhalt:	18	
	Teilaufgabe Mediation/sprachliche Leistung/Darstellung:	27	
	Summe Teilaufgabe Mediation:	45	

	Insgesamt:	150	

Bewertungsschlüssel																	
Punkte = %	29 – 0	39 – 30	48 – 40	57 – 49	67 – 58	74 – 68	82 – 75	89 – 83	97 – 90	104 – 98	112 – 105	119 – 113	127 – 120	134 – 128	142 – 135	150 – 143	**Ziffernote**
Note	6	5-	5	5+	4-	4	4+	3-	3	3+	2-	2	2+	1-	1	1+	

Eine Klausurleistung, die in einem der beiden Anforderungsbereiche, *Inhalt* und *Sprache* eine ungenügende Leistung darstellt, kann insgesamt nicht mit mehr als drei Notenpunkten bewertet werden.

Eine ungenügende Leistung im *inhaltlichen Bereich* liegt vor, wenn in diesem **weniger als 8 Punkte** erreicht werden.

Eine ungenügende Leistung im *sprachlichen Bereich* liegt vor, wenn in ihm **weniger als 12 Punkte** erreicht werden.

Die Klausur wird mit der Note _____ (_____ Punkte) bewertet.

Acknowledgements

Images

front cover: © John R. Rogers Photography; p. 5: © Beeler 2015, The Columbus Dispatch/caglecartoons.com; pp. 186/187: © Loop-Fotolia.com; back cover: © Michel Setboun/Corbis

Texts

p. 38: from The New York Times, 3/7/2015 © 2015 The New York Times. All rights reserved. Used by permission and protected by the Copyright Laws of the United States. The printing, copying, redistribution, or retransmission of this Content without express written permission is prohibited; pp. 83f.: Vox Pops International; p. 94: Deutsche Post DHL Group

All other sources can be found below the texts.

Audios

Track 1: www.youtube.com/watch?v=7SoG4KZOvRc (7 March 2014) [04.04.2015]; Track 2: www.youtube.com/watch?v=DGjWro3CN8s (27 February 2013) [04.04.2015], RT (Russia Today); Track 3: www.youtube.com/watch?v=13kOeTojCBI (28 November) [04.04.2015], RT (Russia Today); Track 4: www.youtube.com/watch?v=ilSU9ENNRZQ (28 March 2015) [04.04.2015], TYT-Network; Track 5: www.youtube.com/watch?v=wWGMvmAlIvA (04.03.2015) [04.04.2015], VPI (Vox Pops International); Track 6: www.youtube.com/watch?v=VE0lPTfsBoI (24.02.2012) [04.04.2015], Deutsche Post DHL Group; Track 7: www.youtube.com/watch?v=oWrzXp2uJRM (23.09.2014) [04.04.2015]; Track 8: www.ted.com/talks/amber_case_we_are_all_cyborgs_now (Dec 2010) [04.04.2015]

Audiovisuals

Track 1: © Kevin Spacey, www.kevinspacey.com/nowthefilm; Track 2: © 1995 Warner Bros. USA

Contents CD-ROM

 01_Film

Track-Nr.	Klausur-Nr.	Dateiname (Material)	Laufzeit in min.
01	1	01_Spacey_Now (Kevin Spacey: Now – Richard III Documentary)	03:18
02	2	02_Shakespeare_Othello (William Shakespeare: Othelo (Act III, Scene 3))	02:59

 02_Audio

Track-Nr.	Klausur-Nr.	Dateiname (Material)	Laufzeit in min.
01	5	01_Obama_Selma Speech (Barack Obama: Selma Speech)	04:59
02	6	02_Firth_Britain's Squeezed Middle Class (William Shakespeare: Othello (Act III, Scene 3))	02:59
03	7	03_Multicultural Society (Multicultural Society – UK Whites and Ethnics Choose to Live Apart)	02:47
04	8	04_The Young Turks_Starbucks (The Young Turks: Starbucks Ends Controversial "Race Together" Campaign)	04:14
05	9	05_Vox Pops International_Britain (Vox Pops International: What Does "Britain" and "Being British" Mean to Millennials?)	02:40
06	10	06_Appel_The World in 2050 (Frank Appel: The World in 2050)	04:58
07	11	07_Obama_2014 UN Climate Summit Speech (Barack Obama: 2014 UN Climate Summit Speech)	04:40
08	12	08_Case_We Are All Cyborgs Now (Amber Case: We Are All Cyborgs Now)	07:50

 03_Bewertungsraster Klausuren pdf

Klausur-Nr.	Dateiname
1	01_Klausur_Bewertungsraster.pdf
2	02_Klausur_Bewertungsraster.pdf
3	03_Klausur_Bewertungsraster.pdf
4	04_Klausur_Bewertungsraster.pdf
5	05_Klausur_Bewertungsraster.pdf
6	06_Klausur_Bewertungsraster.pdf
7	07_Klausur_Bewertungsraster.pdf
8	08_Klausur_Bewertungsraster.pdf
9	09_Klausur_Bewertungsraster.pdf
10	10_Klausur_Bewertungsraster.pdf
11	11_Klausur_Bewertungsraster.pdf
12	12_Klausur_Bewertungsraster.pdf
13	13_Klausur_Bewertungsraster.pdf
14	14_Klausur_Bewertungsraster.pdf
15	15_Klausur_Bewertungsraster.pdf
16	16_Klausur_Bewertungsraster.pdf
17	17_Klausur_Bewertungsraster.pdf
18	18_Klausur_Bewertungsraster.pdf
19	19_Klausur_Bewertungsraster.pdf
20	20_Klausur_Bewertungsraster.pdf

04_Bewertungsraster Appendix pdf

Dateiname
01_Lesen_Sprachliche Leistung Darstellungsleistung.pdf
02_Lesen_Orientierungsangaben Sprachrichtigkeit.pdf
03_Lesen_Gesamtübersicht.pdf
04_Hör- und Hörsehverstehen_Sprachliche Leistung Darstellungsleistung.pdf
05_Hör- und Hörsehverstehen_Orientierungsangaben Sprachrichtigkeit.pdf
06_Hör- und Hörsehverstehen_Gesamtübersicht.pdf
07_Mediation_Sprachliche Leistung Darstellungsleistung.pdf
08_Mediation_Orientierungsangaben Sprachrichtigkeit.pdf
09_Mediation_Gesamtübersicht.pdf

 05_Bewertungsraster Klausuren Word

Klausur-Nr.	Dateiname
1	1_Klausur_Bewertungsraster.docx
2	2_Klausur_Bewertungsraster.docx
3	3_Klausur_Bewertungsraster.docx
4	4_Klausur_Bewertungsraster.docx
5	5_Klausur_Bewertungsraster.docx
6	6_Klausur_Bewertungsraster.docx
7	7_Klausur_Bewertungsraster.docx
8	8_Klausur_Bewertungsraster.docx
9	9_Klausur_Bewertungsraster.docx
10	10_Klausur_Bewertungsraster.docx
11	11_Klausur_Bewertungsraster.docx
12	12_Klausur_Bewertungsraster.docx
13	13_Klausur_Bewertungsraster.docx
14	14_Klausur_Bewertungsraster.docx
15	15_Klausur_Bewertungsraster.docx
16	16_Klausur_Bewertungsraster.docx
17	17_Klausur_Bewertungsraster.docx
18	18_Klausur_Bewertungsraster.docx
19	19_Klausur_Bewertungsraster.docx
20	20_Klausur_Bewertungsraster.docx

 06_Bewertungsraster Appendix Word

Dateiname
01_Lesen_Sprachliche Leistung Darstellungsleistung.docx
02_Lesen_Orientierungsangaben Sprachrichtigkeit.docx
03_Lesen_Gesamtübersicht.docx
04_Hör- und Hörsehverstehen_Sprachliche Leistung Darstellungsleistung.docx
05_Hör- und Hörsehverstehen_Orientierungsangaben Sprachrichtigkeit.docx
06_Hör- und Hörsehverstehen_Gesamtübersicht.docx
07_Mediation_Sprachliche Leistung Darstellungsleistung.docx
08_Mediation_Orientierungsangaben Sprachrichtigkeit.docx
09_Mediation_Gesamtübersicht.docx